1,2,3, 9

2—1,2,3

The Story of Jazz

THE STORY OF JAZZ

MARSHALL W. STEARNS

OXFORD UNIVERSITY PRESS

LONDON   OXFORD   NEW YORK

OXFORD UNIVERSITY PRESS

London   Oxford   New York
Glasgow   Toronto   Melbourne   Wellington
Cape Town   Ibadan   Nairobi   Dar es Salaam   Lusaka   Addis Ababa
Delhi   Bombay   Calcutta   Madras   Karachi   Lahore   Dacca
Kuala Lumpur   Singapore   Hong Kong   Tokyo

To my wife, Betty, who routed the RaRa band under the balcony of the Hotel des Orchidés in Petionville while my daughter and I forgot our fevers and operated the tape recorder (e.g., 'La Fête Rose,' Ethnic Folkways Library, P 432).

Acknowledgments

For the last thirty years—ever since the Hot Five recordings—I have been trying to read all the writings on jazz, listen to all the recordings of jazz, and talk to all the musicians who play jazz that I could possibly discover. This history, then, is a synthesis, and I cannot begin to acknowledge all my indebtedness to others, although I wish I could do so.

Nevertheless, some of my obligations are clear cut. I should like to acknowledge here the material assistance of the Viking Fund, the Center for the Study of Liberal Education for Adults, and the John Simon Guggenheim Memorial Foundation. I should also like to acknowledge the sympathetic understanding and moral support of the Hunter College faculty and staff and President George N. Shuster.

I owe a special debt to the following friends who have been generous enough to read my manuscript, in whole or in part, during the past five years: Donald Allen, George Avakian, Philip Barber, Rudi Blesh, W. Bruce Cameron, Gilbert Chase, Harold Courlander, Ralph Ellison, Leonard Feather, Norman Granz, William Christopher Handy, Don Heckman, Langston Hughes, Willis Laurence James, Roy Lamson, James T. Maher, Tremaine McDowell, Alan

Merriam, Gunther Schuller, Jerome Shipman, Dr. Edmond Souchon, Richard A. Waterman, and Martin Williams.

I have also profited greatly from extensive conversations and correspondence with Arthur S. Alberts, Jean Barnett, Ben Botkin, Sterling Brown, Albert Collins, Henry Cowell, Stuart Davis, Roger Pryor Dodge, Stanley Diamond, Sidney Finkelstein, Bill Grauer, Dr. Maurice Green, S. I. Hayakawa, Melville J. Herskovits, George Herzog, Sheldon Harris, Wilder Hobson, Leon James, Leonard Kunstadt, M. Kolinski, Eric Larrabee, Jacob Lawrence, Alan Lomax, Dr. Norman Margolis, Albert Minns, Alan Morrison, Edward Abbe Niles, Frederic Ramsey, Jr., David Riesman, Boris Rose, Ross Russell, William Russell, Anthony Schwartz, Charles Seeger, Charles Edward Smith, Ernest Smith, Hsio Wen Shih, Harold Thompson, Robert L. Thompson, Lorenzo Turner, Tony Van Dam, Bernard Wolfe, and John W. Work.

I am under a special obligation to Robert George Reisner for preparing the bibliography, and to my editors at the Oxford University Press and the New American Library, Leona Capeless, Carroll Bowen, and Marc Jaffe, for their patience and encouragement.

Above all, my thanks to the many fine musicians whose history this is.

Contents

Introduction

Musicologist Charles Seeger tells the story of a conference of musicologists after which one of the most famous confided: 'You know, I don't hate jazz; I think it's probably very important and it certainly deserves serious study. The trouble is that all the jazz people treat it as holy, holy, holy!' To this, Seeger replied: 'Well, now, don't you consider the area of classical music in which you specialize as holy, too?' 'Ah,' said the musicologist, 'BUT IT *IS!*'

In this book, I have tried not to treat jazz, or any other music, as holy. The reason for this book is quite simple: more people in the United States listen to and enjoy jazz or near-jazz than any other music. Jazz is of tremendous importance for its quantity alone. Because of its all-pervasiveness it has a great influence on most of us. Jazz has played a part, for better or worse, in forming the American character. Jazz is a fact that should be faced—and studied.

Like other musics, however, jazz has its aesthetics and there are crucial qualitative differences. There is good and bad jazz, and all shades between. Further, jazz is a separate and distinct art, to be judged by separate and distinct standards, and comparisons are useful when they help to establish this point. Jazz also has an ancient and honorable history, and this book is designed to deal with these varied questions.

On the other hand, I see no reason to maintain the melancholy pretense of absolute objectivity. I like jazz very much, and I am no doubt biased in its favor—at least to the extent of trying to find out what it is all about. In the process, I find that I have tended to enlarge the usual area covered by the word 'jazz' and to include most of the music created, with the help of the American Negro, in the United States. It is all of a piece, to be sure, but historically the word 'jazz' was used mainly in the 'twenties. I can find no better word, however, to suggest the whole phenomenon.

The aim of *The Story of Jazz* is to outline the main currents of a great tradition.

M. W. S.

New York
June 1956

PART ONE : THE PRE-HISTORY OF JAZZ

1 | Jazz and West African Music

In reply to the sweet old lady's question, 'What is jazz, Mr. Waller?' the late and great Fats is supposed to have sighed: 'Madam, if you don't know by now, DON'T MESS WITH IT!' Fats Waller had a point there. Whether you hear it in New Orleans or Bombay—they play something like it there, too—jazz is a lot easier to recognize than to describe. Suppose we define it temporarily as the result of a 300-year-old blending in the United States of two great musical traditions, the European and the West African. It follows that, in a musical culture predominantly European, the qualities that make jazz a little different and immediately recognizable probably have something to do with West Africa.

What is the connection between jazz and West African music? Perhaps the most obvious similarity is the rhythm —not that a West African tribesman would like jazz, because he wouldn't, the blending has gone too far. But take a tribal ceremony in Dahomey: the musicians are playing rattles, gongs, and other percussion instruments, while the tribesmen are dancing, singing, clapping, and stamping. The main instrument, however, is the drum—usually a set of three drums known to musicologists as a drum choir— because the gods speak through the drums, the dancers face the drums, and the tribe forms a circle around them.

3

At its peak, the sound may seem like a combination of disordered pneumatic drills. The music is polyrhythmic, that is, two or more separate rhythms are being played at the same time, maybe five or six. A common foundation for West African music is a combination of 3/4, 6/8, and 4/4 time signatures. It's as if an orchestra were playing the same tune as a waltz, a one-step, and a fox trot—all at the same time. And of course the singing, clapping, and stamping add further rhythmic complexities.

To a highly trained classical musician this West African music may sound like chaos. For the West Africans have no written music—they play from memory and by ear—and they don't follow anything as regular as the bar-lines of our European system of notation. In fact, in terms of one of our measures their rhythms seem to change right in the middle, a great stumbling block to musicologists when they try to write them down. And yet even the untrained listener can feel the power and drive and can somehow sense that the complicated parts of this rhythmic juggernaut fit together.

By comparison, our jazz rhythms are fairly simple. We've come a long way but we certainly haven't caught up and maybe never will. Down in New Orleans, for example, some of the old-timers are still playing 'Didn't He Ramble' on the way back from a funeral, but it sounds like a march. Jazz is traditionally approximated in notation as 4/4 or duple meter—actually it's more complex—and this march rhythm is basic. You can hear it plainly in the music of a New Orleans brass band, but something new has been added—the music *swings*. And it is apparent that this new ingredient didn't come from Europe.

Theorists tell us that there is no limit to the complexities that can be superimposed upon march rhythm—and that is what jazz is doing. The basis of jazz is a march rhythm but the jazzman puts more complicated rhythms on top of it. He blows a variety of accents between and around, above and below, the march beat. It's a much more complicated process than syncopation, which is usually defined as stressing the normally weak beat, for syncopation sounds unutterably old-fashioned to a jazzman. A regular six-piece band playing in the New Orleans style can create rhythmic complexities which no machine yet invented can fully diagram.

At the start of a recording session Louis Armstrong, handkerchief in one hand and trumpet in the other, stands in front of the microphone and stamps out a steady rhythm. As the band picks it up, Armstrong's foot doubles the beat and starts tapping twice as fast. And as he sings and plays the trumpet he stresses accents *around and between* the taps of his foot. Recorded examples show that he has broken the measure down to sixteenths at least, but this is a standard jazz procedure.

Erroll Garner is justly famous for what jazzmen call 'fooling around with the beat,' because he doesn't seem to let his left hand know what his right hand is doing. In general, his left hand plays a steady 4/4 march rhythm, quite opposite to the modern trend, but his right hand is playing the melody in a variety of changing tempos: first he drags behind and then he more than catches up in constantly varying fractions of the beat. The effect is schizophrenic, like rubbing your stomach in one direction and the top of your head in another. A good example of this is at the beginning of the second chorus of 'What Is This Thing Called Love?' by Garner (Roost 606).

Here is a quality that gives jazz some of its appeal. Psychologically, Garner's steady left hand creates and fulfills the expectancy of a continuous rhythm. His lag-along right hand, however, sets up a contrasting tension which is released when, by means of more unexpected accents, he catches up. It's like a sprinter who saves himself from falling on his face by an extra burst of speed. It's also a kind of rhythmic game. The effect on the listener varies: he may want to sing, dance, shout, or even hit somebody. Somehow he wants to express himself.

Understanding and enjoying this kind of rhythmic complexity is entirely a matter of training. Contrary to the popular notion, nobody is born with a fine sense of rhythm —people simply learn it, sometimes quite unconsciously. The outstanding student of the subject, Richard A. Waterman of Northwestern University, has a phrase for what it takes: 'metronome sense.' [1] If your metronome sense is highly developed, you can *feel* a foundation rhythm when all you hear is a shower of accents being superimposed upon it. The story of the Congo natives being thrilled by the intermittent explosions of a one-cylinder gasoline engine may well be true. Their highly conditioned ears supplied a rhythmic common denominator.

Metronome sense is important in jazz, too. When one jazzman confides that another 'has no beat'—and there is no harsher criticism—he is impugning his metronome sense. The sad plight of the classical musician trying to play jazz is axiomatic, and Mr. José Iturbi's recording of boogie-woogie is a fair example (Victor 10-1127). It doesn't swing. You don't need a highly developed metronome sense in most classical music because this music places primary emphasis upon the up-beat and the down-beat—four to a bar—the accents jazz uses as points of departure.

So something of this engaging rhythm that identifies a lot of jazz for us came from West Africa. It's a survival—diluted, to be sure. There's nothing quite like it in Europe, the source of most of the rest of our music. The intensity and complexity of the rhythm depend on the jazz band you are hearing, of course, but even Guy Lombardo is playing rhythms that were probably unknown to our dance music fifty years ago. As time goes on, jazz rhythms are spreading all over the world and their complexity and intensity are increasing.

Just about every kind of music associated with the American Negro has this rhythmic spark. It also has a second and perhaps just as important quality: the blue note and the blues scale, or to put them both together, blue tonality. At her annual concert at Carnegie Hall, Mahalia Jackson, 'Queen of the Gospel Singers,' creates an almost solid wall of blue tonality. It's not a matter of tempo. She'll sing a slow tune that we all know by heart, 'Silent Night,' for example—adding embellishments that take your breath away. As a member of a Sanctified Church in Mount Vernon once told me: 'Mahalia, she add more flowers and feathers than anybody, and they all is exactly right.' She breaks every rule of concert singing, taking breaths in the middle of a word and sometimes garbling the words altogether, but the full-throated feeling and expression are seraphic.

Here again, we are close to a quality that gives jazz much of its appeal. To be technical, two areas in the octave—the third and the seventh in the scale (E-flat and B-flat in the scale of C)—are attacked with an endless variety of swoops, glides, slurs, smears, and glisses. In other words, a singer, or instrumentalist, takes certain notes and cradles and caresses them lovingly, or fiercely. Of course, you have to know what you're doing. Way back in 1930, Rudy Vallee wrote with what might be called beginner's luck: 'I have played a certain note barbaric in quality on my saxophone very softly, and have watched its effect upon a crowd, the livening up of young legs and feet . . .' [2] He had found one of THE notes, a blue note. (By 1950, the 'flatted fifth' was in the process of becoming a blue note.)

With the addition of a few blue notes, the entire harmony becomes blue, and blue tonality results. It occurs in almost all American Negro music, vocal and instrumental, and especially in jazz. It can be heard in the field-holler and the work song, the spiritual and gospel, minstrelsy and ragtime. Above all, you can hear it in the bittersweet mixture of the blues. But it doesn't stop there. Many Tin-Pan Alley tunes are saturated with it and several classical composers have dabbled in it. Blue tonality has colored America's musical life.

Where does blue tonality come from? It can't be found in Europe. Something very much like it occurs in West Africa, although we don't know how extensive it is. The influence of Arabic music by way of the Moslem penetration of West Africa is a distinct possibility. There are elaborate theories about the superimposition of African pentatonic (5-note) on European diatonic (7-note) scales in the United States that resulted in two 'uncertain' or blue areas. These theories may well be right—although the diatonic scale also occurs in Africa. When Bessie Smith sings (Columbia LP 4810):

> Woke up this mornin', with an awfu' achin' head,
> My good man had lef' me, jes' a room an' a empty bed,

we hear and at once recognize blue tonality and the indis· putable creation of the American Negro. We also share a mood that is just about universal.

Less obvious characteristics of West African music help to give jazz its unique flavor. A real Negro revival meeting, says Alan Lomax, 'is the high point of American folk-theatre.'[3] The tent church of the Rev. A. A. Childs in Harlem during the summer of 1952 furnished a good example. For the Reverend, following a long tradition that goes back before the American Revolution, is a mighty preacher, and his congregation is quick to respond.

A simple form holds the entire performance together: the call-and-response pattern. Known among musicians as antiphony, it combines the preacher's call (variable timing) with the congregation's response (regular timing). Now and then they overlap and accidental harmony results. The words aren't too important, but the preacher's attack varies endlessly. In Buffalo, Elder Beck and his Junior Choir recorded wave after wave of rhythmic sound to the call, 'What do you think of Jesus?' and the high-pitched and fervent response: 'He's all right' (King 4394).

The call-and-response pattern occurs throughout jazz. Bessie Smith's recording of 'Empty Bed Blues' (banned, they say, in Boston) is a classic example. As Miss Smith specifies her woes, Charlie 'Big' Green answers her with interpretative cries and growls on his trombone. He sounds more than sympathetic. The 'chase' choruses of Bix and Tram during the late 'twenties offer another example. In 1953, when the blues shouter Wynonie Harris played the Apollo Theatre in Harlem, he had a tenor saxophonist honking responses that would curdle the blood of a lesser man. In the big bands, the pattern becomes a part of the arrangement. The brass and reed sections in Benny Goodman's swing band of the 'thirties echoed and expanded upon each other's phrases.

In the 'fifties, the small experimental bands used the pattern most clearly when they played 'the fours'—each musician in turn soloing for four bars. An extemporaneous continuity is sometimes established, with each soloist commenting on the phrases of his predecessor. It often becomes competitive. Following trumpeter Dizzy Gillespie, the saxophonist Charlie Parker astonished his colleagues at a Carnegie Hall concert in 1950 by repeating Gillespie's complicated phrases, wringing them out, and hanging them up to dry with additional embellishments—in the same time interval. No one else could have done it. (Part of the performance is preserved on a bootleg label, Black Deuce.)

We find the call-and-response pattern in American Negro music from the early work song on—wherever there are two persons to create a dialogue, or a man and his instrument upon which he can construct a reply. The same pattern is found everywhere in West Africa. There was a musical tradition, however, that confirmed the West African in his use of the call-and-response pattern and hastened the blending: the psalm-singing style of New England (as early as 1650), a style that disappeared in the cities as the country grew but survived in rural areas along the expanding frontier where it had been brought by the Yankee music teacher. Everybody sang his own version of the tune (which thus added improvised embellishments) and the performance was held together by 'lining out,' that is, the preacher spoke the words first and then the congregation sang them. The call-and-response form continued to be employed long after everybody knew the words.[4] When an African heard this folk style, he must have felt at home.

Another characteristic of jazz that probably derives from the music of West Africa may be called the 'falsetto break.' When Blind Sonny Terry is led out on the stage of Town Hall, clutching his precious harmonica, the audience is in for an evening of what he describes as 'whooping.' (Listen to 'Hootin' Blues' on Gramercy 1004.) Whether it's a foxhunt or a lonesome train or simply the blues, Terry laces the music with electrifying falsetto yells. They're something like a cowboy's 'Yippee' except that they can also be far more subtle, varied, and above all, 'bluesy.' The street-cry and field-holler of the American Negro are earlier examples of the same tradition.

In 1955, Count Basie's singer, Joe Williams, explaining the 'yells' he inserts in his vocals, said, 'I heard those street cries on Chicago's South Side.' A 1953 jukebox hit by Tommy Ridgley, 'Looped' (Imperial 5203) was founded upon a convincing mixture of the falsetto break and the hiccup. The falsetto break had been built into instrumental jazz at an early date. Thinking of his instrument as an extension of his voice, the jazzman often employs a similar technical effect. The falsetto break is common, of course, in West Africa and survives in the South today.

To return for a moment to the tribesmen and drums in Dahomey, West Africa, the listener could also have heard —in addition to the complicated rhythms—the use of the falsetto break, blue tonality, and the inevitable call-and-response pattern. They have all survived, in whole or in part, in the music of the United States and may be identified in the new blend—jazz.

Are there any other characteristics of West African music that survive in jazz today? Indeed there are, but they consist of a strange assortment of apparently unrelated details. One characteristic, for example, is simply a matter of the kind of words that go with a song. The New Orleans Creole clarinetist Albert Nicholas still sings this to a rhumba rhythm (Circle 1018): [5]

> Si vous tchoué ain poule pour moi,
> Mêlé li dans ain fricassay,
> Pas blié pou mête la sauce tomate
> Avec ain gros gallon di vin
>
> Sali dame, sali dame, sali dame, un bon jour,
> Sali dame, laissez mo woir, to to, woir to-to.

The language is Creole French and the New Orleans Creoles call it a 'signifying song.'

In spite of its gaiety and rhumba-like rhythms, this song cuts two ways and the *sali dame* (dirty lady) to which it is addressed is about to have her reputation shredded. ('To-to' means both 'toe' and 'backside.') In West Africa, these numbers are called songs of allusion and the people at whom they are directed actually pay the singers to stop singing and go away. A good man who improvises imaginatively can make a fine living out of it. The same kind of song, an archaic and rhythmic type of calypso, pops up in Trinidad as a devastating political weapon.

The lyrics of many jazz tunes are salted with the same loving insults. They occur especially in the blues. Bessie Smith sings 'Dirty No Gooder's Blues,' among others, and Louis Armstrong puts new fire into the standard 'You Rascal You' (Okeh 41504):

> I'll be standing on the corner high,
> When they bring your body by,
> I'll be glad when you're dead
> You rascal you,

while Wynonie Harris shouts 'Don't Roll Those Blood-shot Eyes at Me' (King 4461). For maximum contrast, however, compare Tin-Pan Alley's neurotic statement: 'I Want a Paper Dolly All My Own' with the harsh but healthy billet-doux: 'You Ain't Nothin' But a Hound Dog' (Peacock 1612), as sung by Willie Mae 'Big Mama' Thornton.[6]

A further combination of West African elements has survived almost intact in the ring-shout of the deep South. John and Alan Lomax ran full tilt into one in Jennings, Louisiana, in 1934, and recorded it for the Library of Congress. 'The community had recently re-introduced the ring-shout as a means of attracting and holding in the church the young people who wanted to dance.'[7] Lomax has also seen shouts in Texas, Mrs. Lydia Parrish saw them in Georgia, James Weldon Johnson saw them in Haiti and Florida, and I have seen them in South Carolina, within recent years.

The dancers form a circle in the center of the floor, one in back of another. Then they begin to shuffle in a counter-clockwise direction around and around, arms out and shoulders hunched. A fantastic rhythm is built up by the rest of the group standing back to the walls, who clap their hands and stomp on the floor. Wave after wave of song is led by the shouting preacher, whose varying cry is answered by the regular response of the congregation. Suddenly, sisters and brothers scream and spin, possessed by religious hysteria, like corn starting to pop over a hot fire.

This is actually a West African circle dance. It survived more or less by accident. The Protestant religion discourages dancing and the playing of instruments. But dancing is defined as crossing the feet, and in this religious ceremony of West Africa the dancers never cross their feet anyway. Further, drum rhythms can be easily improvised by clapping and stomping. The only real difference is that the preacher is shouting, moaning, and groaning in English, although the words are sometimes as satirical as they are religious.

In spite of the seeming chaos, everything is under control. Whenever a sister becomes possessed, the people around her take care that she doesn't hurt herself. The same thing occurs in Africa and the West Indies, and I have witnessed it in Haiti. For the whole point of the occasion is to 'get religion' by becoming possessed—but in the correct way. This is a complicated and sacred ritual. It seems to offer, among other things, what the sociologists call an emotional release and perhaps that is why, or so they say, that such a thing as a nervous breakdown is unknown in West Africa.

The continued existence of the ring-shout is of critical importance to jazz, because it means that an assortment of West African musical characteristics are preserved, more or less intact, in the United States—from rhythms and blue tonality, through the falsetto break and the call-and-response pattern, to the songs of allusion and even the motions of the African dance. And an entire way of life has survived with it. Many jazzmen, even among the ultra-moderns, are familiar with all or part of it because they lived with or near one of the Sanctified Churches during childhood. As the Elders of this church are supposed to have observed: 'The Devil shouldn't have all those good rhythms.' The ring-shout is a reservoir of West African qualities that are continually giving new life to jazz.

But how and why did European and West African music blend so easily? The fact is that, unlike other musics of the world, they are very much alike.[8] In ancient times, Europe and Africa were connected—part of the same continent—according to archaeologists. Folk tales, religions, prehistoric arts, and implements of the two areas are similar. So is the music. European and West African music both use the diatonic scale (the white notes on the piano keyboard) in their tunes, and both employ a certain amount of harmony. Now and then, the diatonic scale is found elsewhere in the musics of the world but harmony nowhere else.

This similarity is between European folk music and West African tribal music, however, and does not apply to classical music. The main difference is that European folk music is a little more complicated harmonically and African tribal music is a little more complicated rhythmically. They are about equal in regard to melody. At the extremes, modulation from key to key is unknown in Africa and multiple meters are unknown in Europe, but when the African arrived in the New World the folk music that greeted him must have sounded familiar enough, except for a lack of rhythm. The blending has proceeded on many levels in a variety of ways.

The improvised drum solo is an outstanding example. It occurs in all jazz periods from Baby Dodds to Max Roach. It also occurs in West Africa. It is not found, however, in any European music. So the spectacular drumming of gum-chewing, tousled-haired Gene Krupa, the frantic idol of the bobby-soxers in the 'thirties, for example, is essentially African in concept. The instruments upon which he is pounding are European, but the general idea probably originated in West Africa and nowhere else. And now it has traveled all around the world.

2 | From Africa to the New World

What are the roots of jazz and how did they take hold in the New World? We know quite a bit about the European music that contributed to jazz, but our knowledge of the African music that became an essential part of it is still scanty. Many African musical characteristics survived in the New World—adapted, blended, and changed to fit new conditions. The range and intensity of these survivals, however, is a subject that needs more study. Still and all, we do have enough information at present to indicate certain general patterns. Indeed, some day we may be able to identify the exact rhythms of the particular tribes that helped to create jazz.

It is becoming clear, for example, that the various stages in the development of the slave trade had a decisive influence on what part of Africa the slaves came from, as well as where they were taken in the New World. It was once thought that the slaves came from all over Africa and that only weak and 'inferior' Africans were captured and sold into slavery. Under such conditions, African customs would have a poor chance of survival. But the majority of slaves came from the West coast of Africa—especially Senegal, the Guinea coast, the Niger delta, and the Congo —as anthropologist Melville J. Herskovits has shown,[1] while inter-tribal raids and dynastic wars in West Africa

16

led to the selling of kings and priests into slavery, people who were specialists in their own tribal music and rituals.

Thus, the fact that many West African customs, musical and otherwise, survived in the New World is not surprising. Further, these customs were continually renewed by the arrival of more Africans for, although the slave trade was banned by the United States in 1808, contraband slaves directly from Africa were smuggled into the country as late as Civil War days. At the same time, people from the West Indies with strong African traditions were immigrating to this country as, indeed, they still do to this day. Since West Africa had no literature, customs and rituals were always memorized and handed down by example and word of mouth. And elements of West African music, invisible and preserved in a state of mind that cannot be policed, are still very much with us.

Certain patterns evolved with the slave trade. As the search for slaves advanced down the West coast of Africa from around Dakar all the way to the Congo, first Portuguese traders, then Dutch, and then English—with the French a poor second—dominated the trade. Each European power supplied its own colonies in the New World with slaves from the tribes it had plundered, and the planters in each of the colonies naturally came to prefer the tribesmen supplied by the mother country. England, a partial exception, tended to sell slaves to anyone who would buy, and Spain tended to buy from anyone who would sell. Colonial preferences nevertheless became generally fixed.

Accordingly, Brazilian planters—supplied at an early date with Senegalese slaves by Portuguese traders—preferred Senegalese slaves thereafter. In the same way, Spanish planters came to prefer Yorubas, English planters Ashantis, and French planters Dahomeans. There were many exceptions, of course, but the over-all pattern survives to this day: the predominant African music in Cuba (originally

Spanish) is Yoruban, in Jamaica (British) Ashanti, and in Haiti (formerly French) Dahomean. Now the Dahomeans were the original *vodun* worshippers—the snake god Damballa is one of their deities—and the fact that New Orleans was once a French colony helps to explain why this city is the 'hoodoo' capital of the United States today and may give us a clue as to why jazz was born in New Orleans.

At a later stage, after the Africans had arrived in the New World, the differing environments began to shape new patterns. The African fitted in as best he could and, since it was virtually the West African custom to adopt the deities and attitudes of one's conquerors, he soon began to assimilate the new culture. The colonies reflected the cultures of their mother countries and the slave met with a rather different music, religion, and attitude toward himself in the different colonies.

Much depended, for example, on whether the slave was sold to a British-Protestant or a Latin-Catholic colony. In the first place, the music of the Latin colonies, and especially the Spanish, had more rhythmic life. Perhaps because of the Moorish conquest of Spain in the Middle Ages—the Moors came from North Africa—Spanish music employed elements of improvisation and complex rhythms. An example that survives to this day is the *flamenco* (compare also the *fado* of Portugal). And the numerous church festivals in Latin colonies gave the slaves many opportunities to hear this music.

On the other hand, the Protestant hymns in British colonies were often 'droned out . . . like the braying of asses,' according to John Adams.[2] With the remote exception of the 'Scotch snap,' an elementary bit of syncopation that occurs only incidentally in jazz (hum the tune of 'Gin a Body Meet a Body Comin' thro' the Rye'), the slave heard little or no music with any rhythmic complexity in the African sense of the word. Perhaps the march came as close as any type of music to appealing to the African, simply because it lent itself to the addition of super-imposed rhythms in the African manner.

In the second place, the general attitude and point of view of the Latin-Catholic planters, as contrasted to the attitude of the British-Protestant slave-owners, permitted the survival of more West African traditions. If a planter was Portuguese, Spanish, or French, he dominated the lives of his slaves outwardly—and often with cruelty—but he didn't seem to care about what a slave thought or did in his spare time so long as it didn't interfere with production. Perhaps the attitude of the planters was influenced by centuries of civilized interchange between the Mediterranean countries and North Africa. A kind of cultural *laissez faire* existed whereby the African retained his customs if only by default.

With a British owner, however, a slave was likely to change his ways more quickly, discarding his own traditions and adopting the new. For the British did not specialize in large plantations and each slave-owner possessed fewer slaves. Thus, a slave could come to know his master more easily. Sometimes he was employed as a house slave and, watching his master, became ashamed of his own customs which were thought savage and barbaric. Wanting to improve his condition, he frequently made a point of concealing his own traditions which, in many cases, were consequently forced underground.

Moreover, British-Protestant slave-owners appeared to be much more concerned about what a slave did or thought in his spare time and whether or not he was a Christian. One of the early justifications of slavery argued that it converted the heathen. But then, it followed logically that, once converted, a slave should be a free Christian. The State of Virginia solved this problem as early as 1667 by decreeing: 'Baptism doth not alter the condition of the person as to his bondage or freedom.' Thereafter slaves were permitted to become Christians and remain slaves. By contrast, this problem never bothered Latin colonies. Planters simply assumed, according to the *Code Noir,* that slaves remained slaves whether or not they joined the Catholic Church.

In the third place—and perhaps of greatest importance —whether a slave became a Protestant or a Catholic had a direct effect on the survival of his native music. For a West African in a Latin-Catholic colony soon discovered that a great many Catholic saints bore interesting resemblances to his own gods.[3] The church had pictures of the saints—inexpensive and plentiful chromolithographs— which suggested pointed parallels. St. Patrick, pictured driving the snakes out of Ireland, reminded the slave of his own Damballa, the snake god of the Dahomeans. So on St. Patrick's day, the slaves played the drum rhythms sacred to Damballa and worshipped both Damballa and St. Patrick at the same time and on the same improvised altar.

The ease with which West African and the Catholic religions fused—a process called syncretism by the anthropologists—as well as the extreme flexibility of the slave when it came to adopting new deities is strikingly illustrated in a photograph by Earl Leaf of a Haitian *vodun* altar. Among a variety of African charms and fetishes are several chromolithographs of Catholic saints and religious scenes, plus a forceful photograph of Admiral Ernest J. King of the United States Navy. Clad in a white uniform and staring resolutely forward, the admiral is obviously a powerful antidote to the forces of evil.

In the same manner and in a variety of ways, St. Anthony became associated with Legba, the Dahomean god of the crossroads, since both were imagined and pictured as tattered old men. John the Baptist, portrayed with a shepherd's crook, was identified with Shango, the Yoruban god of thunder whose symbol is the ram. And St. Michael, pictured with a sword, called to mind Ogun, the Yoruban god of war. The identifications varied in different localities—in New Orleans, for example, Limba (Legba?) is still associated with St. Peter—but the over-all process was the same.

These parallels functioned as a kind of bridge to the New World over which West African music could be carried, modified, and preserved. And African rhythms survived more or less by accident. Here again, the Protestant religions of British colonies had no hierarchy of saints and, indeed, forbade any such pictures. The Baptist and Methodist denominations, which most actively proselytized for Negro members, strictly prohibited both dancing and drumming—the two outstanding characteristics of African religion—not so much as a safety precaution against revolts (the usual reason for prohibiting drumming in Catholic colonies) but as a matter of religious principle. So African music either disappeared or went underground.

Parenthetically, the West Africans had no inherent or 'instinctive' sense of rhythm which would have survived in any case. They came from a culture which happened to have fantastically complicated rhythms but only those rhythms survived which in one way or another were permitted to do so. A good part of the West African musical heritage, however, survived unconsciously—through attitudes, motions, habits, points of view, mannerisms, and gestures carried down from generation to generation without thought or plan.

A child might absorb some part of African rhythms, for example, simply by watching and listening to his mother sweep the floor. In her *Slave Songs of the Georgia Sea Islands,* Lydia Parrish prints parallel photographs of three native women in West Africa pounding corn in a pestle and three American Negro women in Georgia pounding rice. The sticks and the pestles are very similar but the important point is that both groups appear to be singing rhythmically as they pound. In the Georgia photograph, a little child is standing close by in rapt attention, absorbing the entire performance.

What light do these general patterns, formed in connection with the development of the slave trade and the changed New World environment, throw on the origins of jazz? We are still in the process of filling out the patterns which helped and hindered the survival of African music in the New World, but we can already pin down the dominant tribal style that existed in certain areas. Further, we know that these musical characteristics tended to survive in Latin-Catholic colonies and to disappear or go underground in British-Protestant colonies.

This is not to say that jazz evolved in Latin-Catholic surroundings because of the greater prevalence of African music, or even that going underground in British-Protestant surroundings contributed indirectly to the evolution of jazz—although, as we shall see, there may be some truth in both hypotheses. It is enough to observe that the elements of West African music which contributed to the blend that became jazz were certainly present and active in the New World. In the following pages we shall examine a variety of musical blendings in various parts of the New World in an effort to reconstruct the pattern that led to jazz.

3 | The West Indies and the United States

Each island in the West Indies is a sort of musical test-tube in which West African and European music have been mixed in more or less known quantities, thus furnishing possible clues to what must have happened in the United States. No one island, of course, has exactly the same combination of ingredients, and the United States has a still different and perhaps more complicated mixture of its own. Although the results vary, the over-all pattern of blending is the same.

At one extreme is Dutch Guiana, located in the northern part of South America, where the Bush-Negroes live. It is jungle country and, from the first, many slaves escaped inland where they flourished. A wide sampling of the music of Dutch Guiana has been recorded by Herskovits and analyzed by Kolinski, who found: 'With the exception of a few songs, the music of the Bush-Negroes displays traits that are essentially African.'[1] In fact, since African music has been influenced by ours in recent times, Bush-Negro music, it has been suggested, is more African than African music today. Kolinski also discovered that the songs of the coastal Negroes, who lived in a predominantly European culture, were about 23 per cent African. Thus, in Dutch Guiana we find a pattern of survival ranging from a little less than one-quarter to almost total retention.

Haiti is a more complicated but more illuminating example. Haiti was supplied with slaves by French traders, among others, and the French planters preferred Dahomeans. Hence it is not surprising that although Courlander found traces of at least thirty-seven African tribes in Haiti, he found the dominant culture to be Dahomean.[2] Today Haiti is probably the most 'primitive' island this side of Africa. As Courlander says: [3]

On the plantations and off, the Negroes never forgot the drum rhythms of their own countries, nor their ancestors and deities. They never forgot how to make fine drums. And whether the drum was of a Congo pattern, or Ibo, or Arada, all men listened to it, and danced in the light of the smoking oil lamps.

The Arada tribe is Dahomean and its members are practitioners of *vodun*. (For twelve years, from 1847 to 1859, *vodun* was virtually the official religion of Haiti.) At the same time, just about everyone in Haiti is a member of the Catholic Church. *Vodun* and Catholicism have merged, for the Haitian peasant gladly adopts the Catholic religion to reinforce his African beliefs.

On a field trip to Haiti in 1953, I witnessed a *vodun* ceremony presided over by a young *houngan*, or priest, named Dr. Jean Dieudonné. He looked so much like the late saxophonist Charlie Parker that it made me uneasy. For three or more hours, the *hounsis*, or priestesses, danced and sang a regular response to the *houngan's* cries, while the drum trio pounded away hypnotically. In a back room was an oven-like altar. Within the oven was a tank of water containing a snake, sacred to Damballa, and on top of this altar was a second, smaller one, containing a blond baby doll of the Coney Island variety and a statuette of the Madonna, twin symbols of Ezulie, goddess of fertility and chastity.

About eleven o'clock the lid blew off. Drinking from a paper-wrapped bottle, the *houngan* sprayed some liquid out of his mouth in a fine mist and the *mambos*, or women dancers, became seized with religious hysteria, or 'possessed,' much like an epileptic fit. The rest of the group kept the 'possessed' ones from hurting themselves. I saw one young and stately priestess, who had earlier impressed me with the poise and dignity of her dancing, bumping across the dirt floor in time with the drums. The spirit of Damballa, the snake god, had entered her.

I shall never know how much of the performance was authentic. The drums, and the rhythms played upon them, were Dahomean. The whole ceremony was similar to, but decidedly more orderly than, some revival meetings—both white and Negro—that I have observed in the United States. This was probably because in Haiti they had a formal goal, namely, possession, and it was reached in a highly ritualized fashion. I noticed that several *mambos*, emerging from possession, simply sat down and fell into a peaceful sleep.

Secular African rhythms have survived in Haiti, too, in the *coumbite* (Dahomean: 'dokpwe'), or communal work-group. Their songs are similar to our own work songs. On the other hand, predominantly European mixtures, such as the *meringue* with its French folk melodies, also occur in Haiti. The Haitian *meringues* sometimes sound a little like our ragtime without the force and drive.

These parallels between Haitian and American music help to establish an over-all pattern. Both Haiti and New Orleans, for example, were Latin-colonial—French and Spanish—until the early 1800's. Africans from the same tribes arrived in both areas. In fact, many slaves came to New Orleans direct from Haiti during the revolution, brought there by fleeing French planters. The chief difference is that, from this time on, New Orleans but not Haiti

felt the influence of British Protestantism, American variety, and sudden prosperity.

In 1885, a correspondent of the New York *World,* watching the dancing of the Negroes in New Orleans' Congo
Square, asked a colored lady what the dance was. 'C'est le
Congo,' she replied.[4] The Congo, as such, is no longer
danced in New Orleans, but it is still danced in Haiti, along
with the Bamboula, the Juba, the Calinda, and the Coun-
jaille—dances that are mentioned frequently by early vis-
itors to New Orleans. The Haitian versions, which have
remained more or less untouched, are probably similar to
the early New Orleans dances which have disappeared.

Another pattern for comparison occurs in Cuba.[5] The
music varies from Yoruba rhythms to Spanish songs. This
wide range reflects Cuba's historical background accurately. For many years a Spanish possession, into which
Africans were smuggled as late as the 1880's, Cuba became
a republic in 1902. Unlike Haiti, Cuba welcomed outside
influences, in particular American capital, and has become
prosperous more recently.

We are better acquainted with certain Cuban music because Cuba has its own Tin-Pan Alley, which in recent
years has been closely linked with our own. The tango and
its rhythms, which became the rage of New York City in
1914 over the protests of educators and clergymen, are a
development of the Habanera (Havana). The word 'tango'
is of African origin and the dance, according to Slonimsky,
illustrates what the Africans in Cuba could do with an
English country dance.

Of the native Cuban dances, the Habanera, Guajira,
Punto, and Guaracha contain strong Spanish elements,
while the Rhumba, Conga, Son Afro-Cubano, Mambo, and
Cha-Cha are predominantly African. The chief difference,
of course, is in the rhythm. And even the amount of rhythm
in any one dance can vary. The rhumba, which is by far

the most popular outside of Cuba, is consistently diluted for Western ears and has become a fixture at fashionable American night clubs. Played by a real Afro-Cuban band, however, the true rhumba can develop into a rhythmic holocaust.

These dances and their rhythms show us only the surface of Cuban music. There is a lively religious group in Cuba known as Los Santos, or The Saints, which is quite similar to the following of Daddy Grace and Father Divine in the United States. The Saints, dressed in pure white, stage elaborate religious rituals which culminate in possession, much like our own revival meetings. But the musical instruments for such occasions consist of Yoruban drums, shaped like hour glasses, and the drumming and singing are in the Yoruban style.

Another and more important brand of West African music is sung, danced, and played by secret societies, or *cabildos*, in Cuba.[6] The chief cults are the Arara from Dahomey (Haitian 'Arada,' the practitioners of *vodun*), the Kimbisa from the Congo, the Lucumi from the Slave Coast, and the Abakwa from the region of the Niger River. Each has its own type of West African instrument, rhythm, and dialect. The Abakwa, members of which are slightingly known as 'Nanigos,' is the most important and includes members of other cults and even a few whites.

These secret societies actually continue organizations that existed in Africa. They have been outlawed, whenever the political situation needed a scapegoat, but on the other hand they are also asked to furnish the rhythmic propulsion for the annual Mardi Gras. The Cuban dancer, drummer, and composer, Chano Pozo, was a member of the Abakwa and became the hit of Mardi Gras. Pozo had a direct impact on jazz when he joined the Dizzy Gillespie band in 1947.

In a search for Pozo's antecedents I was taken to the Cayo Hueso, or slum district, of Havana. I met his grandmother in a narrow, crowded alley where dozens of families live outdoors all the year round. As the only white man and in the company of a brown-skinned guide, I met with silent hostility. My guide actually did not dare to ask the pipe-smoking old lady if she was born in Africa. Later, I met Pozo's father, a shoeshine 'boy,' and learned that the son was two generations from Africa. Puzzled tears came to the father's eyes as he asked me why his oldest and last son had been murdered in Harlem.

It was not difficult to find drummers in Cuba. In a bare tenement room I recorded the songs and rhythms of the various secret societies. The drummers knew most of them, but their favorites were Yoruban and derived from the Lucumi cult. The most impressive number was dedicated to Chango, the Yoruban thunder god, known as Shango in Trinidad. Another, in praise of 'Legua,' was similar to the rhythms of the Dahomean Legba, the guardian of the cross-roads in Haiti.

What patterns occur in Cuba? Like Haiti, Cuba dupli-cates the Latin-Catholic background of New Orleans up to 1803. Unlike Haiti, Cuba has become relatively prosperous in recent years. Neither Haiti nor Cuba, however, felt the influence of British Protestantism until very recently. No jazz evolved in Cuba, and yet Cuban popular music and the dances associated with it have spread over the Western world. The mixture of Spanish and African music, in vary-ing amounts, seems to be a highly palatable product.

Perhaps a more significant pattern for comparison occurs in Trinidad, for here we find the additional influence of British Protestantism.[7] Originally Spanish, Trinidad admit-ted Catholic colonists—mostly French—from 1783 to 1797, when it became a British colony and English planters moved in. Thus, the aristocracy of the island still consists of Span-ish, French, and British families, in that order. In our time, laborers have been imported from the Orient—Chinese and

East Indians—and with the discovery of oil, Trinidad has prospered.

The music of Trinidad runs the gamut from predominantly European to essentially West African. The calypso, Trinidad's best-known creation, can be heard in the United States in a diluted version in such popular hits as 'Rum and Coca-Cola,' or in Trinidad in a more rhythmic version in a West African style. It is derived, in part, from the biting West African songs of ridicule and is still used as a political weapon when more direct means would bring reprisal. It also contains, according to some theorists, the melody and harmony of French folk songs, a dialect of several languages, and African rhythms. Its influence is now felt throughout the West Indies.

Like Haiti and Cuba, nevertheless, Trinidad has its African cult, or secret society, music. Much of this is Yoruban and dedicated to Shango, the god of thunder. The instruments have changed, however, for when drums were banned Trinidad Negroes adopted tambos—bamboo sticks tapped on the ground one at a time. When tambos were banned —with some reason, for they made formidable weapons— Trinidadians invented the steel band. The vogue of the steel band has invaded many other islands in the West Indies, and has even reached New York. (After hearing a steel band at the Jazz Roundtable at Music Inn, composer Henry Cowell scored part of a new symphony for steel drums.) Just one type of instrument is used: a drum made from the top of a huge oil barrel, heated and hammered until it responds with a variety of notes when struck in certain spots. Trinidad drummers march a hundred strong during a festival, playing the latest pop tune amidst a boiler factory of sound.

The special significance of Trinidad's background, however, lies in the rather early existence of Protestantism. When England took over in 1797, Catholicism and African fetish were already partly fused. The northern religion did not make much headway except with a small group of converts to the Baptist faith in Toco, a village in the northeastern part of the island. They are called Shouters with some accuracy, for they generated enough excitement and noise to be officially banned. Unlike The Saints in Cuba, the Trinidad Shouters banned dancing and drumming, according to the Baptist rules. Hand-clapping and foot-stamping evolved to take the place of the drums, and the ceremonies became famous for their revivalist power and frenzy. Complaints poured in for a radius of several miles whenever the Shouters held a meeting. Here is a new pattern: Protestantism superimposed upon a mixture of African and Catholic ritual, leading to revival music such as is found in the United States.

A recording of the Shouters, made by Herskovits, furnishes an amazing parallel. The tune is 'Jesus Lover of My Soul,' a standard hymn from the Moody and Sankey hymnbook. Beginning in a very stolid manner, the Shouters intone the tune 'as written.' Gradually, rhythms are introduced; one singer starts to imitate a drum, another begins to clap on the off-beat, a third introduces a falsetto cry. Soon the call-and-response pattern dominates the performance, which builds into a rhythmic jamboree of such intensity that it might well produce religious possession.[8]

The recording is a capsule demonstration of the Africanization of a British hymn. In the space of four minutes, the European elements are transformed into African elements. Thus, when people of African descent perform European hymns, according to the prohibitions of Protestant religion, the music seems to bear a strong resemblance to one of the precursors of jazz in the United States—the shouting spiritual. Add European instruments and you have something very near to early jazz.

Another pattern for comparison occurs in the Bahamas,

which had little or no Latin-Catholic influence. The out-standing fact about the Bahamas is their poverty, relieved in recent years by the tourist business. Their contact with the United States has been close for a century and a half. Bimini was a busy port during Prohibition and, in 1954, I found that the latest rhythm-and-blues hits from Harlem were played on juke boxes in the Negro section of Nassau. The keen admiration for the United States is symbolized by the fact that the so-called 'natives' prefer a Buick to a Rolls-Royce. Social distinctions are hard and fast, neverthe-less, for the Bahamas are a typical British colony.

The music of the Bahamas is very similar to the music of the United States.[9] There are, however, subtle differences. The calypso influence is stronger but its current exponent, Blind Blake, acknowledges the early influence of Bessie Smith. Spirituals called 'ant'hems' are still sung in the old American style, as well as the latest gospel songs. Except for the addition of a formidable Salvation Army band accom-paniment, the services of the Sanctified Church are similar to those held in the United States, where the denomination originated.

And yet drumming on native drums in the African manner still flourishes (Folkways LP 440), although all the jazz in the Bahamas came from the United States. Why? Perhaps because there was no Latin-Catholic background to assist in a blending. Perhaps because the United States emerged from colonial status at an early date. This meant social upheaval which broke down colonial attitudes, sharp-ened awareness of Negro-white relationships, and permitted the Negro to integrate himself more completely with the dominant culture. In the stable British colonial relation-ships of the Bahamas, unchanged because of one ruling class, poverty, and a lack of industrial development, class distinctions insulated Negro from white. African drumming may have survived simply by default, but later, it became an asset to festivals and the tourist trade, and was encouraged.

Martinique, on the other hand, was colonized by the French in 1635 and has remained a French colony ever since. The music of the island, much like that of Haiti, runs the gamut from West African cult music to French folk songs. Unlike Haiti, Martinique remained a French colonial possession, and a musical blending resulted that is very close to New Orleans Creole music, even to the clarinet and trombone style and instrumentation. Music from the Select Tango dance-hall in Fort de France documents the Bechet-like clarinet, the Ory-like trombone, and the raggy piano, playing waltzes, galops, and mazurkas with a kind of 'jazzy' rhythm (Dial LP 402). This Martinique music is slightly less martial, more complex rhythmically, and a little lighter than the Creole music of New Orleans, which is a demonstrable component of jazz.

What conclusions can we draw from the known patterns in Dutch Guiana, Haiti, Cuba, Trinidad, the Bahamas, and Martinique? West African religious music such as *vodun* survived best of all, because it was highly formalized and could mix with elements of Christianity, especially Catholicism. Where Protestantism existed, the blending took the direction of shouting revival music. Above all, a Latin-Catholic environment appears to have assisted the survival of African qualities.

In general, the cities and especially New Orleans (but cf. also Mobile and Charleston) seem to have evolved a blend of march music and satirical love song similar—even in instrumentation—to the Afro-French music of Martinique. On the other hand, the countryside, dominated by Protestant religions in the United States, seems to have evolved the style of the preacher and shouting congregation as in Toco, Trinidad. And then, of course, both traditions began to mix and blend in the southern United States in an endless variety of ways.

Living in New Orleans in 1880, Lafcadio Hearn wrote: 'the melancholy, quavering beauty and weirdness of the Negro chant are lightened by the French influence, or subdued and deepened by the Spanish.' [10] The contrasting music of Cuba and Martinique seems to bear out this insight—the former blending Spanish and the latter French music with West African. Again, prosperity certainly hastened the development and extended the influence of the merging wherever it occurred. Could it be that the Latin-Catholic background of New Orleans gave the West African musical heritage a head start in the blending of European and African musics, which was later slowed down and forced underground by the gradual advent of Protestantism after the Louisiana Purchase? Then, in turn, could this double process of speed-up and slow-down have forced a more radical integration, creating a new combination and a new music? In the following pages, we shall investigate this hypothesis.

PART TWO : **NEW ORLEANS**

4 | The New Orleans Background

New Orleans has a special place in the story of jazz. A Latin-Catholic possession for eighty-two years, it became part of a predominantly British-Protestant country after the Louisiana Purchase. At times, the patterns of music in New Orleans resembled those of different islands in the West Indies. The combination and the timing in the blend of West African music with European was unique, however, and led to the birth of a new music. For the New Orleans environment was decidedly different from that of the rest of the United States.

For its first forty-six years New Orleans was a French possession and customs were established that have endured to this day. The city was ceded by France to Spain in 1764, and the Spanish governed it for the next thirty-six years; New Orleans nevertheless remained fundamentally French in thought and feeling.[1] At this stage, it resembled the French West Indies, with music that probably was similar to Martinique's or Haiti's today. The big change, political and economic, came at the turn of the century. In 1800, Napoleon forced Spain to return the territory to France, and for three years no one in New Orleans was quite sure whether the city belonged to France or Spain. Then, in 1803, Napoleon sold the territory to the United States.

The prosperity that resulted in the city of New Orleans

37

and which played its part in shaping New Orleans music was due in part to the Western migration of Americans to the valleys of the Ohio and Mississippi rivers. Between the years 1776 and 1820, the number of settlers west of the Allegheny Mountains increased from 12,000 to 2,000,000. They needed supplies, and the cheapest way to transport the supplies to them was by riverboat from New Orleans. On the other hand, flatboats floated raw materials down from the newly settled lands to the port city. In 1803, the tonnage of ships using the port increased 50 per cent. The population of the city at this time was approximately 10,000—half white and half Negro. With the opening of the Louisiana Territory to Americans, a great influx of people into New Orleans began. The population doubled in seven years. The demand for entertainment—musical and otherwise—increased accordingly. And at the same time the invasion of British-Protestant culture commenced. New Orleans became a boom town and one of the chief cities of the New World.

The Negroes, of course, participated in the development of the city and its music. From what part of West Africa did they come and what elements of their customs survived? We may never know the whole story, but we do have several clues. Many came from the West Indies. The editors of *Gumbo Ya-Ya* state that 500 slaves from Martinique, Guadeloupe, and San Domingo (part of which later became Haiti) were imported into Louisiana in 1776, and 3,000 more the following year.[2] These islands were French possessions at the time, and the slaves were mainly Yorubas and Dahomeans, worshippers of *vodun*. From 1809 to 1810, more than 3,000 arrived from San Domingo, by way of Cuba, their French masters having fled the Haitian revolution.

Many more had come directly from West Africa. Not long after the Civil War, Africans from a variety of tribes could be identified in New Orleans. An essay by G. W. Cable, who lived in New Orleans before and after the Civil War, gives us the observations of an acute eyewitness: [3]

See them . . . tall, well-knit Senegalese from Cape Verde, black as ebony, with intelligent, kindly eyes and long, straight, shapely noses; Mandingoes, from the Gambia River, lighter of color, of cruder form, and a cunning that shows in the countenance; whose enslavement seems specially a shame, their nation the 'merchants of Africa,' dwelling in towns, industrious, thrifty, skilled in commerce and husbandry, and expert in the working of metals, even to silver and gold; and Foulahs, playfully miscalled '*Poulards*,'—fat chickens—of goodly stature, and with a perceptible rose tint in the cheeks; and Sosos, famous warriors, dexterous with the African targe; and in contrast to these, with small ears, thick eyebrows, bright eyes, flat, upturned noses, shining skin, wide mouths and white teeth, the Negroes of Guinea, true and unmixed, from the Gold Coast, the Slave Coast, and the Cape of Palms—not from the Grain Coast; the English had that trade. See them come! Popoes, Cotocolies, Fidas, Socoes, Agwas, short, copper-colored Mines—what havoc the slavers did make—and from interior Africa others equally proud and warlike: fierce Nagoes and Fonds; tawny Awassas; Iboes, so light colored that one could not tell them from mulattoes but for their national tattooing; and the half-civilized and quick-witted but ferocious Arada, the original Voudou worshipper. And how many more! For here come, also, men and women from all the great Congo coast—Angola, Malimbe, Ambrice, etc. . . . the most numerous sort of negro in the colonies, the Congoes and Franc-Congoes, and though serpent worshippers, yet the gentlest and kindliest natures that came from Africa.

Some eighteen tribal names and localities, many of which are now known by other names, are listed here.

Cable has done a pretty systematic job in listing African tribes from Dakar to the Congo. The Mandingoes, Senegalese, Foulahs, and Sosos came from northwest Africa around and below Dakar. He explicitly excludes the Grain Coast (now Sierra Leone and Liberia). The Agwas and, perhaps, the Socoes came from the Ivory and Gold Coasts, in and near Ashanti territory. The Popes, Fidas, Cotocolies, and Aradas came from in and around Dahomey. The Nagoes, Fonds, Awassas, and Iboes came from Nigeria, home of the Yorubas, and adjoining lands. And the Angolas, Malimbes, and Ambrices came from the Congo.

The emphasis here is upon the four areas that Herskovits specifies: Senegal, the Guinea coast, the Niger delta, and the Congo. The Ashantis (preferred by the British) are not well represented, while the Congo tribes, which arrived late, are referred to as the most numerous. Four tribes each from the vicinity of Nigeria and Dahomey are specified, however, which bears out the preferences of French and Spanish planters. Further, Cable mentions the Slave Coast, which included Dahomey, and singles out for comment 'the half-civilized and quick-witted but ferocious Arada, the original Voudou worshipper,' a Dahomean tribesman.

Since *vodun* (or voodoo or hoodoo) has survived in the United States to this day, the mention of the Arada tribe— as we have discovered—is significant. Speaking of the parallel example of Haiti, Courlander says, 'The Iboes learned the dances of the Congos, the Arada of the Senegalese. And yet, one culture came to dominate the whole, that of the Dahomeans.'

For the Dahomean religion of *vodun* gave its name and served as a focal point for a constellation of similar rituals from a variety of West African tribes. The combination was both powerful and enduring, and it surfaced later in Congo Square. Herskovits, referring to Cable's novel, *The Grandissimes,* a story of (white) Creole life in ante-bellum New Orleans, carries the point a step further: [4]

The names of several deities which figure in the *vodun* cults of Haiti and Dahomey are mentioned in Cable's novel. Papa Lébat [Legba] . . . Danny [Damballa] . . . Agoussou . . . M.

Assouquer . . . the familiar pouring of a libation . . . the concept of the *zombi* as spirit . . . the magic charm embodied in the term *ouangan* . . . these are familiar aspects of Haitian terminology and important elements in Haitian no less than West African life.

In fact, Cable's stories of the French aristocrats in New Orleans leave the impression that these people spent a good part of each day casting spells or counter-spells on one another according to the Dahomean or *vodun* rituals they had absorbed from the Africans.

The environment in which the African found himself in New Orleans was diverse and changing. Thomas Ashe, who visited the city in 1806, comments on the economic structure in terms of national origin:[5]

The trade of the city is conducted, for the most part, by four classes of men. Virginians and Kentuckians reign over the brokerage and commission business; the Scotch and Irish absorb all the respectable commerce of exportation and importation; the French keep magazines and stores; and the Spaniards do all the small retail trade of grocer's shops, cabants, and the lowest order of drinking houses. People of colour, and free negroes, also keep inferior shops, and sell goods and fruits.

The French and Spanish aristocrats of Latin-Catholic days, it seems, were ill-equipped to compete with the invasion of Yankee traders which followed the Louisiana Purchase, and British-Protestant customs were beginning to make themselves felt.

Yet New Orleans remained—and remains to this day—a preponderantly Latin-Catholic town, a factor which aided the survival of African music. As late as 1846, when geologist Charles Lyell visited the city, he was told that 'in spite of the increase of Protestants . . . there had been quite as much "flour and fun" ' at Mardi Gras.[6] And the music that the African heard in New Orleans was rather congenial as contrasted to the music he might have heard in the rest of the United States. In addition, Africans from the French West Indies, who had already absorbed something of European music, continued to arrive and a further blending was under way.

Again, the range of music with which people of varying degrees of African descent became familiar was unique. On the one hand, the Creoles of Color, who combined Spanish, French, and African ancestry, attained considerable social status for a while and absorbed much of the best European music. They sent their children to Paris to be educated and they had their own opera in New Orleans with a conductor celebrated in Europe. After the Civil War and with the arrival of Northern prejudice, their downfall was slow but complete. They were forced to join their darker brothers and—as we shall see—they had much to contribute, perhaps most clearly by way of technique, to the birth of jazz.

On the other hand, the slaves on the large plantations in the vicinity of New Orleans heard little or no European music. Left pretty much to themselves, these field hands were able to retain much of their musical heritage and the plantations became a reservoir of African music. Between these two extremes, many slaves and free men of color were scattered through the city—a legal measure to discourage rebellion which incidentally reduced segregation. This tendency to make social distinctions along economic rather than racial lines, which later lost its force, also helped to accelerate a blending of musics.

The changing factors that set New Orleans apart from the rest of the United States made for a powerful survival of West African music and an early blending of this music with European music. West African music—and we can pinpoint the dominant tribe and document the high intensity of *vodun* ritual—had a unique measure of survival because of the Latin-Catholic environment. The blending of West

African and European music had a pronounced head start because of the wide range of assimilation by people of color amidst unusual business prosperity. For during its early years, New Orleans was a musical melting pot *par excellence* with a large component of West African ingredients simmering to a boil over the forced draft of a financial boom.

5 | The Transition to Jazz

How did the West African influence survive in New Orleans and blend with European music? Two steps in the process seem to be clear: private *vodun* ceremonies and public performances in Congo Square. The first preserved African music—and especially rhythm—in the midst of its rituals; and the second forced the same music—without as much of the ritual—out into the open where it could easily influence and be influenced by European music.

The Black Code of 1724 forbade all forms of worship except Catholicism. The prevalence of *vodun* among the slaves, however, presented a continual problem. In 1782, Governor Galvez banned the admission of Negroes from Martinique because they practiced voodoo and would 'make the lives of the citizens unsafe.' [1] Others were sent back in 1792. As late as 1803, the Municipal Council banned a shipload of Santo Domingo slaves on the same grounds. *Vodun* was spreading even among the whites.

After the Louisiana Purchase of 1803, the United States lifted all restrictions and immigration boomed. So did *vodun*. Tallant remarks that the Sunday dances of the slaves in Congo Square, legalized by the Municipal Council in 1817, were an attempt 'of the city authorities to combat Voodooism.' [2] They were supposed to act as a kind of safety valve to keep the slaves contented. The dances also became a remunerative tourist attraction at which *vodun* music happened to be played.

Trustworthy early accounts of *vodun* ceremonies are rare. They are also exaggerated. J. W. Buel tells the story of a friend who saw a *vodun* ceremony in 1825, led by the first of the voodoo queens, Sanite Dede:[3]

> . . . I recognized an old negro by the name of Zozo, well-known in New Orleans as a vender of palmetto and sassafras roots . . . He was astride of a cylinder made of thin cypress staves hooped with brass and headed by a sheepskin. With two sticks he droned away a monotonous ra-ta-ta, ra-ta-ta-ta, while on his left sat a negro on a low stool, who with two sheep shank bones, and a negress with the leg-bones of a buzzard or turkey, beat an accompaniment on the sides of the cylinder . . . Some two feet from these arch-musicians squatted a young negro vigorously twirling a long calabash.

These instruments and the style of drumming are still used in the West Indies for the Juba and Bamboula dances. And the 'ra-ta-ta, ra-ta-ta-ta' is a good approximation of one of the rhythms I heard at *vodun* ceremonies in Haiti.

A later account from the New Orleans *Times* (21 March 1869) describes a public ceremony at Lake Ponchatrain. Marie Laveau, the most famous of all voodoo queens, presided. The presence of a reporter shows her belief in the value of publicity, as well as indicating that elements of *vodun* were becoming an accepted part of New Orleans life. According to this report,[4]

> . . . an elderly turbaned female dressed in yellow and red, ascended a sort of dais and chanted a wild sort of fetish song, to which the others kept up an accompaniment with their voices and with a drum-like beat of their hands and feet. At the same time they commenced to move in a circle, while gradually increasing the time.

The drum-like rhythms of the clapping and stamping, the accelerated tempo, the circle dance, and the call-and-response pattern are essentially West African.

A more trustworthy account was written by Charles Dudley Warner in the 'eighties. (It was Warner who collaborated with Mark Twain on *The Gilded Age*.) This illegal affair took place on the second floor of a house near Congo Square. It began with a recitation of the Apostles' Creed, followed by prayers to the Virgin Mary, whose statue stood upon an altar crowded with *vodun* fetishes. Then the singing began: [5]

The chant grew, the single line was enunciated in stronger pulsations, and other voices joined in the wild refrain,

> 'Danse Calinda, boudoum, boudoum!
> Danse Calinda, boudoum, boudoum!'

Bodies swayed, the hands kept time in soft patpatting, and the feet in muffled accentuation.

As the singing became wilder, the 'witch doctor' ignited some brandy and performed a dance with a flaming dish.

The rhythm switched during the dance and a new and more powerful rhythm began:

. . . the chant had been changed for the wild *canga*, more rapid in movement than the *chanson Africaine*:

> Eh! Eh! Bomba, hen! hen!
> Canga bafio, té
> Canga moune dé lé
> Canga do ki la
> Canga li

. . . During his dancing and whirling he frequently filled his mouth with liquid, and discharged it in a spray . . . Having extinguished the candles of the suppliants, he scooped the liquid from the bowl, flaming or not as it might seem, and with his hands vigorously scrubbed their faces and heads . . . While the victim was still sputtering and choking he seized him by the right hand, lifted him up, spun him round a half dozen times, and then sent him whirling.

Here, the ritual details—the changing of rhythm, the spraying of spirits, the spinning of devotees, as well as the igniting of the brandy—are identical with the details of *vodun* ceremonies. Mr. Warner could hardly have invented the real thing. (The words, in an African-Creole dialect, are quite another matter—originally authentic perhaps, they had been reprinted more or less intact by a series of authors over the preceding hundred years.)

A mixture of African gods and Catholic saints took place in New Orleans, too. For example, Legba is the Dahomean god of the crossroads, of luck and fertility, and *vodun* ceremonies in West Africa usually begin with an invocation to him. In New Orleans, Legba was identified with St. Peter, perhaps because St. Peter is represented as carrying keys, which suggest the omniscient powers of Legba. Thus, the sanctity of St. Peter helped to preserve the rituals and rhythms connected with Legba.

For example, recalling stories of Marie Laveau, the late Josephine Green told interviewers: [6]

It was back before the war what they had here wit' the Northerners. My ma heard a noise on Frenchman street where she lived at and she start to go outside. Her pa say, 'Where you goin'? Stay in the house!' She say, 'Marie Laveau is comin' and I gotta see her.' She went outside and here come Marie Laveau wit' a big crowd of people followin' her. My ma say that woman used to strut like she owned the city, and she was tall and good-lookin' and wore her hair hangin' down her back. She looked just like a Indian or one of them Gypsy ladies. She wore big full skirts and lots of jewelry hangin' all over her. All the people wit' her was hollerin' and screamin', 'We is goin' to see Papa Limba! We is goin' to see Papa Limba!' My grandpa go runnin' after my ma then, yellin' at her, 'You come on in here, Eunice! Don't you know Papa

Limba is the devil?' But after that my ma find out Papa Limba means St. Peter, and her pa was jest foolin' her.

Stories about *vodun* in New Orleans are full of garbled references to Legba. Old-timer Alexander Augustin remarked that 'oldtime Voodoos always talked about Papa La Bas,' and another informant named Mary Ellis remembered that 'Marie Laveau used to call St. Peter somethin' like "Laba." '[7]

The Bible itself became a great 'conjur' book, along with a text ascribed to Albertus Magnus which was banned in Haiti and which is available in Harlem bookstores today. For *vodun* is still with us. Anthropologist Zora Neal Hurston, who joined several New Orleans cults in the 'twenties, declares: [8]

New Orleans is now and has ever been the hoodoo capital of America. Great names in rites that vie with those of Hayti in deeds that keep alive the powers of Africa. Hoodoo, or Voodoo, as pronounced by the whites, is burning with a flame in America, with all the intensity of a suppressed religion. It has its thousands of secret adherents.

She participated in a ceremony which was intended to bring death to its victim. No white people were present, and the music consisted of chanting, clapping, and stamping. 'The heel-patting was a perfect drum rhythm,' while 'the hand-clapping had various stimulating breaks,' and the 'fury of the rhythm' kept the dancers going until they became possessed.

As time went on, elements of *vodun* came to the surface under various guises. Even today, voodoo drugstores in New Orleans are doing a profitable business in *gris-gris* or magic charms. Among the voodoo paraphernalia for sale are pictures of Catholic saints, and in his *Voodoo in New Orleans*, Robert Tallant states: [9]

To certain Roman Catholic saints particular Voodoo power has been attributed: St. Michael is thought best able to aid in conquering enemies; St. Anthony de Padua is invoked for 'luck'; St. Mary Magdalene is popular with women who are in love; St. Joseph (holding the Infant Jesus) is used to get a job. Many Voodoos believe a picture of the Virgin Mary in their homes will prevent illness, and that one of St. Peter (with the Key to Heaven) will bring great and speedy success in financial matters (without the Key to Heaven, St. Peter is still reliable in helping in the achievement of minor successes; the *power* of the picture is less, however). Pictures of the Sacred Heart of Jesus are believed to have the ability to cure organic diseases.

'Lodestones,' which are like Haitian loa or fetishes, are also considered powerful charms. More recently, 'John the Conqueror'—good for both love and gambling—is highly popular. (It is manufactured in Chicago.)

Another facet of *vodun* has come to the surface as 'spiritualism.' The 16 May 1953 edition of the *Amsterdam News* of New York, for example, contains twenty-nine advertisements of spiritualists. One mentions Africa as his place of origin and nine name New Orleans. Here is a sample:

QUICK ACTION

Troubled, unlucky, need money? Regardless of what your troubles are I can help any human on earth. Do something about it. 25 years experience searching in Kentucky, South Carolina, Virginia, Birmingham, New Orleans. Learn the secret from old folks in these states who know how to do things. My method brings amazingly quick results. Work guaranteed. A word from three of the thousands of people that I have helped. A.W., New York: I was blessed $500.00 R.P.: I have a new 1953 Mercury. D.M., New York: I never in all my life knew anyone who has helped me as much as you have. Bishop Moody, 3420 Park Ave., Bronx. Hours 2 to 8 P.M. Phone MO. 5-4487.

This is the 'legitimate' side of a big industry.

The famous Ferdinand 'Jelly Roll' Morton was a devout believer. Although removed from the strongest influences by his Creole ancestry, Morton was brought up by his aunt, Eulalie Echo, whom he quite casually calls a 'voodoo witch.' As a youth, he was cured of some illness by voodoo. Later on, during a stay in New York, he burned up a dozen or so new suits at the suggestion of a 'voodoo doctor.' 'I spent thousands of dollars,' says Morton in the book by Alan Lomax, 'trying to get this spell taken off me.' Similarly when questioned about 'voodoo' in his interview with Larry Gara, Baby Dodds replied, 'That's all bosh. Sure I heard of it . . . Practically all people from New Orleans take that seriously. Very much yet.' The attitude of several modern jazzmen, born and bred in the South, is striking: 'This hoodoo jive is nowhere,' they say, 'but man, watch out!'

Other evidences of the survival of *vodun* in our culture keep popping up. Courlander noted *vodun* phrases in a Creole song recorded by John and Alan Lomax for the Library of Congress. Nobody had noticed it. References to 'goofer dust' and other fetishes are preserved in many recorded blues from Cripple Clarence Lofton to Willie Mabon and blues singer Bo Diddley. In 1953, Mr. Anthony Schwartz recorded *vodun* drumming and chanting in New York City.

These scattered examples probably represent the small part of the *vodun* iceberg that shows above water. Secret and illegal, *vodun* preserves elements of African ritual. Among other things, it is a reservoir of rhythm in our culture. In the early days, its greatest influence was felt among the less-educated and darker-skinned Negroes of uptown New Orleans. It is probably no accident that, when jazz began, it came from that part of town.

Public performances by Negroes in an empty lot known as Congo Square occurred off and on from 1817 to 1885.

These brought the sound and a little of the ritual of *vodun* out into the open—speeding up the blending of African with European music. In *The French Quarter*, Herbert Asbury describes the early days: [10]

At a signal from a police official, the slaves were summoned to the center of the square by the prolonged rattling of two huge beef bones upon the head of a cask, out of which had been fashioned a sort of drum or tambourine called the bamboula . . . The favorite dances of the slaves were the Calinda, a variation of which was also used in the Voodoo ceremonies, and the Dance of the Bamboula, both of which were primarily based on the primitive dances of the African jungle . . . the entire square was an almost solid mass of black bodies stamping and swaying to the rhythmic beat of the bones on the cask, the frenzied chanting of the women, and the clanging of pieces of metal which dangled from the ankles of the men.

The Calinda dance is connected with zombiism in Haiti; the Bamboula dance, named perhaps after the material of the drum, is an ancient dance once found in Martinique, Haiti, and the Virgin Islands. Both the instruments and music used in these dances are clearly West African.

An architect named Benjamin Henry Latrobe visited Congo Square in 1819 and described the instruments that he saw: [11]

The music consisted of two drums and a stringed instrument. An old man sat astride of a cylindrical drum about a foot in diameter, & beat it with incredible quickness with the edge of his hand & fingers. The other drum was an open staved thing held between the knees & beaten in the same manner . . . The most curious instrument, however, was a stringed instrument which no doubt was imported from Africa. On the top of the finger board was the rude figure of a man in a sitting posture, & two pegs behind him to which the strings were fastened. The body was a calabash . . . One, which from the color of the wood seemed new, consisted of a block cut into something of the form of a cricket bat with a long & deep mortice down the center . . . being beaten lustily on the side by a short stick. In the same orchestra was a square drum, looking like a stool . . . also a calabash with a round hole in it, the hole studded with brass nails, which was beaten by a woman with two short sticks.

These instruments are found in West Africa, but they may occur in more than one area. Dr. Curt Sachs writes that 'the elaborately carved long-neck lute . . . hints at the Congo, and so does the hobby-horse drum.' Harold Courlander has seen instruments like the 'cricket bat' in Cuba and suspects Yoruban origin. He adds that the square drum is found in Jamaica, and may be Ashanti. Professor Alan P. Merriam, on the other hand, ran across a reference to square drums 'among the Ijaw of South East Nigeria,' while Professor Lorenzo D. Turner of Roosevelt University says that all these instruments can be found among the Hausa or the Yoruba tribes of Nigeria.

By 1886, when G. W. Cable wrote about Congo Square, important changes were taking place: [12]

The drums were very long, hollowed, often from a single piece of wood, open at one end and having a sheep or goat skin stretched across the other. One was large, the other much smaller. The tight skin heads were not held up to be struck; the drums were laid along on the turf and the drummers bestrode them, and beat them on the head madly with fingers, fists, and feet, with slow vehemence on the great drum, and fiercely and rapidly on the small one. Sometimes an extra performer sat on the ground behind the larger drum, at its open end, and 'beat upon the wooden sides of it with two sticks.'

So far, this description of instruments and techniques could apply equally to West Africa or the West Indies.

The fact that the drums were 'laid along on the turf' and also beaten with two sticks indicates a close resemblance to the Juba or Martinique dance still current in Haiti where, according to Courlander, 'the Haitians . . . say it was one of the first African dances in the New World.' (I have witnessed the dance in Haiti, but the drummer damped the head of the drum with his heel rather than kicking it, as Cable relates.) Early accounts of New Orleans mention the Juba, and the term became a commonplace in minstrelsy.

Cable's description continues:

One important instrument was a gourd partly filled with pebbles or grains of corn, flourished violently at the end of a stout staff with one hand and beaten upon the palm of the other. Other performers rang triangles, and others twanged from jew's harps an astonishing amount of sound. Another instrument was the jawbone of some ox, horse, or mule, and a key rattled rhythmically along its weather-beaten teeth. At times, the drums were reinforced by one or more empty barrels or casks beaten on the head with the shankbones of cattle.

The typically African instruments, such as drums, gourd rattles, and scrapers, contrast here with the European jew's harp and triangle. A blending of instruments had begun.

The next instrument that Cable describes is rather unusual and certainly not European:

. . . the Marimba brett, a union of reed and string principles. A single strand of wire ran lengthwise of a bit of wooden board, sometimes a shallow box of thin wood, some eight inches long by four or five in width, across which, under the wire, were several joints of reed about a quarter of an inch in diameter and of graduated lengths. The performer, sitting cross-legged, held the board in both hands and plucked the ends of the reeds with his thumb-nails.

The 'marimba brett' is a descendant of the African 'thumb piano,' known throughout West Africa and common in the jungle belt. It still exists in Haiti, where it is called the 'malimba.'

The climax of Cable's description gives us further clues concerning the musical blending that has taken place:

But the grand instrument . . . was the banjo. It had but four strings, not six . . . for the true African dance, a dance not so much of legs and feet as of the upper half of the body . . . there was wanted the dark inspiration of African drums and the banjo's thrump and strum.

And then there was that long-drawn cry of tremendous volume, richness, and resound, to which no instrument within their reach could make the faintest approach:

> *'Eh! pou' la belle Layotte*
> *ma mourri 'nocent*
> *Qui 'nocent ma mourri!'*

all the instruments silent while it rises and swells with mighty energy and dies away distinctly, 'Yea-a-a-a-a-a!'—Then the crash of savage drums, horns, and rattles. To all this there was sometimes added a Pan's pipe of but three reeds . . . called by English-speaking negroes 'the quills.'

Quite possibly the banjo came from Africa. Writing about the Negroes in 1781-2, Thomas Jefferson observed: 'The instrument proper to them is the banjor, which they brought hither from Africa.' [13] On the other hand, the Pan's pipes or quills (New Orleans drummer Baby Dodds said his father could make and play them) trace back to antiquity.

The most notable fact, however, is that the slaves are apparently singing a French-Creole tune in the French-Creole patois. And the melody is sung in the call-and-response pattern. A few European instruments and a European melody—no doubt modified—exist in the middle of this predominantly African performance. The blending of European and West African music is well under way, therefore, and the transition to jazz has begun.

6 | Jazz Begins

If something of the West African musical influence survived secretly in *vodun* and surfaced at Congo Square, how then did it contribute to the birth of jazz? Two factors aided this evolution: the tremendous popularity of the military band and the gradual adoption of European instruments. Beneath it all, of course, was the powerful and constant desire of the American Negro to make his mark, to belong, to participate effectively in a predominantly white culture. And music was one of the few avenues to fame and fortune.

The popularity of the military band reached its peak in the France of Napoleon. Parades and concerts soon became one of America's favorite outdoor sports. The Negroes had their bands, too. Writing about his trip to the South in 1853, F. L. Olmsted says 'in all of the Southern cities, there are music bands, composed of negroes, often of great excellence. The military parades are usually accompanied by a Negro brass band.'[1] Olmsted's standards of excellence are European and he is speaking here of European march music, played by the Negro freedman or house-slave. The field-slave working on the plantation had no such opportunity until after the Civil War. When the opportunity arrived, however, he brought less diluted West African influences with him and it made a decided difference.

As a former colony, New Orleans followed the French fashion in military bands closely and became justly famous for them. (Much later, in 1891, according to clarinetist Ed Hall, whose father was a member, the Onward Brass Band, composed of Negroes from New Orleans, won contests in New York.) Bands were employed on almost all occasions— parades, picnics, concerts, riverboat excursions, dances, funerals—and they were a sure-fire attraction. In 1871, no fewer than thirteen Negro organizations in New Orleans were represented by their own bands at the funeral cere- monies for President Garfield.[2]

What is the explanation for the pre-eminence and fre- quency of Negro bands in New Orleans? In addition to the close ties with France and the general popularity of brass bands, New Orleans had a special kind of organization to give them employment and an unusual tradition that welcomed their presence on a wide range of occasions. This combination helped to produce the first bands that began to swing.

The special kind of organization was the secret society. Negro life in New Orleans was honeycombed with them. 'Perhaps no phase of Negro life,' writes H. W. Odum, 'is so characteristic of the race and had developed so rapidly as that which centers around secret societies and fraternal orders.' They pay 'burial expenses, sick benefits, and small amounts to beneficiaries of deceased members.'[3] They also, adds W. E. B. Du Bois, 'furnish pastime from the mo- notony of work, a field of ambition and intrigue, a chance for parade, and insurance against misfortune.'[4]

Louis Armstrong mentions the names of twenty-two fraternal organizations in his book, *Satchmo,* and adds that his lodge is the Knights of Pythias. Papa Celestin, who died in 1954 at the probable age of seventy, belonged to 'Prince Hall affiliation of Richmond Lodge No. 1, F & AM; Eureka Consistory No. 7, ASRFM; and Radiant Chapter

No. 1, RAM,' according to the *Times Picayune* (17 December 1954). 'Two or three guys would get together, you know,' explains Danny Barker in *Hear Me Talkin' to Ya,* 'and make up the club and it would grow.'

These secret societies, far more numerous than similar white organizations, laid the economic foundation for the Negro brass bands by offering intermittent but frequent employment for musicians. Why were they so numerous? There was a powerful precedent in West Africa. Describing the *gbĕ* in Dahomey, Herskovits writes: [5]

With elected membership and with ritual secrets in the manner of American lodges, such groups often have large followings and persist over long periods of time. Their primary purpose is to provide their members with adequate financial assistance so that at the funeral of a member's relative . . . he can make a showing in competitive giving that will bring prestige to himself and to his group. Each member must swear a blood oath on joining, and there are adequate controls over the treasurer. Each society has its banner, and indulges in public display of its power and resources in its processions, especially when it goes as a body to the funeral rituals.

Similar societies exist wherever the African landed in the New World. In Trinidad, for example, they are known as 'susu,' from the 'esusu' of the Yoruba tribe in Nigeria.

The parallel to Negro life in New Orleans is very close. When Major Adolphe J. Osey, a member of more than twenty secret societies, died in 1937, the editors of *Gumbo Ya-Ya* report that he was 'waked' for five days and nights and a thirteen-piece band accompanied his coffin to the cemetery.[6] The great importance and the intense appeal of the secret societies are explained in the same book by Sister Johnson: [7]

A woman's got to belong to at least seven secret societies if she 'spects to get buried with any style . . . And the more lodges you belongs to, the more music you gits when you goes to meet your Maker. I belongs to enough now to have shoes on my feets. I knows right now what I'm gonna have at my wake. I already done checked off chicken salad and coffee.

I'm sure lookin' forward to my wake. They is wakin' me for four nights and I is gonna have the biggest funeral the church ever had. That's why everything I makes goes to the church and them societies.

The drive beneath this explanation, transposed and disguised, seems to be based on the powerful West African custom of ancestor-worship—the spirit of the departed is still very active and must, above all, be appeased.

More particularly, there was a tradition that led to the employment of brass bands at Negro funerals. With the mild exception of the Irish wake, there is nothing in the United States like a New Orleans funeral. But Jelly Roll Morton, born and bred in the Crescent City, saw nothing unusual about it. 'Everybody in the City of New Orleans was always organization minded . . . and a dead man always belonged to several organizations, secret orders . . . We would often wonder where a dead person was located . . . we knew we had plenty of good food that night.' [8]

A Negro funeral in New Orleans is a major celebration. At the end of his description of a funeral, Morton makes a hair-raising pun without conscious irreverence, 'It was the end of a perfect death.' In fact, he summarizes the West African point of view when he concludes (attributing the expression incorrectly to the Bible): 'Rejoice at the death and cry at the birth.' For the rejoicing inevitably included the music of a brass band. 'There were many funerals,' adds Danny Barker, 'that had three or four bands of music.'

Describing the funeral of Sister Cordelia, the editors of *Gumbo Ya-Ya* report: [9]

The wake was anything but dull. One of the sisters described it, 'We had solos and duets and hymn-singin' all night long. The womens was passin' out right and left. A doctor was kept busy and the smellin' salts was more popular than the food.'

The husband and two daughters made a most spectacular entrance at the funeral, coming up the stairs and into the room, screaming and moaning, alternately. The daughter who hadn't seen her mother for nine years made the most noise . . . She fell to her knees, rocked back and forth, tearing at her hair with her hands. . . .

The church service was just as eventful. After the preaching and the praying and the psalm-singing, members of the various societies circled the casket. Some of them would shout and scream hysterically, finally fainting and having to be carried out. One huge woman taxed the strength of five men. Other sisters just kept walking up and down, releasing screams periodically. This is called the 'walkin' spirits.' One immense sister almost tore down the church when she had a sudden attack of the 'runnin' spirits.' Some of the women trucked, others shook all over, one kept knocking off as many hats as she could possibly reach. . . .

Marching to the cemetery is a mournful and sad affair, but it's an important kind of mournfulness and an impressive kind of sadness . . . they marched with solemnity, with dignity, and gusto . . . The organization banner was red-lined in silver and bore the words 'Young and True Friends' in huge letters of gold. . . .

The ceremonies at the grave were short and simple, but everybody stayed until the last clod of dirt was put on the casket. A sister of the deceased waited until everyone else reached the grave before she began a slow march forward, the crowd parting to let her through; she was supported on each side by a woman, in a condition of semi-prostration, and moaned over and over again, 'I can't stand it!' . . . As she reached the hole in the ground, her knees buckled under her and she collapsed completely.

But when the procession was half a block from the cemetery, en route home, the band burst into 'Just Stay a Little While,' and all the True Friends performed individual and various dances, and the sister, but lately unconscious with grief, was soon trucking with the rest of them.

The conduct of the mourners at this funeral incidentally is quite formal and ritualized. Take, for example, the hysterical scene at the graveside, performed by the next of kin, and suddenly transformed into a happy, dancing return to town. Latrobe witnessed a part of the same thing in New Orleans in 1819: [10]

The parade of funerals is still a thing which is peculiar to New Orleans . . . As soon as the priests, who were 5 in number, had entered the cemetery, preceded by three boys carrying the usual pair of urns & crucifix on staves, they began their chant, lazily enough, & continued it till they arrived at the grave . . . One of the negro women, who seemed more particularly affected, threw herself into the grave upon the Coffin . . . [I] asked one of the mourners in white . . . if her granddaughter who threw herself into the grave could possibly have felt such excessive distress . . . She shrugged her shoulders two or three times, & then said, 'Je n'en sçais rien, cela est *une manière.*'

The graveside scene was a *'manière,'* or custom, which is more West African than European.

The New Orleans drummer, Warren 'Baby' Dodds, once impressed upon me, in conversation, the crucial importance of starting a drum-roll at the correct moment toward the end of the relative's performance at the grave. 'They used to hire me,' said Dodds with some pride, 'because I knew just when to cut in and start the real jazz home.' Old-timers on Wilmington Island, Georgia, remember similar ceremonies with drums only: 'Wen a pusson die, we beat duh drum tuh let ebrybody know . . . we beat duh drum agen at duh fewnul . . . wen we beat duh drum we mahch [march] roun duh grabe in a ring.' [11] The employment of brass bands at funerals in New Orleans, however, began some time after 1819, for Latrobe speaks only of chanting in the cemetery.

From the point of view of a jazzman, the best part of a funeral took place after the burial. Trumpeter Bunk Johnson's description of the ceremony, recorded by Bill Russell, is unsurpassed: [12]

On the way to the cemetery with an Odd Fellow or a Mason —they always buried with music you see—we would always use slow, slow numbers such as 'Nearer My God to Thee,' 'Flee as a Bird to the Mountains,' 'Come Thee Disconsolate.' We would use most any 4/4, played very slow; they walked very slow behind the body.

After we would get to the cemetery, and after that particular person were put away, the band would come on to the front, out of the graveyard. Then the lodge would come out . . . and they called roll—fall in line, and then we'd march away from the cemetery by the snare drum only, until we got about a block or two blocks from the cemetery. Then we'd go right on into ragtime—what the people call today swing—ragtime. We would play 'Didn't He Ramble,' or we'd take all those spiritual hymns and turn them into ragtime—2/4 movements, you know, step lively everybody. 'Didn't He Ramble,' 'When the Saints Go Marching In,' that good old piece 'Ain't Gonna Study War No More,' and several others we would have and we'd play them just for that effect.

We would have a second line there that was 'most equivalent to King Rex parade—Mardi Gras Carnival parade. The police were unable to keep the second line back—all in the street, all on the sidewalks, in front of the band, and behind the lodge, in front of the lodge. We'd have some immense crowds following. They would follow the funeral up to the cemetery just to get this ragtime music comin' back. Some of the women would have beer cans on their arm. They'd stop and get a half can of beer and drink that to freshen up and follow the band for miles—in the dust, in the dirt, in the street, on the sidewalk, and the Law was trying not to gang the thoroughfare, but just let them have their way. There wouldn't be any fight or anything of that kind; it would just be dancin' in the street. Even police horse—mounted police—their horse would prance. Music done them all the good in the world. That's the class of music we used on funerals.

Bunk mentions the second line, or dancing followers recruited from the crowd, and many a New Orleans jazzman as a youngster went to school in the second line.

Is there any precedent in the customs of West Africa for the Negro funeral in New Orleans? Indeed there is. Describing a funeral in Dahomey, Herskovits reports: [13]

When the grave is finished, it is left with a mat over its opening. Every morning thereafter, until the body is buried, the children and wives of the deceased enter the house of the dead, fall across the body and weep . . . [after the funeral] Throughout the night, and until an hour or two before dawn, there is drinking and dancing and singing. Tales are recounted dealing with themes of the broadest sexual innuendo, for the native view is that this is the time to amuse the dead, for to moralize to a dead person is both indelicate and senseless.

'Tradition has set it down as bad form,' Herskovits notes, 'to continue to remind an acquaintance of an affliction.'

Something of the West African tradition behind the New Orleans Negro funeral is explained by Herskovits' comments on the significance of funerals in Dahomey: [14]

The Dahomean funeral thus furnishes a point of contact between many aspects of Dahomean life. It is a veritable climax to the life of the individual; the source from which the ancestral cult arises and the sib maintains its supply of souls for future generations. Because of the expenditure of food, money, and materials which it entails, it is connected with the economic life of Dahomey. Indeed, it may be said to be one of the focal institutions which leads to an integrated understanding of Dahomean culture.

Talbot makes a similar point about the Sudanese of Southern Nigeria, Leonard about the Ibos of the lower Niger, and Rattray about the Ashanti. Funerals were a high point in West African life.

As time goes on and New Orleans becomes more like any other American city, the Negro funeral is disappearing. At the funeral of trumpeter 'Papa' Celestin *Ebony* magazine reports (March 1955) that no jazz was played— 'out of respect for Papa.' The Catholic Church frowns upon the custom—with some reason. Who ever heard of such 'carryings on' over a corpse? A deep-rooted tradition from West Africa is being modified.

In 1874, the White League was organized to throw out the Yankee carpetbaggers and keep the Negro in his place. 'Discrimination came in 1889,' said Bunk Johnson flatly. The Creoles of Color were hard hit. Bit by bit, they were pushed out of any job a white man could use, and they lost their place in the downtown parade. 'Quite naturally,' says drummer Baby Dodds in Larry Gara's biography, 'the colored fellows didn't get any of the better jobs.' Eventually and against their will, they went uptown and 'sat in' with their darker brothers. They could play European instruments correctly and they could read music. But, at first, they couldn't play jazz.

Where did the Creoles of Color come from? The Black Code of 1724 made provision for the manumission, or freeing, of slaves. Children shared the status of their mother. When a white aristocrat died, according to Asbury, his will frequently provided that his part-African mistress and slave should be freed. His children by the same woman were automatically free. A class known as Creoles of Color grew up with French and Spanish as well as African blood in their veins.

Sometimes the part-African children of wealthy planters were given all the advantages that the family could provide. Charles Gayarré writes: [15]

By 1830, some of these *gens de couleur* had arrived at such a degree of wealth as to own cotton and sugar plantations with numerous slaves. They educated their children, as they had been educated, in France. Those who chose to remain there, attained, many of them, distinction in scientific and literary circles. In New Orleans they became musicians, merchants, and money and real estate brokers. The humbler classes were mechanics; they monopolized the trade of shoemakers, a trade for which, even to this day, they have a special vocation; they were barbers, tailors, carpenters, upholsterers. They were notably successful hunters and supplied the city with game. As tailors, they were almost exclusively patronized by the *élite,* so much so that the Legoasters', the Dumas', the Clovis', the Lacroix', acquired individually fortunes of several hundred thousands of dollars. . . . At the Orleans theatre they attended their mothers, wives, and sisters in the second tier reserved exclusively for them, and where no white person of either sex would have been permitted to intrude.

The Creoles of Color, Asbury adds, 'in the Southern phrase, knew their places,' although their role in the strict caste system was precarious. Cable's novel, *The Grandissimes,* deals with the tragedy of the darker brother caught in this inter-racial no-man's-land.

The fall of the Creoles of Color was gradual but complete. As Lomax demonstrates in *Mister Jelly Roll,* the ancestry of Morton is a case in point. His grandfather was a member of the Louisiana Constitutional Convention of 1868, his father (according to Morton) was a small business man, and Morton himself worked as a manual laborer in a barrel factory before he escaped to the red-light district of Storyville. His Creole grandmother immediately disowned him but Morton was making big money. A familiarity with light classical music and European technique was part of his Creole background and helped him to contribute new elements to jazz.

The Creoles of Color had much to learn about jazz

which their academic training could not give them. The light-skinned Creole clarinetist, Alphonse Picou, who was seventy-three years old in 1953 when I interviewed him, could still remember the difficulties he had. 'When I was very young,' he told me, 'I took lessons from the flute player at the French Opera House. He made me practice fingering for six months before I was permitted to play a note.' While still in his teens, Picou was invited to play in the jazz orchestra of his friend, the trombone player Bouboul Augustat. Picou was shocked when he discovered that they had no written music. He was expected to improvise. 'Bouboul told me, "Just listen," and I sat there not knowing what to do. After a while I caught on and started playing two or three notes for one.'

It was Picou who first adapted the piccolo part from the march version of 'High Society' to jazz—a technical but not very creative feat. It has become a standard solo for jazz clarinet whenever the tune is played, and modern jazz musicians such as Charlie Parker have quoted parts of it in the course of their improvising. Picou's eyes light up as he remembers the first time. 'I just happened to think of playing it that way one night and the crowd went wild. They kept requesting it over and over and wouldn't let me stop.' To this day, Picou retains a semi-legitimate tone and style without the vitality of a Johnny Dodds.

The Creole violinist, Paul Dominguez, explained to Alan Lomax how his friends had to compete with the darker Negroes uptown: [16]

See, us Downtown people, we didn't think so much of this rough Uptown jazz until we couldn't make a living otherwise . . . they made a fiddler out of a violinist—me, I'm talking about. A fiddler is *not* a violinist but a violinist can be a fiddler. If I wanted to make a living, I had to be rowdy like the other group. I had to jazz it or rag it or any other damn thing . . . Bolden cause all that. He cause these younger Creoles, men like Bechet and Keppard, to have a different style altogether from the old heads like Tio and Perez. I don't know how they do it. But goddam, they'll do it. Can't tell you what's there on the paper, but just play the hell out of it.

Dominguez had been left stranded with his Creole prejudices. And yet the chronicles of jazz are crowded with the names of Creoles of Color who made the jump to jazz successfully: Ory, Bechet, Bigard, Celestin, Dutrey, Picou, Robichaux, Simeon, St. Cyr, and so forth.

They brought their knowledge of European instruments and technique with them and merged with the darker pioneers who thought of any instrument simply as an extension of the human voice. 'If you can't sing it,' says New Orleans trumpeter Mutt Carey in *Hear Me Talkin' to Ya,* 'you can't play it. When I'm improvising, I'm singing in my mind. I sing what I feel and then try to reproduce it on the horn.' And all of it blended with the thriving brass bands employed by the fraternal societies. The result was a competently played march music that had also begun to swing, an elementary kind of jazz that would still be recognizable as such today.

7 | Buddy Bolden and the Growth of Jazz

Battles of music, once known as 'carving contests,' have occurred—and still occur—frequently in the history of jazz. In early New Orleans days, they say it was Armstrong versus Kid Rena (this is pure legend), or Red Allen versus Guy Kelly, or Joe Oliver (later, 'King') versus Freddie Keppard. 'If you couldn't blow a man down with your horn,' declares trumpeter Mutt Carey in *Hear Me Talkin' to Ya,* 'at least you could use it to hit him alongside the head.' In the 'thirties in Kansas City it was saxophonist Coleman Hawkins versus Lester Young, while in New York it was trombonist Big Green versus Jimmy Harrison. (At the Bandbox in 1953 it was the entire bands of Count Basie and Duke Ellington.) In a free-wheeling music such as jazz, a musician is judged by his capacity for sustained and swinging improvisation.

The first and archetypical legend in jazz is the life of Charles 'Buddy' Bolden, who never lost a carving contest. He was almost eight years old before the dances at Congo Square came to an end, and he probably knew all about *vodun* and attended his share of secret meetings. He grew up in the midst of the brass-band craze and he mastered a European instrument, the cornet. As a child, he was a part of a shouting congregation in church. He was heir to all the musical influences that survived in and around

New Orleans. And the sounds that burst from his cornet helped to establish a new music.

Bolden was born in 1868 in the rough-and-ready uptown section of New Orleans. He ran a barber shop, edited a scandal sheet called 'The Cricket,' and around 1897 organized the first out-and-out jazz band. He was the first jazzman to earn the title 'King' by popular acclaim. For seven years he was the undisputed champ. Then, at the age of twenty-nine, he ran amuck during a parade and was committed to the State Hospital at Angola on 5 June 1907. He died twenty-four years later.

Six years before his death, Bolden was given a routine examination by Dr. S. B. Hays: [1]

Accessible and answers fairly well. Paranoid delusions, also grandiosed. Auditory hallucinations and visual. Talks to self. Much reaction. Picks things off the wall. Tears his clothes. Insight and judgment lacking. Looks deteriorated but memory is good. . . . Has a string of talk that is incoherent. Hears the voices of people that bothered him before he came here. History of one month in House of Detention on account of alcohol. Diagnosis: Dementia praecox, paranoid type.

In the official records there is no inkling of the fact that women once fought for the privilege of carrying Buddy's cornet.

The folk heroes of jazz have often been celebrated for enormous appetites of all kinds, and Bolden set a pattern that has been followed by many young men with horns. He lived hard and he 'died' young. Old-timer Albert Glenny remembers Bolden as a 'good dresser,' while Jelly Roll Morton says that 'he drink all the whiskey he could find . . . always having a ball.' Above all, Bolden was a ladies' man, and in the words of the Belgian author Robert Goffin, 'Il doit encore rendre les femmes rouges-chaudes!' [2]

Bolden probably never recorded, although the wishful

thought of ancient Edison cylinders keeps circulating, but we know that at one time his band consisted of cornet, clarinet, trombone, violin, guitar, string bass, and drums. They played at saloons, dance halls, parades, picnics, lawn parties, carnivals, and parks. (When the band came through Plaquemine, Louisiana, on an excursion sometime before 1906, thirteen-year-old Clarence Williams ran away from home to New Orleans. 'I had never heard anything like that before in my whole life.') Tin Type Hall on Liberty Street in uptown New Orleans was the band's favorite location. And they played polkas, quadrilles, ragtime tunes, and blues—all by ear.

But Bolden's specialty was the blues. An uptown dance at Tin Type Hall is described in *Jazzmen*: ³

In the daytime, Tin Type Hall was used as a sort of morgue, for here the hustlers and roustabouts were always laid out when they were killed. The hustlers, gamblers, and race track followers were often hard-working musicians in their off seasons, or when luck turned and they needed a little ready cash. At night, however, the Tin Type trembled with life and activity, especially when Bolden was 'socking it out.' The 'high class' or 'dicty' people didn't go to such lowdown affairs as the Tin Type dances. At about twelve o'clock, when the ball was getting right, the more respectable Negroes who did attend went home. Then Bolden played a number called *Don't Go Away Nobody,* and the dancing got rough. When the orchestra settled down to the slow blues, the music was mean and dirty, as Tin Type roared full blast.

On slow blues, such as 'Careless Love' and '2:19 Took My Baby Away,' Bolden was at his best. 'Bolden went to church,' Bud Scott claims, 'and that's where he got his idea of jazz music. Negro religious music and blues were always closely related.

All the musicians who heard Bolden agree on two things: Buddy couldn't read a note and he played the most powerful horn of all time. Louis Armstrong (who was seven years old when Bolden ran amuck and therefore a not too reliable witness) speaks of Bolden's style as 'a little too rough,' while Morton says: [4]

Buddy Bolden was the most powerful trumpet in history. I remember we'd be hanging around some corner, wouldn't know that there was going to be a dance out at Lincoln Park. Then we'd hear old Buddy's trumpet coming on and we'd all start. Any time it was a quiet night at Lincoln Park because maybe the affair hadn't been so well publicized, Buddy Bolden would publicize it! He'd turn his big trumpet around toward the city and blow his blues, calling his children home, as he used to say. The whole town would know Buddy Bolden was at the Park, ten or twelve miles from the center of town. He was the blowingest man ever lived since Gabriel.

Albert Glenny, who once played bass with Bolden, estimates that 'Buddy was louder than Louis Armstrong with the microphone turned on.' Thus, Fred Ramsey suggests that the term 'loud,' so frequently used to describe Bolden's playing by those who actually heard him, may be a way of saying that the music as a whole was rough and unfamiliar—with 'hoarseness, a notable lack of harmony, and a high level of heterophony' (voices close to but not quite in unison)—in other words, a way of describing *a new manner of playing*. This interesting speculation makes excellent sense in connection with the very early brass band music Ramsey located in the Southern countryside.

Did Bolden play ragtime or jazz? Would he sound old-fashioned or modern today? Glenny says that he was 'the best for ragtime,' but Bunk Johnson insisted that Bolden 'could step out right today, play his own style, and be called "hot." ' Wallace Collins, who played tuba with Bolden, told Rudi Blesh that Buddy would 'take one note and put two or three to it.' That sounds like ragtime. But then, trombonist Willy Cornish, speaking of the rhythms, says, 'when we got going good, they'd cross three times at once.' That sounds like jazz. The truth is that Bolden probably played a transitional style that could be either 'raggy' or 'hot.' When he played a ragtime tune such as 'Maple Leaf Rag' by Scott Joplin, which he memorized, he followed a syncopated melody which gave the music a 'raggy' sound. When he played the blues, however, he probably used blue tonality and the flowing rhythms that crossed 'three times at once.'

Before Buddy Bolden was put away in 1907, New Orleans saw the rise of many other jazzmen. They were using European instruments without benefit of orthodox instruction, and they were playing European tunes. But their conception of how these instruments and tunes should be played was influenced by their West African heritage. The tunes were a point of departure for endless variations, instruments were an extension of the human voice, and both were welded together by a propulsive march rhythm.

In Bolden's day, playing jazz was usually an avocation, a part-time job, integrated with the everyday life of the Negro community. 'Most of the musicians had day jobs,' says Zutty Singleton. It was a folk music and the distinction between performer and audience was shadowy. But with the opening of Storyville, the official red-light district, in 1897, things began to change. Playing jazz became a full-time profession for some, and the occupational hazards of working while others enjoyed themselves became more or less standardized.

In 1910, there were 'almost two hundred houses of pleasure,' according to *Jazzmen,* as well as 'nine cabarets, many "dance schools," innumerable honky-tonks, barrelhouses, and gambling joints.' The 101 Ranch, a cabaret which employed many jazzbands, was particularly famous, and it was there that trombonist Preston Jackson recalls seeing the white kids who later became world-famous as the Original Dixieland Jazz Band, hanging around and listening open-mouthed to the music. The changes of personnel and location were endless, but Storyville kept a dozen or so bands working every night.

'Jazz wasn't born in Storyville,' said old-time school teacher and trumpeter Johnny Wiggs in an interview, 'it came long before that.' Storyville helped to establish a special kind of jazzman: the solo pianist. He made more money than an entire jazzband. Jelly Roll Morton took in fifteen or eighteen dollars a night at Lulu White's, while the band musicians got from one to two-and-a-half dollars apiece at the cabarets. (It was poetic justice of a sort because the New Orleans jazzbands, with their marching-band tradition, did not use a piano in the early days.) 'You never had to [could] figure on getting work in the District,' says guitarist Danny Barker, 'so it wasn't so important when it closed [in 1917].' Very few jazzmen ever played in a brothel out of choice.

At the same time, the solo pianists of Storyville were assimilating the rolling rhythms of the brass bands. In so doing they went a step beyond the ragtime style of the day. A transitional figure in this sense, Morton helped to spread the newer style in the course of his endless travels, while the band rhythms made him the victor in 'carving contests' all over the country. By 1917, Storyville was closed, New Orleans was sunk in a business depression, and jazzmen were looking north for employment.

From around 1900, a music that we should probably recognize today as jazz began to be played in New Orleans. We have been stressing the West African elements in the blend, since they determined the unique character of the music, but what were the European influences? Echoes of almost any Old World music can be found in New Orleans jazz. Bit by bit, the Protestant folk manner of singing psalms and hymns, with its free embellishments, lining-out form, and non-harmonic horizontal feeling made itself felt in and around Latin-Catholic New Orleans—especially in revival singing—and dove-tailed neatly with the over-all development. The American Negro did not need to borrow any rhythms, but rather adapted and limited himself to the European march beat, building upon it. He cheerfully borrowed European melodies and transformed them by improvisation. Above all, he gradually mastered European harmony—an element which was not entirely new to him—and proceeded to color it with blue tonality.

Tracing specific European melodies in jazz is a thankless task. British ballads, for example, were no doubt played by jazzmen, but the emphasis was upon the manner of playing while the tunes themselves were quickly transformed into something else. Spanish melodies were more hardy, frequently because they had already blended with West African influences in the West Indies. A large borrowing consisted of Afro-Spanish rhythms such as the tango and rhumba, which Jelly Roll Morton called the 'Spanish tinge.' By 1914, when W. C. Handy composed 'St. Louis Blues,' he used a *tangana* rhythm in the verse. By then, however, the tango had been the craze for some time in New York City.

As might be expected, the French influence is perhaps the greatest European influence on New Orleans jazz. It merged with rhumba rhythms to produce Creole songs, some of which were published as early as 1867 in *Slave Songs of the United States*. (Eighty years later, the rhumba became a Tin-Pan Alley commodity.) Jelly Roll Morton demonstrates how a French quadrille was adapted to the jazz idiom (Circle JM 1-2). The name of the quadrille was 'La Marseillaise' (not the French national anthem), and the contrasting time signatures of its five sections were changed to duple rhythm—with appropriate embellishments.

The fortunes of this quadrille in New Orleans are legendary. Originally called 'Praline'—a ragged kind of candy—it was known in Storyville as 'Get Out of Here and Go Home.' Later, it was entitled 'Jack Carey' and then 'Number Two Rag' when the Dixieland Five played it around 1914. The Original Dixieland Jass (sic) Band, a white group from New Orleans, made the first recording of it in 1917 under the name of 'Tiger Rag,' and the title stuck.

Confirmation of the French origin of 'Tiger Rag' comes from an unexpected source. The Belgian author, Robert Goffin, identifies the number as 'the distorted theme of the second tableau of a quadrille I used to hear as a boy, at all the balls of Walloon, Belgium.' Further, he adds that the military bands of every French village played two marches that can be easily identified as the New Orleans jazz standards, 'Panama' and 'High Society.' In these rare cases, the actual melody was retained, probably because it was so well known, although in actual performance the variations were—and still are—practically endless.

Finally, if we had to choose a date when the over-all direction switched from European elements *dominating* African elements to European elements *being influenced* by a new combination dominated by African elements, it would be around 1900. It is a question of the general trend. European and African music continued to blend, of course, but something unusual had occurred. From the previous blending, a music had evolved in New Orleans with a distinct character of its own. It struck the public, and quite rightly, as something entirely new, and it began to spread, grow, and influence all American popular music.

The general style later became known as 'Dixieland,' especially when played by white musicians, and it spread fan-wise to the North until it became the rage of the Jazz Age. In the meantime, the Great Awakening, minstrelsy, the spiritual, and ragtime had evolved outside of New Orleans. They all borrowed certain African elements in turn and paved the way for the acceptance of jazz. They were a little more European in feeling, however, while jazz was something else again—a new music.

PART THREE : THE AMERICAN

BACKGROUND

8 | The Great Awakening

Around 1800, a religious mass movement in the United States known as 'The Great Awakening' produced a frontier revival and a music that was of, by, and for the people. At a series of hysterical camp meetings from Northampton, Massachusetts, to Cane Ridge, Kentucky, spiritual songs and revival hymns were re-created in a new form and spirit. The poor and lowly people who attended the camp meetings preferred a style which happened to fit the over-all feeling of brotherhood and the general urge for freedom of expression. And a new kind of mass blending of the two musical traditions of Europe and West Africa took place in the United States.

There had been famous Negro preachers before the American Revolution. James Weldon Johnson writes: [1]

The history of the Negro preacher reaches back to Colonial days. Before the Revolutionary War, when slavery had not yet taken on its more grim and heartless economic aspects, there were famed black preachers who preached to both whites and blacks. George Liele was preaching to whites and blacks at Augusta, Ga., as far back as 1773, and Andrew Bryan at Savannah a few years later. The most famous of these earliest preachers was Black Harry, who during the Revolutionary period accompanied Bishop Asbury as a drawing card and preached from the same platform with other founders of the

Methodist Church. Of him, John Ledman in his *History of the Rise of Methodism in America* says, 'The truth was that Harry was a more popular speaker than Mr. Asbury or almost anyone else in his day.'

A rhythmic style of preaching made Black Harry the real attraction. Carter G. Woodson tells an anecdote about Black Harry's tours with Bishop Asbury: [2]

On one occasion in Wilmington, Delaware, where the cause of the Methodist was unpopular, a large number of persons came out of curiosity to hear Bishop Asbury. But, as the auditorium was already taxed to its fullest capacity, they could only hear from the outside. At the conclusion of the exercises, they said, without having seen the speaker: 'If all Methodist preachers can preach like the Bishop, we should like to be constant hearers.' Some one present replied: 'That was not the Bishop, but the Bishop's servant that you heard.' This to be sure, had the desired effect, for these inquiries concluded: 'If such be the servant, what must the master be?'

The techniques of these early Negro preachers and their effects on the audience are revealed in a description of preacher John Jasper at a funeral. 'His vivid and spectacular eloquence resulted in an uproar of groans, shouts, fainting women, and people who were swept to the ground to lie in a trance-like state sometimes for hours.' [3]

As the plantations grew larger and slavery became a grim and profitable business, these Negro preachers disappeared because their very presence made the slaves restless and interfered with work. Much later, after the Civil War, they reappeared in segregated churches of their own, and are thriving to this day.

The slaves as well as the Negro preachers seem to have shared in the religious music of the United States before the American Revolution. But it was a special kind of religious music. In the mid-eighteenth century, the Virginia evangelist John Davies was preaching to the slaves with great success and noted their taste in a letter to John Wesley: [4]

All the books were very acceptable, but none more so than the Psalms and Hymns, which enabled them to gratify their peculiar taste for psalmody . . . and sometimes when I have awaked, at two or three in the morning, a torrent of sacred psalmody has poured into my chamber. In this exercise some of them spend the whole night . . .

In another letter, he says: [5]

. . . the Negroes, above all of the human species I ever knew, have the nicest ear for music. They have a kind of ecstatic delight in psalmody . . .

This psalmody, or singing the words of Biblical psalms, frequently employed a style of its own, a style which appealed to the Negroes.

In a chapter on the 'Early New England Folk Style' of psalmody, Gilbert Chase in his *America's Music* describes the style: [6]

. . . its main characteristics are singing by ear rather than by note or 'rule'; the raising or lowering of notes at will; the adding of grace notes, turns, and other embellishments; the 'sliding' from one note to another; the adding of parts at the intervals of a fourth, a fifth, and an octave; and the practice of 'lining out,' with the leader reading or chanting the verses of the psalm, one or two lines at a time, and the congregation singing them afterward.

This series of characteristics parallel many characteristics of West African music—with the notable exception of the rhythm. To the newly arrived African, then, this music furnished something to build on.

Take the custom of 'lining out,' which lent itself so easily to the West African call-and-response pattern. We can trace the former to the British Isles where, in 1644, the Westminster Assembly recommended the adoption of the practice in English churches because the congregation couldn't read. A hundred years later, churches in Scotland refused to give up the procedure even though the congregation knew all the words by heart. 'Lining out' had become an organic part of the style. Musical reformers disapproved of the practice, however, and in 1699 it was abolished in the fashionable Brattle Square Church in Cambridge. Even though the big cities gave it up, 'lining out' spread to the rural areas south and west (by way of the itinerant Yankee music teacher) and established itself among the folk where it still exists.

Later on, during the Great Awakening, the folk hymn became popular. A ballad tune with religious words, the folk hymn often adopted the call-and-response pattern in order to answer the needs of outdoor preaching and shouting congregations. Harmony in the European sense was neglected. The hymn books of the day stressed part-singing which harmonized only by accident, and the 'shape-note' and 'fasola' systems of notation emphasized interesting, horizontal parts for each singer, rather than vertical chords combining all the voices. The days of barbershop harmony were far in the future and, meanwhile, the freedom from harmony gave a melodic and rhythmic liberty which proved attractive to the West African ear. In this way the blending of African and British folk style was accelerated.

An example of this merging is the tune of 'Wondrous Love,' which was taken from the ballad of 'The Wicked Captain Kidd.' In these early days, hymn books printed only the words, *not* the music—a situation that encouraged improvisation. As G. G. Johnson says: [7]

Camp meeting leaders abandoned the usual church hymns and composed, sometimes extemporaneously, songs which more nearly suited the spirit of the meeting.

This extemporaneous composition, whereby 'the volume of song burst all bonds of guidance and control,' also transformed the melody into a blend of European and West African qualities. Gilbert Chase adds that the tune we know as 'The Battle Hymn of the Republic' was a jumping revival number with a 'Hallelujah' response long before Julia Ward Howe wrote 'Mine eyes have seen the glory . . .' A key to the general process is revealed by Professor John W. Work's discovery of a variant version of 'Rock of Ages,' which was radically changed at a revival meeting where tunes were freely embellished in the folk style.

Consider the situation: the preacher wants more mass participation with music, outdoors. The call-and-response pattern and a compelling rhythm are therefore essential. After each line of Charles Wesley's hymn, 'He comes, he comes, the Judge severe,' for example, revivalists added the refrain, 'Roll, Jordan, roll!' Similarly, march rather than waltz rhythms were employed and the words subordinated to an impromptu expressiveness which favored improvisation and 'composing' on the spot. In short, the blend of British hymn and folk song became partly Africanized.

Why did the Great Awakening spread so rapidly and reach its peak in the South? The reasons are fairly simple. In New England such Puritan preachers as Jonathan Edwards, who signed his letters 'Yours in the bowels of Christ,' were terrifying their contemporaries with threats of inescapable hell-fire. According to Calvinist beliefs, only a very, very few were among the elect and would go to heaven; the great majority were horribly doomed and would go straight to hell. Edwards' sermons were frightening—people fainted in terror—but the sermons were also discouraging and depressing.

In contrast, we have the dissenting preachers who broke

away from Calvinism and journeyed South to more fertile fields announcing that grace was free and everyone had a good chance of eternal life. Before the American Revolution, such renegade preachers were jailed; afterwards, they were let alone and religious freedom became a fact. Among the pioneering settlers of what was then the West —Kentucky and Tennessee—these preachers were naturally popular. The poor, the social outcast, and the Negro flocked to hear the new and democratic gospel.

One of these preachers, Shubal Stearns, called the 'Boston Baptist Branerges' by G. P. Jackson, was a distant ancestor of my own. He took the Separate Baptist creed, based on 'conviction and conversion,' from New England to Sandy Creek, North Carolina, in 1755. An eyewitness, Morgan Edwards, who visited North Carolina in 1771 and 1772, remarks that 'the neighborhood was alarmed and the Spirit of God listed to blow as a mighty rushing wind.' Within three years, the Separates had three churches and over nine hundred members. Describing Stearns' technique, Edwards writes: [8]

His voice was musical and strong, which he managed in such a manner, as, one while, to make soft impressions on the heart, and fetch tears from the eyes in a mechanical way; and anon, to shake the very nerves and throw the animal system into tumults and perturbations.

Edwards also noted 'crying out . . . falling down as in fits, and awakening in ecstasies.'

Although white men played a leading role in these early revivals, the Negro also participated fully. In *White and Negro Spirituals*, G. P. Jackson says: [9]

. . . the negro found himself among real friends—among those who, by reason of their ethnic, social and economic background, harbored a minimum of racial prejudice; among those whose religious practices came nearest to what he—by nature a religious person—could understand and participate in. He found himself a churchless pioneer among those white people who built meeting houses and invited him not only to attend their services and sing their songs but also to join with them in full membership; white people who were concerned not only with his soul's welfare but also even with his release from slavery.

These preachers were potential Abolitionists, preaching a gospel of equality before God, and white man and Negro sang their religious music standing side by side, their voices blending.

One of the high points of the Great Awakening occurred in the summer of 1801 at the Cane Ridge camp meeting, about twenty-five miles north of Lexington, Kentucky. A composite picture of the meeting is drawn by F. M. Davenport from various accounts of eyewitnesses in his *Primitive Traits in Religious Revivals:* [10]

It was at night that the most terrible scenes were witnessed, when the camp-fires blazed in a mighty circle around the vast audience of pioneers . . . As the darkness deepened, the exhortations of the preachers became more fervent and impassioned, their picturesque prophecies of doom more lurid and alarming, the volume of song burst all bonds of guidance and control, and broke again and again from the throats of the people, while over all, at intervals, there rang out the shout of ecstasy, the sob and the groan . . . Men and women shouted aloud during the sermon, and shook hands all around at the close in what was termed 'the singing ecstasy' . . . the crowd at Cane Ridge [went] rushing from preacher to preacher if it were whispered that it was 'more lively' at some other point, swarming enthusiastically around a 'fallen' brother, laughing, leaping, sobbing, shouting, swooning . . . The whole body of persons who actually fell helpless to the earth during the progress of the meeting was computed . . . to be three thousand . . . Those who fell were carried to the meeting-house near by. 'At no time was the floor less than half covered. Some lay quiet, unable to move or speak. Some talked, but could not move . . . Some, shrieking in agony, bounded about like a live fish out of water. Many lay down and rolled over and over for hours at a time. Others rushed wildly over the stumps and benches, and then plunged, shouting, "Lost! Lost!" into the forest.'

Offhand, this sounds like a West African religious ceremony—gone mad. There are, in fact, more than a few resemblances.

A gradual change was taking place in the British-Protestant religions and new fashions in the manner of religious worship were developing. A person's social status came to be judged—and quite accurately—by the symptoms of his religious hysteria. Of course the rich plantation owners, who possessed the best tobacco land and most of the slaves, disapproved of camp meetings. Camp meetings made slaves unruly. G. G. Johnson says: [11]

Many educated ministers and laymen were from the first opposed to the Great Revival . . . the gentry, as a rule, held aloof from camp meetings . . . A revival usually met with some active opposition.

The Reverend Samuel McCorkle, for example, couldn't make up his mind whether or not the Great Awakening was an act of God. He was a Presbyterian.

Reverend McCorkle was also disturbed by the class of people who were enjoying the camp meetings. He noted that persons with weak nerves, women, adolescents, and Negroes were most frequently moved to hysteria of an unregulated nature. On the other hand, the Reverend Joseph Travis saw certain notables 'stricken to the floor, as if shot by a deadly arrow,' who 'for an hour or so remained speechless, breathless, pulseless, and, to all appearances, perfectly dead.' Then with a heavenly smile, they would 'look up, stand up, and shout aloud, "Glory, glory to God! My soul is converted, and I am happy." ' This was the way of the grand and wealthy.

The vast majority had other symptoms, known as 'exercises,' which came to be classified under such titles as laughing, dancing, wheeling, barking, and jerking. Preacher Lorenzo Dow (1777–1834), who carried the gospel all over the United States and even to England, writes in his *Journal:* [12]

I have seen Presbyterians, Methodists, Quakers, Baptists, Church of England, and Independents, exercized with the *jerks;* Gentleman and Lady, black and white, the aged and the youth, rich and poor, without exception . . .

(Dow, like other Northern preachers, was heckled now and then because he openly condemned mistreatment of the Negro.) Perhaps jerking was considered the most vulgar of the exercises, but it gradually came to be the most widespread. G. G. Johnson says: [13]

The jerking exercise, or the jerks, as it was commonly called, together with the dancing and barking exercises, did not appear at the beginning of the Great Revival. The Reverend Eli Caruthers refers to these phenomena as '*fungi,* which grew out of the revival in its state of decay.' At first, the jerks were manifested by an involuntary twitching of the arms; later this twitching spread over all the body. It was perhaps the most contagious of the exercises. Sometimes the mere mention of it was enough to set most of a congregation to jerking . . .

Whenever a woman was taken with the jerks at a camp meeting her friends formed a circle about her, for the exercise was so violent that she could scarcely maintain a correct posture. Men would go bumping about over benches, into trees, bruising and cutting themselves, if friends did not catch and hold them. Some were ashamed of having the jerks, but most persons agreed that it was impossible to resist them.

I have witnessed these symptoms, even to the circle of friends protecting the one possessed, at *vodun* ceremonies in Haiti, where the music was more exciting and the behavior of the participants was more controlled.

Where did 'the jerks' come from? In the Ulster revival of 1755, the symptoms were different. F. M. Davenport was puzzled by it: [14]

In Kentucky the motor automatisms, the voluntary muscles in violent action, were the prevailing type, although there were many of the sensory. On the other hand, in Ulster the sensory automatisms, trance, vision, the physical disability and the sinking of muscular energy were the prevailing type, although there were many of the motor. I do not mean that I can explain it.

In other words, in the Old World revivalists went to sleep; in the New World they woke up, violently. 'It is just in the forms of motor behavior remarked on as characteristic of the "automatisms" of the . . . Kentucky revivals,' says Professor Herskovits, 'that aboriginal modes of African worship are to be marked off from the those of Europe.' [15]

By 1820 there were about 40,000 Negro Methodists and 60,000 Negro Baptists. The Baptist Church had the greatest appeal for Negroes because of its informal organization. A group of four was enough to constitute a congregation and anyone who felt the call might preach. A poor but fervent denomination, the Baptists were closest to the economic level of the Negro, while Baptist religious practices happened to duplicate certain African customs, including 'total immersion' which corresponded to customs of the West African river cults, and the uninhibited manner of 'getting religion' which is similar to West African spirit possession.

Today, the wheel has come full circle and white revival meetings have adopted Negro songs, styles, and rhythms. A gap still remains. Comparing white and Negro camp meetings, Dr. Hortense Powdermaker comments: [16]

A further, less definable difference seems due to an impression of greater rhythm and spontaneity in the Negro revival, not wholly accounted for by the greater participation of the audience. The rhythm of the white minister's speech was more halting than that of the Negro minister, and shaped to a less vigorous melodic line. The movements of the white congregation were more convulsive and jerky than those of the Negroes.

It should not be surprising that the Negro excels in a manner of worship that is a central part of his heritage.

The Great Awakening, then, led to the first extensive blending in the United States—outside of New Orleans—of European and West African music. It was a grass-roots phenomenon that took place mainly within a shifting frontier population, although the aristocrats of the East coast were also touched by it. One of its by-products was a subtle education for many Americans in West African musical characteristics, which sold themselves on their own merits. When the next step in the over-all process took place, the blending could start on a more advanced level.

9 | The Work Song

With the Great Awakening, the blend of European and West African elements in religious music becomes evident; with the work song a similar blend in secular music begins. Perhaps because it was associated (among other things) with labor and not the church, the work song did not enter and influence the widening stream of American popular music as quickly or as noticeably as, say, the spiritual. It remained in the background, beyond earshot of most white people, a mixture that preserved and fostered a number of West African qualities.

The machine is probably the greatest enemy of the work song, which survives best today in Southern penitentiaries where forced manual labor is still used. The function of the work song, as the name indicates, is purely utilitarian—to co-ordinate the efforts of the workers. The chain gang is the clearest example. Bound together, the men must move together, and the work song furnishes a rhythmic cue. In such a situation, the plantation overseer was hardly interested in the style of singing, and many African characteristics are preserved by default.

A good work-song leader, as Leadbelly once boasted, was always in demand. To the worker, it meant passing the time more bearably; to the boss, it meant a more efficient team. The performance of a talented leader of work songs sometimes resembles a strenuous tightrope act. He can don the mask of apparent conformity to the 'Cap'n,' or white boss, and at the same time entertain the gang by embroidering upon the mask with extemporaneous satire, *double-entendre*, and even veiled threats of escape.

Alan Lomax calls the work song a 'spiritual speed-up,' which is literally the case when the gang—as they often did—adapted a religious tune to their own requirements. It was also a morale-building vehicle of not-so-passive resistance, which reinforced the impulse to employ African idioms by the need for concealing open hostility. As a result, the work song to this day shows little European influence and retains a great many West African qualities.

If we examine the music of West Africa, we find that the work song is almost universal. The African musicologist, Nicholas Ballanta-Taylor, describes it: [1]

Music in Africa is not cultivated for its own sake. It is always used in connection with dances or to accompany workmen. The rhythmic interest of the songs impels them to work and takes away the feeling of drudgery . . .

[The work song is] mainly rhythmic—short phrases mostly of two or three bars; solo and chorus follow each other instantly; the chorus is in many instances composed of two or three ejaculatory words, answered by the workmen.

The importance of the rhythm and the continuous play of the call-and-response pattern is clear.

In all parts of the New World, the work song is sung wherever Africans are found, for this type of music is an integral part of an African tradition of mutual help. Herskovits, for example, explains how widespread this tradition is: [2]

The tradition of cooperation in the field of economic endeavor is outstanding in Negro cultures everywhere . . . This tradition, carried over into the New World, is manifest in the tree-felling parties of the Suriname Bush Negroes, the *combites* of the Haitian peasant, and in various forms of group labor in agriculture, fishing, house-raising, and the like encountered in Jamaica, Trinidad, the French West Indies, and elsewhere.

This African tradition found a congenial counterpart in the plantation system; and when freedom came, its original form of voluntary cooperation was reestablished. It is said to have reappeared in the Sea Islands [South Carolina and Georgia] immediately after the Civil War, but its outstanding present form is gang labor.

All of the groups mentioned used work songs.

Within the United States, the work song was probably sung as soon as the first slaves were landed and put to work. The first type of work song described by early travelers, however, is the rowing song, perhaps because boats were the most practical form of transportation on the East coast at that time. From the 1820's on, observers such as Basil Hall, Fanny Kemble, and Charles Lyell write of the 'weird and wild' songs of Negro oarsmen which impressed them deeply.

In 1845, Lyell told of songs that he had heard on a boat trip: [3]

. . . our black oarsmen made the woods echo to their song. One of them taking the lead, first improvised a verse, paying compliments to his master's family, and to a celebrated black beauty of the neighborhood, who was compared to the 'red bird.' The other five then joined in the chorus, always repeating the same words. Occasionally they struck up a hymn . . .

This is a description of both the call-and-response pattern and the use of a hymn as a work song, but perhaps the most noteworthy fact is the extemporaneous nature of the whole performance. The words most certainly and the music quite probably were improvised.

The first published collection which included work

songs appeared in 1867. It was *Slave Songs of the United States,* edited by Allen, Ware, and Garrison, who make the point that it is impossible to set them down exactly. Of one song, the editors say that it is 'still heard upon the Mississippi steamboats—wild and strangely fascinating': [4]

> I'm gwine to Alabamy, *Oh* . . . .
> For to see my mammy, *Ah* . . . .
> She went from Ole Virginny, *Oh* . . . . .
> And I'm her pickaninny, *Ah* . . . .
> She lives on the Tombigbee, *Oh* . . . . . .
> I wish I had her wid me, *Ah*. . . . .

The words are apparently the leader's lines, while the 'Ohs' and 'Ahs'—which are long-drawn-out—indicate the response and the moment at which group action begins, perhaps pulling a rope. Another work song in the collection is taken from the repertoire of Negro firemen in Savannah. 'Each company has its own set of tunes,' says the informant, 'its own leader': [5]

> . . . I'd rather court a yellow gal
> Than work for Henry Clay,
> *Heave away, heave away!* . . .
> I'd rather court a yellow gal
> Than work for Henry Clay,
> *Heave away, heave away!* . . . [my italics]

Here the distinction between leader and chorus is clear.

Allen, Ware, and Garrison also print the interesting reminiscences of 'a gentleman from Delaware': [6]

Some of the best *pure Negro* songs I have ever heard were those that used to be sung by the black stevedores, or perhaps the crews themselves, of the West India vessels, loading and unloading at the wharves in Philadelphia and Baltimore. I have stood for more than an hour, often, listening to them, as they hoisted and lowered the hogsheads and boxes of their cargoes; one man taking the burden of the song (and the slack of the rope) and the others striking in with the chorus.

This pre-Civil War observer was no doubt hearing a sea shanty, a type of work song that made contact with popular music by way of the minstrel show.

The story of jazz and the sea shanty has never been told. The invention of the cotton gin had made a profitable business of exporting American cotton to British mills. Annual shipments of cotton rose from 96 million pounds in 1815 to 444 million pounds in 1837, and American ships began to carry more and more world trade. Ships called at cotton ports from Savannah to New Orleans, and the popularity of the sea shanty reached its peak.

Because of sailors' varied national origins and far-flung ports of call, the sea shanty traveled all over the world. By 1845, when minstrel shows were beginning to prosper, sea shanties were frequently presented and—an interesting exchange—minstrel tunes such as 'Gimme de Banjo,' 'Do John Boker,' and 'De Camptown Races' became well-known sea shanties. Since many of these tunes were originally adaptations of Negro folk music, however, we often cannot tell whether they were taken to sea in their folk or minstrel versions.

'There were no finer shantymen,' writes Doerflinger, '. . . than the Negroes.' [7] Laboring as roustabouts on the Mississippi, working as stevedores along the Eastern coast, or shipping out from the Gulf ports as members of a crew, Negroes set an indelible stamp upon such shanties as 'Roll the Cotton Down,' 'A Long Time Ago,' and 'Shallo Brown.' It was the custom to set sail with a starboard watch of Negroes and a port watch of whites, but the work-song leader was usually a Negro.

The leader had to give the song enough lift and drive to get the work done: [8]

Way down South where I was born,
  Roll the cotton down:
I worked in the cotton and the corn,
  Oh, roll the cotton down.
When I was young and in my prime,
  Roll the cotton down:
I thought I'd go and join the Line,
  Oh, roll the cotton down.
And for a sailor caught a shine,
  Roll the cotton down:
I joined on a ship of the Black Ball Line,
  Oh, roll the cotton down.

—and so on, with the leader improvising whatever words and melody came to mind and the crew roaring out the refrain in steady chorus as they bent to their task.

Although we are dealing primarily with a manner and style of singing, the general outlines of a few melodies can be traced back to earlier sources. The shanty 'Lowlands,' which satirized working conditions among stevedores in Mobile, is taken from a British ballad dealing with a domestic tragedy. Many shanties were also taken from the English Music Hall tradition. On the other hand, another shanty, 'Rock About My Saro Jane,' sung by roustabouts on the Mississippi, is very close to the blues—the backbone of jazz. The amount of European or West African influence on any one shanty depended pretty much on who was singing it at the time, but as a type of work song the sea shanty furnishes an example of an early and world-wide blending of Euro-African musical qualities.

The sea shanty has practically disappeared, although it is still sung, as Tony Schwartz has demonstrated, by the menhaden fishermen off Barnegat Light. In other contexts, however, the work song is still very much with us. In 1924–5, Odum and Johnson collected a large assortment from many occupations, which they edited in *Negro Workaday Songs:* [9]

Whoever has seen a railroad section gang of five score Negroes working with pick and shovel and hammer and bars and other tools, and has heard them singing together will scarcely question the effectiveness of the scene . . .

Four pickmen of the road sing, swinging pick up, whirling it now round and round and now down again, movement well punctuated with nasal grunt and swelling song. Another group unloading coal, another asphalt, another lime, or sand, sing unnumbered songs and improvisations. Another group sings as workers rush wheelbarrows loaded with stone or sand or dirt or concrete, or still again line up on the roadside with picks and shovels. And of course there are the songs of the chain gangs . . .

All these singers constitute the great body of workers and singers who sing apparently with unlimited repertoire.

Whereas early travelers heard rowing songs and sea shanties, later specialists found work songs wherever group labor existed.

The classic description of a work song in full blast occurs in John and Alan Lomax's *Folk Song U.S.A.*[10]

The hot Southern sun shines down on the brown and glossy muscles of the work gang. The picks make whirling rainbow arcs around the shoulders of the singers. As the picks dig into the rock, the men give a deep, guttural grunt; their pent-up strength flows through the pick handle and they relax their bodies and prepare for the next blow.

The song leader now begins—pick handle twirling in his palms, the pickhead flashing in the sun:

Take this hammo—Huh!

The men grunt as the picks bite in together. They join the leader on his line, trailing in, one in harmony, one talking the words, another grunting them out between clenched teeth, another throwing out a high, thin falsetto cry above the rest.

On the final syllable, the picks are descending and again they bite a chip out of the rock and again there is a grunting exhalation of breath:

Carry it to my Captain—Huh!

The picks whirl up together in the sunlight and down again, they ring on the earth together, with maybe one or two bouncing a couple of times in a sort of syncopation. When the leader comes to the third—

Carry it to my Captain—

he holds on to the word 'captain' as long as he can, looks around at the boss and grins; his buddies chuckle and relax for a moment, knowing that he is giving them a little rest; then, 'wham' the steel bites at the rock and the whole gang roars out the final line, so that the hill gives back the sound . . .

The Lomaxes add that 'the way of singing is unique, the way of using the voice and attacking the tones of the melody have to be heard to be understood.'

The unique way of singing to which the Lomaxes refer is probably a result of West African influence: an over-all blue tonality and an expressiveness due to the relatively free use of the human voice. European harmony is almost entirely absent and the melody is similar to the street-cry or field-holler. The rhythmic accenting in the voices as well as in the bouncing of the pickax is polyrhythmic. At the same time, the manner in which the gang responds to the leader—with a grunt, talking, a trace of harmony, and a falsetto cry—is a variation on the West African call-and-response pattern. Even the concealed humor has its African counterpart.

(Perhaps the best recorded work songs available today are found in Tony Schwartz' privately issued LP entitled 'If He Asks You Was I Laughing.' Other examples occur in Albums III and VIII of the Music Division of the Library of Congress, including 'Long John,' 'Jumpin' Judy,' and

'Hammer Ring.' Recorded by the Lomaxes in the deep South, these songs are authentic and demonstrably West African in style. The chain-gang songs of Josh White are a bit mannered but Leadbelly's work songs ring true. Leadbelly's recording of 'Looky Looky Yonder' and 'Black Betty' (the whip) illustrates something of the rhythmic complexity of the work song on a minor scale. In the first tune, the hammer falls on the first beat of a 2/4 march tempo; in the second tune, the hammer falls on an off-beat —the sixth in an 8/8 tempo.)

Because of the lowly and isolated role played by the work song in American life, it survived relatively untouched in the nooks and crannies of the rural Negro South, especially where men work together. At the same time, it offered a semi-concealed avenue of expression which encouraged the preservation of West African elements. To this day the work song is an important part of a disappearing reservoir of African musical qualities deep in the heart of the United States.

10 | The Blues

Although they did not come into public notice until after the First World War, the blues are at the center of the jazz tradition and date back to the earliest days of jazz. From 1917 on, blues, near-blues, and non-blues-called-blues penetrated our popular music through and through. Almost everyone, for example, knows W. C. Handy's 'St. Louis Blues.' The general public thinks of the blues, however, as any popular music that is slow and sad. Actually, they are a separate and distinct form of jazz, and when a musician says, 'Let's play the blues,' he means something quite specific.

With the exception of the rhythm, perhaps the most important single element in the blues is the cry or holler, which has come to characterize much of jazz. It is part and parcel of the blue note and blue tonality. The cry has been described by John W. Work of Fisk University as 'a fragmentary bit of yodel, half sung, half yelled': [1]

Approaching his house or that of his sweetheart in the evening, or sometimes out of sheer lonesomeness, he would emit his 'holler.' Listeners would say, 'Here comes Sam,' or 'Will Jackson's coming,' or 'I just heard Archie down the road' . . .

In these 'hollers' the idiomatic material found in the blues is readily seen; the excessive portament, the slow time, the preference for the flatted third [or blue note], the melancholy type of tune, . . . many . . . could serve as lines of blues.

In the cry we have the basis of the ever-changing pitch in the melody of the blues.

In the Georgia Sea Islands, Lydia Parrish was fascinated by the same sound: [2]

In the old days, before Negroes rode to work in automobiles, they sang as they walked, and most of their tasks were lightened with song. One of my pleasantest memories is of hearing them singing in the early morning and at sundown, and—during the heat of the day—calling to each other across wide fields. The call was peculiar, and I always wondered how they came by such a strange form of vocal gymnastics, since I never heard a white person do anything like it.

She adds that these cries reminded her of a Bantu rain song, recorded in Africa, which had the same 'upward break in the voice.'

An early illustration of the process by which the cry was incorporated into a group song is furnished by F. L. Olmsted, who traveled in the South before the Civil War. He was sleeping in a railroad passenger car at the time: [3]

At midnight I was awakened by loud laughter, and, looking out, saw that the loading gang of negroes had made a fire, and were enjoying a right merry repast. Suddenly, one raised such a sound as I never heard before; a long, loud, musical shout, rising and falling, and breaking into falsetto, his voice ringing through the woods in the clear, frosty night air, like a bugle call. As he finished, the melody was caught up by another, and then, by several in chorus . . .

After a few minutes I could hear one urging the rest to come to work again, and soon he stepped towards the cotton bales, saying, 'Come, bredern, come; let's go at it; come now, eoho! roll away! eeoho—eeoho—weeioho—i!!—and the rest taking it up as before, in a few moments they all had their shoulders to a bale of cotton, and were rolling it up the embankment.

Here the cry leads first to group singing and then to a work song.

Experts have attempted to analyze the unusual manner of vocalization in the cry and holler. In their *Negro Workaday Songs,* Odum and Johnson print four detailed graphs of the sound waves of a holler, prepared by a phonophotographic process of recording. The editors are the first to admit that these sounds are unique and defy complete analysis, but they note an unusually warm vibrato and sudden changes of pitch. They conclude that 'the vocal chords must undergo a snap.' [4]

This 'snap' is what Harold Courlander calls 'the falsetto voice,' adding that it originated in West Africa. Professor Waterman, too, speaks of 'the custom of singing in falsetto . . . common (among Negroes) both in West Africa and in the New World.' Much more prolonged and complex than the cowboy's, or roisterer's, 'Yippee,' traces of the cry or holler can be heard in most of jazz. It exists virtually intact in the work song, the shouting spiritual, and above all, the blues.

Examples of cries or hollers can be heard in Album VIII of the Library of Congress recordings. ('Arwhoolie' is one of the most interesting since it employs falsetto, portamento, or sliding from note to note, and blue tonality; in fact, it is a blues without the rhythm and the European harmony.) Leadbelly recorded a similar holler which he called 'Ain't Goin' Down to the Well No Mo' ' (Musicraft 224). Identical melodic phrases occur on a 1947 recording by Chano Pozo, who belonged to a Nigerian cult in Havana.

The harmony employed in the blues is another matter. It is pretty clearly derived from European music although colored by the blue tonality of the cry. At its simplest, the harmony of the blues consists of the three basic chords in our musical language. The same chords, for example, are used in the accompaniment to 'Yankee Doodle,' 'Silent Night,' and 'Swanee River.' These chords are technically known as the 'tonic,' the 'sub-dominant,' and the 'dominant'—in all keys—and you can hear them in the right order if you listen to the background of a simple version of 'Careless Love.'

How did the blues happen to adopt this harmony? It probably came from our religious music, which employed these chords. Says guitar-picker T-Bone Walker: [5]

Of course, the blues comes a lot from the church, too. The first time I ever heard a boogie-woogie piano was the first time I went to church. That was the Holy Ghost Church in Dallas, Texas. That boogie-woogie was a kind of blues, I guess.

'How Long Blues' is derived from a spiritual, says Rudi Blesh in *Shining Trumpets,* and the spirituals 'Precious Lord Hold My Hand' and 'Nobody's Fault but Mine' are essentially blues. Parallel examples also occur where the harmony and even part of the melody is retained. Thus, 'St. James Infirmary' owes much to the spiritual 'Hold On, Keep Your Hands on the Plow,' and the last chorus of 'St. Louis Blues' owes its melody to the exhortations of Brother Lazarus Gardner, Presiding Elder of the A.M.E. Church of Florence, Alabama, according to W. C. Handy. Here, again, we are close to the cry.

There were blues singers on recordings in 1955, however, who still did not employ European harmony. It is generally possible to date a blues style by the complexity of the harmony. Guitarist John Lee Hooker, whose recordings are made for the Negro trade exclusively, employs a drone which sounds very much like the skirl of a bagpipe and he says his grandfather played that way. His rhythms, however, are very complicated. With Big Bill Broonzy it's a matter of pride not to employ European harmony, although he doesn't think of it in those terms: [6]

. . . for me to really sing the old blues that I learned in Mississippi I have to go back to my sound and not the right chords as the musicians have told me to make. They just don't work with the real blues . . . the blues didn't come out of no book and them real chords did . . . the real blues is played and sung the way you feel and no man or woman feels the same way every day . . .

Other favorites in 1955 such as Muddy Waters, Smokey Hogg, and Lil' Son Jackson employ some harmony, but often without any consistent plan.

This non-harmonic style is archaic and may well date back to pre-Civil War days. Wilder Hobson in his *American Jazz Music* suggests: [7]

. . . the blues may originally have consisted merely in the singing, over a steady, percussive rhythm, of lines of variable length, the length being determined by what phrase the singer had in mind, with equally variable pauses (the accompanying rhythm continuing) determined by how long it took the singer to think up another phrase.

With this early style, in other words, the singer didn't need a pre-arranged series of chords as long as he performed by himself.

When the blues became a group performance some pre-conceived plan was needed, for everyone had to agree on when to start and stop. Leadbelly furnishes an example of an intermediate stage. Performing alone on recordings, he sometimes disregards what have become the conventional chord 'changes' and the usual duration of each chord, strumming along until he remembers the words that come next. Perhaps he is searching his memory, but as long as he is alone it makes little difference. On the other hand, when Leadbelly plays with a group he automatically adopts a common harmony and timing.

The form of the blues is a mixture. The over-all length and general proportions are derived from European harmony; the inner form is taken from the West African call-and-response pattern. As in the work song, which probably contributed to the formation of the blues, the call-and-response pattern came first and was employed intact. European harmony and the forms it favored came later and were absorbed gradually. In our own day, the European-derived form has become the most easily recognized characteristic of the blues.

The length of blues form varied originally, as we have seen, but today among jazzmen it has become fixed at 12 bars. These bars are divided into three equal parts, with a different chord for each. The words themselves illustrate this division:

> I'm goin' down and lay my head on the railroad track,
> I'm goin' down and lay my head on the railroad track,
> When the train come along, I'm gonna snatch it back.

Roughly speaking, the time taken in singing the words of each line is a little more than one half of each of the three equal (musical) parts, which leaves considerable room for an instrumental response after each line. Here is the call-and-response pattern again, and Joe Smith's cornet accompaniment of Bessie Smith on 'Young Woman's Blues' is a classic example.

The unusual fact about this blues form is that it consists of three parts, instead of two or four. This stanza form is quite rare in English literature and may have originated with the American Negro. Like the ballad stanza, it furnishes a good vehicle for a narrative of any length. At the same time, it is more dramatic: the first two lines set the stage clearly by repetition and the third line delivers the punch. The blues stanza is capsule communication, tailored for live performance among a participating, dancing audience.

The date of the first blues will probably never be known. The more we learn, the earlier it seems to have been. 'African songs of proverbial wit and ridicule were one likely source,' says Russell Ames, 'and African songs of pity and sorrow another.' [8] Old-timers in New Orleans, a few born as early as the 1860's, say 'the blues was here when I come.' Gertrude 'Ma' Rainey, one of the greatest of blues singers, told Professor Work that she heard the blues in 1902 and sang them from then on. W. C. Handy reports that he heard the blues in 1903. Baby Dodds (born in 1894) says: 'The blues were played in New Orleans in the early days.' Jelly Roll Morton gives the impression that just about everyone within reach of a piano in New Orleans worked out his own version of the blues in a barrelhouse style that later became known as boogie-woogie. 'They couldn't play anything else,' he reports disparagingly.

Morton was inclined to look down on the blues—a perennial attitude—as crude and unpolished. At the same time, he made fine arrangements of the blues and played exquisite blues himself. In retrospect, it seems clear that Morton disapproved only of the boogie-woogie style of the blues, which is indeed archaic. For the blues form is simply a frame for the musical picture, a mold into which the jazzman pours his creative energy. The melody, harmony, and rhythm can become infinitely complicated, depending upon the performer's sophistication. Hence playing the blues is still an acid test for a jazzman.

Among musicians the use of the words, 'the blues,' to refer specifically to the 12-bar form came late in the day. Among music publishing houses this form was so unusual that W. C. Handy's 'Memphis Blues' (which may have helped establish the pattern) had been turned down by several publishers because of its form before being issued in 1912. Count Basie, who played piano in New York City in 1925, told me that he does not remember hearing this use of the phrase until he arrived in Oklahoma City in 1926, when he met the vocalist Jimmy Rushing, who had been taught by an uncle from the deep South around 1915 that 'the blues means twelve bars.' When Jack Teagarden arrived in New York City much later (1927), he was the only known white musician who could sing the blues in an 'authentic' manner. It was not until the 1930's that recorded performances by Fats Waller, Artie Shaw, and a few others were first labeled—quite accurately—'The Blues.'

Although the popular market was flooded with highly inaccurate imitations of the blues before 1920, the real thing was more or less unknown and the spread of any one blues was slow. It took place, if at all, among Negroes. One focal point was the T.O.B.A. circuit (Theatre Owners and Bookers Association) which operated a chain of theaters for the Negro trade in the South. Sterling Brown's poem, 'Ma Rainey,' communicates the feeling of excitement that the arrival of a blues singer caused in those days. And whatever blues she sang, the people took them over as their own—thus, partially composed music became folk music overnight. At the same time, the difference between the blues and religious music was never sharp. Only the words differed in many cases, and sometimes even they were alike. We have recordings from the late 'twenties of Mamie Forehand and Blind Willie Johnson singing spirituals in the form of 12-bar blues. Similarly, the Reverend McGhee and his congregation recorded music in blues form as a shouting spiritual. In West Africa, as in the United States, there is little or no technical distinction between secular and religious music.

By 1920, phonograph companies discovered that there

was a market among Negroes for the blues. The first hit—but not the best—was Mamie Smith's 'Crazy Blues.' Bootleg copies sold for three times list price. A Negro undergraduate in a Northern university, now a well-known professor at Howard University, recalls buying a copy and playing it late at night with the curtains drawn. He knew that his uninitiated white classmates would consider it crude and vulgar.

During the 'twenties, a special category called 'Race Recordings' was issued for the Negro public. With the Depression, this market almost disappeared until 1945 when the large sales of Cecil Gant's 'I Wonder' made record companies sit up and take notice again. Categorized as 'Rhythm and Blues' in 1950, a hit sold about 100,000 copies and commercial white bands often recorded their own diluted versions afterwards. The next big step was the 'Rock and Roll' music of the 1955 period—simplified but rhythmic blues—which white youngsters en masse heard for the first time in a tasteless version of the real thing.

The mood of the blues is difficult to assess. Arriving after World War I, when our popular music was either sad and sentimental or glad and boisterous, the bittersweet blues mixture founded a new tradition. 'The blues singer,' says Professor Work, 'translates every happening into his own intimate inconvenience.' There is a stoic humor: 'I'm laughing,' says the blues singer, 'just to keep from crying,' or 'Got the blues, but I'm too damn mean to cry.' A few are desperate: 'I used to love you, but oh, God damn you now!' The language is deceptively simple. Beneath it all, there is a lean matter-of-fact skepticism that penetrates the florid façade of our culture like a knife.

The blues are still very much with us. Our popular music is increasingly permeated with blue tonality. Composers such as Hoagy Carmichael, Johnny Mercer, and George Gershwin have been saturated in it. 'If there is a national American form of song,' says Russell Ames, 'it is the blues.' [9] And the 12-bar blues are still at the heart of modern jazz. Duke Ellington's best compositions are usually transformations of the blues. The most influential of modern jazzmen, Charlie Parker, recorded more versions of the blues (under a variety of titles) than any other form. As long as improvisation is a vital element in jazz, the blues will probably be the prime form for its expression.

11 | Minstrelsy

Minstrelsy reigned supreme in the American entertainment world from about 1845 to 1900. Unlike the work song or the blues, it contributed no particularly outstanding characteristics to the development of jazz. Yet it is of vast importance to the history of jazz because it served as a vehicle for the spread of American Negro music. During its fifty-year reign, minstrelsy furnished an introduction to the general public of a type of entertainment based upon Negro elements of story, dance, and song. For minstrelsy educated the general ear, preparing the way for the introduction of jazz.

At its best, minstrelsy was more of a burlesque than a truthful imitation of Negro life. Its appeal was enormous, however, and it became a big business—joining forces with the music business and borrowing material from every conceivable source. In its heyday, minstrelsy featured, among other attractions, circus acrobats, Chinese giants, parodies of *Hamlet*, African villages, and always, the Negro. In turn it gave birth to vaudeville, burlesque (in the original meaning), and musical comedy. Three big minstrel companies were on tour in 1919 and small companies were still playing the South in 1955.

Why was minstrelsy so popular? The American public loved it, says the brilliant historian Constance Rourke, because it reflected their point of view. Minstrel players acted the role of Negroes with an air of comic triumph, irreverent wisdom, and an underlying note of rebellion. Perhaps the combination appealed to a practical people in a new country. It was no accident that minstrelsy was born during the unsettled era of Jacksonian Democracy and grew as the Abolitionist movement prospered.

Constance Rourke supports her conclusions with evidence. In her reading of early American almanacs, jokebooks, theatrical posters, memoirs, travel accounts, tracts, sermons, and pamphlets, she found that the American people tended to think of the typical American as a Yankee peddler, a backwoodsman, or a Negro. (Just as we in 1955 thought of Wally Cox, Molly Berg, or Amos and Andy as typical Americans.) She concludes that, of these three types, 'none left a deeper imprint than the Negro in minstrelsy,' who provided a sympathetic symbol 'for a pioneer people who required resilience as a prime trait.' [1]

Minstrelsy began gradually enough. Before 1800, there were occasional solo performances by white men in blackface inserted between intermissions of plays. The general conception of the Negro appears to have been partly a carry-over from seventeenth-century England. In Aphra Behn's novelette *Oroonoko* (1688) and the popular play based upon it, the later stereotypes of the 'regal slave' of colonial fiction and the 'noble savage' of Rousseau were inextricably mixed. Neither bore any true resemblance to the American Negro, but the Abolitionists, for example, seemed to believe it.

By 1810, blackface impersonations with titles such as 'A Negro Boy' were being presented by clowns of sorts to the accompaniment of jigs and clogs. This was before the circus, as we know it, was organized. A little later, solo blackface acts with bone-clappers, tambourines, and banjos became popular. These instruments, which probably have their prototypes in West Africa, had long been used by Negroes in the South and they became the customary instruments of minstrelsy. Essentially percussive, they helped to establish the rhythmic foundation of minstrel shows.

Using these instruments, among others, various acts were booked on rough-and-ready theatrical tours through the newly settled frontier country of Kentucky, Tennessee, and Ohio. The entertainers came into direct contact with the fiery camp meetings and the powerful music which played so large a part in frontier revivals. Negroes, as we have seen, were very active in these religious gatherings. So members of these touring shows, ever alert to discover new material, hit upon a mine of inspiration in the Negro and his folkways.

The man who may have struck the spark that ignited the minstrel era was raised in frontier territory. He was Thomas D. Rice, professionally known as Daddy 'Jim Crow' Rice. A professed eyewitness, Edmon S. Conner, recalls how it all began around the years 1828–9: [2]

N. M. Ludlow took a Summer company to Louisville. Among the members were Sol Smith . . . and Tom Rice. It was the first regular theatre in that city. Back of the theatre was a livery stable kept by a man named Crow. The actors would look into the stable yard from the theatre, and were particularly amused by an old decrepit negro, who used to do odd jobs for Crow. As was then usual with slaves, they called themselves after their owner, so that old Daddy had assumed the name of Jim Crow. He was very much deformed, the right shoulder being drawn high up, the left leg stiff and crooked at the knee, giving him a painful, but at the same time laughable limp. He used to croon a queer old tune with words of his own, and at the end of each verse would give a little jump, and when he came down he set his 'heel a-rockin'.' He called it 'jumping Jim Crow.' The words of the refrain were:

'Wheel about, turn about,
Do jis so,
An' ebery time I wheel about,
I jump Jim Crow!'

Rice watched him closely, and saw that here was a character unknown to the stage. He wrote several verses, changed the air somewhat, quickened it a good deal, made up exactly like Daddy, and sang it to a Louisville audience. They were wild with delight, and on the first night he was recalled twenty times.

One of several commentators on this incident, Conner's memory appears to be sharp, his observation keen. The words of the song reflect the close observation of animal life found in Negro folklore. A crow, for example, hops or jumps rather than walks. The identification with the color black adds another clue to its origin.

'Jump Jim Crow' became a tremendous hit. It swept this country and later became the greatest song of the century in London. Bayard Taylor, according to Wittke in *Tambo and Bones,* heard the tune sung by Hindu minstrels in Delhi. By 1840, blackface imitators of Daddy Rice —and, indirectly or directly, the Negro—were on every type of playbill in the country. Sometime in 1843, these various specialties were combined into one big show by the Virginia Minstrels in New York. E. P. Christy in the following year worked out the minstrel formula of presentation. Its success was amazing. Another company, Bryant's Minstrels, charging twenty-five cents admission, ran for sixteen uninterrupted years in New York City.

Although Negro minstrel troupes did not appear until after the Civil War, certain individual Negroes became famous before then. William Henry Lane (c. 1825–62), billed as 'Juba,' was universally conceded to be the greatest minstrel dancer.[3] In 1845 he actually received top billing with a white company. In two contests, he defeated

Jack Diamond, who was considered the best white dancer. Lane's specialty was an imitation of the steps of other well-known dancers topped by his own dance routine which always brought down the house.

In his *American Notes* (1842), Charles Dickens is said to be describing Juba: [4]

Single shuffle, double shuffle, cut and cross-cut; snapping his fingers, rolling his eyes, turning in his knees, presenting the backs of his legs in front, spinning about on his toes and heels like nothing but the man's fingers on the tambourine; dancing with two left legs, two right legs, two wooden legs, two wire legs, two spring legs—all sorts of legs and no legs—what is this to him?

In comparing Lane's dancing to the rhythms of 'fingers on a tambourine,' Dickens hits upon an important element in the world-wide appeal of minstrelsy.

More specifically, a critic in Liverpool compared Juba's dancing to the rhythms of the banjo and bones, adding that 'this youth is the delight and astonishment of all who witness his extraordinary dancing; to our mind he dances demisemi, semi, and quavers, as well as the slower steps.' [5] (A 'quaver' is the British word for our eighth note and a 'demisemi' is 1/32 of a whole note, next to the smallest rhythmic unit our system of notation uses.) English audiences were hearing, seeing, and enjoying much more complicated dance rhythms than were common in Europe.

Of course, there was more to minstrelsy than the complex rhythms. Another critic in the *Theatrical Times* (August 1848) tried to explain it: [6]

The performances of this young man are far above the common performances of the mountebanks who give imitations of American and Negro character; there is an ideality in what he does that makes his efforts at once grotesque and poetical, without losing sight of the reality of the representation.

Separated by the Atlantic Ocean from the birthplace of minstrelsy, the British press was in a position to analyze the phenomenon a little more objectively. In this case, the critic had seen Juba—not the usual white imitator—and a significant difference was apparent to him.

A blending had taken place, and minstrel music and dance were something new under the sun. Perhaps William Makepeace Thackeray expresses its spirit most clearly: [7]

I heard a humorous balladist not long ago, a minstrel with wool on his head and an ultra-Ethiopian complexion, who performed a negro ballad that I confess moistened these spectacles in a most unexpected manner. I have gazed at thousands of tragedy queens dying on the stage, and expiring in appropriate blank verse, and I never wanted to wipe them. They have looked up, be it said, at many scores of clergymen without being dimmed, and behold! a vagabond with a corked face and a banjo sings a little song, strikes a wild note, which sets the heart thrilling with happy pity.

The 'wild note' may have been descended from a field-holler. For the appeal of this music was real and lasting. Whatever the mixed impulses beneath Thackeray's emotional response, he and millions of others were moved by minstrelsy.

The influence of minstrelsy in England went deep. Years later, 'English clowns, such as Majiltons and Hanlon-Lees, returned to whiteface,' says Marion Winter in *Chronicles of the American Dance,* 'but kept certain characteristics of blackface performers—the manic gaiety, he-who-gets-slapped apprehensions, and dance acrobatics—evolving thereby a slightly macabre, almost surrealist personage.' [8] Charlie Chaplin, for example, owes something to the same tradition. 'Christies' became the British name for minstrel shows, after the famous impresario E. P. Christy, and the hero of D. H. Lawrence's *Sons and Lovers*

(1916) speaks of taking the evening off and going to a 'Christy' (cf. also 'The Dead' in James Joyce's *Dubliners*).

Back in the United States, minstrelsy spread together with the expanding frontier. During the Gold Rush of 1849, it reached the mining camps and mushroom towns of California where, a little later, minstrel troupes featured spirituals as well as camp-meeting songs with huge success. In the early 'fifties, for example, a young dancer named Ralph Keeler was touring with a minstrel company on a Mississippi showboat: '. . . we steamed thousands of miles on the Western and Southern rivers,' he writes. 'We went, for instance, the entire navigable lengths of the Cumberland and Tennessee.' [9]

On another occasion, Keeler and a minstrel troupe started in New Orleans on a showboat which paddled north, while they gave performances along the way wherever an audience could be found. They even played prisons, perhaps entertaining guitar-picking forerunners of Leadbelly: 'From motives of curiosity, charity, and advertisement combined, we always visited the state prisons . . . and sang and played to the prisoners.' In his wide-ranging travels, Keeler must have influenced and been influenced by a great variety of American Negro music.

After the Civil War, minstrelsy boomed. The financial panic of '57 had had little effect on its rapid growth, and the post-bellum organization of Negro troupes, such as the Georgia Minstrels in 1865, further stimulated the trade. Horace Weston, Billy Kersands, Sam Lucas, James Bland (composer of 'Carry Me Back to Old Virginny'), Billy Speed, the Bohee brothers, and many other Negro performers became famous in the United States. These men all had white managers and played in blackface. Many of them toured Europe with Haverley's European Minstrels. James Bohee, for example, gave banjo lessons to the Prince of Wales. By the 'nineties, the burnt-cork make-up was dropped and three crack Negro troupes were touring the country: Hicks and Sawyer Minstrels, Richards and Pringle Minstrels, and McCabe and Young Minstrels.

Based upon Negro characteristics of story, dance, and song, the minstrel show presented endless opportunities for the use of American Negro music and related elements. The formula of presentation consisted of three more-or-less unrelated parts: the show proper, the olio, and sometimes a parody playlet. The first part, or show proper, began with the usual half circle of players with the end-men and interlocutor cracking jokes and doing their various specialties. It ended with the Walk Around, a grand finale in which everyone joined.

The Walk Around, at the height of minstrelsy, was simply the cakewalk. Couples promenaded grandly with a high kickstep, waving canes, doffing hats, and bowing low. The cakewalk, as Shephard Edmunds testifies in *They All Played Ragtime,* originated on the plantation: 'They did a take-off on the high manners of the white folks in the "big house," but their masters, who gathered around to watch the fun, missed the point.' [10] (It may also be that the Walk Around owes something to the ring-shout in origin.) This finale of the first part was enlivened by Negro song and dance. Dan Emmett, a white composer and impresario, always insisted that the Walk Around be performed in as authentic a Negro manner as possible. And it was accompanied by ragtime.

The second part, or olio (a word derived from the Spanish *olla,* meaning mixture), consisted of a series of solo acts that later evolved into variety or vaudeville. It too was usually climaxed by 'a genuine, hilarious darkey "hoe-down," ' as Wittke writes, 'in which every member of the company did a dance at the center of the stage, while the others sang and vigorously clapped their hands to emphasize the rhythm.' [11] This custom of circling a solo dancer

and clapping encouragement survives to this day and may
be seen any night at the Savoy Ballroom in Harlem.

The hoe-down incorporated a variety of American Negro
elements, from hand-clapping and foot-patting to characteristics of ring games and shouting spirituals. Considerable rhythmic complexity was built up by the bones,
tambourines, and banjos, and the call-and-response pattern dominated the performance:

> Darkies hear dat banjo ring,
> Yoe! Ha! Yoe!
> Listen to the fiddle sing,
> Yoe! Ha! Yoe!
> Dee dah doo dah dum,
> Aha! Aha! . . .

As usual, the words are unimportant and simply serve to
embellish the roll of the rhythm.

The third part, or parody playlet, often as not consisted
of a burlesque of *Uncle Tom's Cabin*—the most frequently performed work in the American theater. (*Mac-
beth* was presented as *Bad Breath, the Crane of Chowder*.)
Yet even in this part of the show, groups of Jubilee Singers
were often introduced at various points, singing 'plantation' songs. In 1875, for example, the 'North Carolinians'
were similarly presented at Case Hall in Cleveland. They
were described as 'a company of genuine field hands from
the Southern plantations, male and female, who were formerly slaves. Their music is . . . weird, grotesque, but generally melodious . . .' [12] In this way, camp-meeting songs
and even field-hollers and work songs obtained a wide
hearing.

By the 'nineties, minstrelsy was suffering from galloping
elephantiasis. Buffalo Bill's agent, Nate Salsbury, produced a spectacle called 'Black America' at Ambrose Park
in Brooklyn, New York. It included a Negro village with

cabins, mules, washtubs (probably *not* used as musical instruments), a meetinghouse, and a preacher. Introduced by 'African tribal episodes and a war dance,' the show featured a choir of five hundred voices recruited from 'the farm and mill hands of Georgia, Alabama, and Florida.' This was in 1894. In 1902, A. W. Martin produced 'a spectacular scene of Voodoo worship' in New York City as an intermission between the acts of a comic parody of *Uncle Tom's Cabin*. Wildly unauthentic as these shows must have been, they and their music made a deep impression on the public.

The penetration into our popular culture—by way of minstrelsy—of American Negro musical characteristics can be documented by certain tunes. This is unusual, because the main contribution of the Negro consists in the intangibles of performance, fleeting improvisations, and extemporaneous embellishments. Nevertheless, many of the songs of Stephen Foster show a strong camp-meeting influence. Foster was brought up by a mulatto nurse and as a child learned to love Negro music. His most enduring songs, which have become part of our folk music, are of the minstrel type with lyrics in Negro dialect such as 'Swanee River,' 'Old Black Joe,' 'My Old Kentucky Home,' and 'Massa's in the Cold, Cold Ground.' ('Old Folks at Home' has the same three opening notes as the Negro spiritual 'Deep River,' and the same early jump of an octave. 'Camptown Races' owes much to 'Lord, Remember Me' and 'Roll Jordan Roll,' and so on.)

Another famous composer, Dan Emmett, used the Jordan theme again and again in his minstrel music. The composer of 'Dixie,' Emmett was white and claimed credit for the hit 'Old Dan Tucker.' The original words, however, describe a Negro and (as Constance Rourke points out) the beast-fable lyrics, the call-and-response pattern, and the tune itself betray strong Negro influence. It is probable that many minstrel hits, just as 'Jump Jim Crow,' were taken over wholly or in part from the Negro. As usual, white men were in a better position to cash in on them. And yet it was a Negro composer, James Bland, who wrote 'In the Evening by the Moonlight,' 'Oh Dem Golden Slippers,' and 'Carry Me Back to Old Virginny.' Here, the contribution is direct but the Negro musical characteristics are few.

On the other hand, 'Zip Coon,' better known today as 'Turkey in the Straw,' has been traced back to a Mississippi river-boat breakdown, or dance, called 'Natchez under the Hill.' In an old version, it tells the story of an old Negro. Another minstrel hit, 'Clare de Kitchen,' was apparently the creation of Negro firemen on the river boats. Later successes such as 'Ta-ra-ra-boom-de-ay!,' 'The Bully Song,' and 'A Hot Time in the Old Town' are supposed to have originated in a famous Negro cabaret in St. Louis named *Babe Connor's*. In most cases, of course, the amount of American Negro qualities in any one song varied with the interpretation.

Minstrelsy and the beginnings of jazz collided in the 'nineties. Besides carrying American Negro music to the public, minstrelsy also served as a training ground for early jazzmen. Or perhaps it would be more accurate to say that many minstrel musicians simply turned to ragtime and then to jazz as minstrelsy declined. The jazz musician Jack Laine was leading a minstrel band in and around New Orleans in 1895. Stale Bread (Emile Lacoume) and his Spasm Band joined Doc Malney's Minstrels in the following year. 'All the minstrel shows, like the Rabbit Foot Minstrels and Silas Green and the Georgia Minstrels,' says New Orleans guitarist Danny Barker, 'used New Orleans musicians year in and year out.'

W. C. Handy had joined Mahara's Minstrels in 1896 and in the next year, which saw the end of the depression and election of McKinley, became cornet soloist and leader. It had been the custom since about 1850 for newly arrived minstrel troupes to put on a parade to stir up interest in the show to follow—a device also used by the circus. In his *Father of the Blues*, Handy writes: [13]

> We used the heaviest works of W. P. Chambers, C. W. Dalbey and C. L. Barnhouse; even the stiff composition *Alvin Joslin* by Pettee was not beyond us. It was only when we were lip-weary that we eased off on the light, swingy marches of R. B. Hall and John Philip Sousa.

Mahara's was a famous troupe and the musicians prided themselves on their up-to-date classical repertory. A Sousa march, however, when played with a little verve, can come very close to jazz.

Later, in the public square, the band would play 'Brudder Gardner's Picnic,' a medley of Stephen Foster hits. As a specialty, they might perform 'The Musicians' Strike' to the dismay and then delight of the innocent townspeople: one by one the musicians would quarrel with each other and desert the band, only to re-assemble around the corner and suddenly 'cut loose with one of the most sizzling tunes of the day,' as Handy says, 'perhaps "Creole Belles," "Georgia Camp Meeting," or "A Hot Time in the Old Town Tonight." ' [14] At this point, the presence of a few potential jazzmen was essential and the sound may well have approximated the music of a New Orleans marching band.

By the turn of the century, jazzmen could be found in almost any minstrel troupe. The old-time pianist, Clarence Williams, ran away from home at the age of twelve to join a show. The great blues singer, Gertrude 'Ma' Rainey, was one of the star attractions in Rainey's Rabbit Foot Minstrels. Jelly Roll Morton was working with the McCabe and Young Minstrels in 1910—they say he was the world's worst comedian—and James P. Johnson played ragtime with an amateur minstrel group at Public School 69 in New York City. Trumpeter Bunk Johnson, rediscovered in the 'forties, was on tour with various minstrel shows from 1903, when he joined Holecamp's Georgia Smart Set, until 1931, when he went back to work in the fields. And even jazz-men of more recent years, such as Hot Lips Page and Les-ter Young, played with minstrel shows when they were first starting out. 'A lot of men,' observes drummer Jo Jones, quoted in *Hear Me Talkin' to Ya,* 'came up through the minstrel shows.'

Minstrelsy, however, was doomed. It was meeting stiff competition from the Harrigan and Hart shows (spurred by importations of Gilbert and Sullivan), vaudeville, caba-rets, the early movies, and by 1917, from jazz itself. The minstrel dance was siphoned off into social dancing by the dance team of Vernon and Irene Castle and the fox trot. Old-time minstrel men blamed one thing. Back in 1902, when the successful impresario Lew Dockstader was asked why minstrelsy was slipping, he replied that the essential Negro qualities had become dated and lost.[15] Time and again, experienced observers make the same point: the contribution of the American Negro, directly and in-directly, gave minstrelsy its vitality. When the basic Negro qualities became diluted and the stock characters lost any relation to real life, minstrelsy died.

American popular entertainment is still riddled with debts to minstrelsy. Joseph Jefferson, Edwin Booth, Chauncey Olcott, and Al Jolson were minstrel men. So were Fred Stone, Benny Field, and Eddie Cantor. The dancing of Bill Robinson and others derived from min-strelsy. Minstrel tunes even appear on the Hit Parade. The Andrews Sisters' 'Dance with a Dolly,' for example, was entitled 'Lubly Fan' when it was composed for a min-strel show by John Hodges in the 1840's. More recently, loyal alumni of Cornell discovered that their Alma Mater song was originally a minstrel tune having little to do with 'Cayuga's Waters.'

The effect of minstrelsy upon American culture is almost inestimable. The basis upon which the Negro built, of course, was European and American popular music. Fiddle tunes, jigs, hornpipes, and square dances were standard fare, but they were all gradually transformed by the American Negro manner and style of performance. The blending was broad and lasting if not very deep. In the process, minstrelsy once and for all acquainted the general public with something of the music of the American Negro.

12 | The Spiritual

Spirituals have been a cherished part of our musical culture for nearly a hundred years. Who has not heard and enjoyed 'Swing Low, Sweet Chariot'? And spirituals, or something very much like them, were probably sung during the Great Awakening of the early nineteenth century. In contrast to minstrelsy, they present the Negro as a thoughtful human being, and reveal some of his aspirations to those who care to listen. They were an early and impressive means for making the United States, and indeed the whole world, conscious of the Negro and his music. The process also helped make familiar something of the rhythmic idiom and, especially, the blue tonality which became important to jazz.

Spirituals came to the attention of the public after the Civil War. Northerners such as Colonel T. W. Higginson, who had led a Negro regiment, wrote about them in the *Atlantic Monthly*. They were included in the first collection of Negro tunes, *Slave Songs of the United States*, edited by Allen, Ware, and Garrison in 1867. Then, in 1871, the Fisk Jubilee Singers began their famous tours at home and abroad, establishing spirituals once and for all as respectable music.[1]

How old are the spirituals? Professor John W. Work of Fisk University argues that some of them go back before

1800. He points out, for example, that a group of Negro freedmen from Kentucky, Pennsylvania, and South Carolina migrated in 1824 to Haiti, where 'Roll Jordan Roll' is still sung. The emigrants must have taken the song with them and so, allowing time for its composition and growth in the United States, Professor Work feels that this particular spiritual dates back at least to the turn of the century.[2] Similar examples in the Bahamas indicate 1780 or earlier.

The religious music of the American Negro ranges wide and deep. In addition to spirituals, it includes other kinds or types such as the ring-shout, the song-sermon, the jubilee, and the gospel song (the label 'anthem' is a general term which is applied to any church singing). Each of these has its own characteristics and is still being sung in various parts of the United States today.

Professor Work divides this music into three types, according to the way the melody is handled: (1) the call-and-response or back-and-forth melody (ring-shout, song-sermon, and—sometimes—jubilee and gospel song); (2) the short, rhythmic melody (gospel song—usually—and jubilee —sometimes); and (3) the long, sustained melody (spiritual). On the other hand, Professor W. L. James of Spelman College, Atlanta, told me that he divides this music, according to mood and other qualities, from enthusiastic rejoicing (jubilee) to deep reverence (spiritual). There is also a vast difference, of course, between the folk and concert manner of performance of any one type.

What we know as the spiritual is really a very rare type. Probably the greatest number of religious songs of the American Negro employ the call-and-response pattern and have a cheerful mood. But the spirituals with which the general public is most familiar, such as 'Nobody Knows the Trouble I've Seen,' 'Go Down Moses,' and 'Swing Low, Sweet Chariot,' do not usually employ the call-and-response pattern. They are the least African and most European of all Afro-American religious music, and—perhaps for this reason—to a great many people they represent the crowning glory of Negro music.

Where did the spirituals come from? There are two diametrically opposed views. The first is that the spiritual was created out of nowhere by a sort of spontaneous combustion of the Negro's genius; the second is that the spiritual was taken entirely from European music, especially the hymn, since there could be no other source. Each of these views is probably half right. But they both fail to take into account the existence of an African musical tradition and the blending with European music that was bound to occur.

A third and middle-of-the-road view is that the spiritual is a varying mixture of European and African music. There was plenty of reason for such a merging. Behind the Negro spirituals, as Gilbert Chase observes, was a 'century-long tradition of "ecstatic delight in psalmody." ' [3] The African arriving in the United States was not influenced by hymns sung in fashionable churches by city dwellers. He was attracted to the folk hymn, which started in early New England but was soon followed in the towns by a more modern style with which most Northerners are still familiar. The folk hymn survived only in rural districts.

Certain occasional elements in the style of the folk hymn made it attractive to the West African. As mentioned in the chapter on the Great Awakening, one style of folk hymn is sung by ear with each singer improvising as many embellishments as he pleases. Slurs, glides, flourishes, and turns are expected of everybody. Added to this was the custom of 'lining out,' whereby the preacher reads the words before the congregation sings them. This custom started in the British Isles and lasted over three hundred years, even when the congregation had learned the words by heart. It became an organic part of the music and dovetailed neatly with the African custom of employing the call-and-response pattern.

Further, this folk style of singing hymns dispensed with all but accidental harmony. Everybody sang the tune—in unison. Nobody, however, sang exactly the same notes and the result was heterophony, or different versions of the same melody. Similarly, when Yankee singing masters invaded rural areas with their 'fasola' and 'shape-note' systems of reading music, they taught folk hymns that consisted of part-singing rather than conventional harmonizing. Everybody had an interesting part, for the idea was to move horizontally rather than vertically. To the West African only blue notes and rhythm were lacking.

We know little enough about the West African musical tradition, but one example of it, the circle dance, has survived in this country as the ring-shout. This is the dance, described in Chapter One, which happened not to violate Protestant prohibitions against dancing and drumming. Anthropologist Ernest Borneman calls it 'a straight adaptation of African ceremonialism to Christian liturgy.' [4]

Describing the ring-shout, Alan Lomax writes: [5]

We have seen 'shouts' in Louisiana, in Texas, in Georgia, and in the Bahamas; we have seen vaudou dancing in Haiti; we have read accounts of similar rites in works upon Negro life in other parts of the Western hemisphere.

All share basic similarities: (1) the song is 'danced' with the whole body, with hands, feet, belly, and hips; (2) the worship is, basically, a dancing-singing phenomenon; (3) the dancers always move counter-clockwise around the ring; (4) the song has the leader-chorus form, with much repetition, with a focus on rhythm rather than on melody, that is, with a form that invites and ultimately enforces cooperative group activity; (5) the song continues to be repeated for sometimes more than an hour, steadily increasing in intensity and gradually accelerating, until a sort of mass hypnosis ensues . . .

This shout pattern . . . is demonstrably West African in origin.

In 1934, John and Alan Lomax recorded an excellent ring-shout and song-sermon in Jennings, Louisiana, entitled 'Run Old Jeremiah.'

In the ring-shout, we find the basic combination of qualities that appears throughout the music of the American Negro. Lomax stresses the fundamental importance of the rhythm and the consistent use of the call-and-response pattern. He might also have commented upon the melody, which employs the blue tonality of the cry. All of these qualities—variously diluted—occur in most of the religious music of the Negro, as well as in the work song, the blues, minstrelsy, ragtime, and the wide expanse of jazz.

The ring-shout had been noted and described as early as Civil War days. A rare description by H. G. Spaulding appeared in the *Continental Monthly* as early as 1863: [6]

At the 'praise meetings' on the plantations, one of the elders usually presides . . . Passages of Scripture are quoted from memory, and the hymns, which constitute the principal feature of the meeting, are deaconed off as at church . . . After the praise meeting is over, there usually follows the very singular and impressive performance of the *'Shout'* or religious dance of the negroes. Three or four, standing still, clapping their hands and beating time with their feet, commence singing in unison one of the peculiar shout melodies, while the others walk round in a ring, in single file, joining also in the song. Soon those in the ring leave off their singing, the others keeping it up the while with increased vigor, and strike into the shout step, observing most accurate time with the music. This step is sometimes halfway between a shuffle and a dance, as difficult for an uninitiated person to describe as to imitate. At the end of each stanza of the song the dancers stop short with a slight stamp on the last note, and then, putting the other foot forward, proceed through the next verse. They will often dance to the same song for twenty or thirty minutes, once or twice, perhaps, varying the monotony of their movement by walking for a little while and joining in the singing. The physical exertion, which is really very great, as the dance calls into play nearly every muscle of the body, seems never to weary them in the least, and they frequently keep up a shout for hours, resting only for brief intervals between the different songs. Yet in trying to imitate them, I was completely tired out in a very short time. The children are the best dancers, and are allowed by their parents to have a shout at any time, though, with the adults, the shout always follows a religious meeting, and none but church members are expected to join . . .

The negroes never indulge in it when, for any reason, they feel down-hearted or sad at their meetings. The shout is a simple outburst and manifestation of religious fervor . . .

The tunes to which these songs are sung, are some of them weird and wild—'barbaric madrigals'—while others are sweet and impressive melodies. The most striking of their barbaric airs it would be impossible to write out, but many of their more common melodies are easily caught upon being heard a few times.

Another and better-known description of the 'praise meeting' appeared in *The Nation* four years later.[7]

This is a ceremony which the white clergymen are inclined to discountenance, and even of the colored elders some of the more discreet try sometimes to put on a face of discouragement; and, although if pressed for Biblical warrant for the shout, they generally seem to think, 'he in de Book,' or, 'he dere-da in Matchew,' still it is not considered blasphemous or improper if 'de chillen' and 'dem young gal' carry it on in the evening for amusement's sake, and with no well-defined intention of 'praise.' But the true 'shout' takes place on Sundays, or on 'praise' nights through the week, and either in the praise-house or in some cabin in which a regular religious

meeting has been held. Very likely more than half the population of the plantation is gathered together; let it be in the
evening, and a light-wood fire burns red before the door of
the house and on the hearth. For some time one can hear,
though at a good distance, the vociferous exhortation or
prayer of the presiding elder or of the brother who has a gift
that way and who is not 'on the back seat'—a phrase the interpretation of which is 'under the censure of the church authorities for bad behavior'—and at regular intervals one hears
the elder 'deaconing' [i.e. lining out] a hymn-book hymn,
which is sung two lines at a time, and whose wailing cadences,
borne on the night air, are indescribably melancholy. But the
benches are pushed back to the wall when the formal meeting
is over, and old and young, men and women, sprucely-dressed
young men, grotesquely half-clad field-hands—the women generally with gay handkerchiefs twisted about their heads and
with short skirts, boys with tattered shirts and men's trousers,
young girls bare-footed—all stand up in the middle of the
floor, and when the 'sperichil' is struck up, begin first walking
and by-and-by shuffling round, one after the other, in a ring.
The foot is hardly taken from the floor, and the progression
is mainly due to a jerking, hitching motion which agitates the
entire shouter, and soon brings out streams of perspiration.
Sometimes he dances silently, sometimes as he shuffles he sings
the chorus of the spiritual, and sometimes the song itself is
also sung by the dancers. But more frequently a band, composed of some of the best singers and of tired shouters, stand
at the side of the room to 'base' the others, singing the body
of the song and clapping their hands together or on the knees.
Song and dance are alike extremely energetic, and often, when
the shout lasts into the middle of the night, the monotonous
thud, thud of the feet prevents sleep within half a mile of the
praise-house.

Although the reporter refers to this music as a 'sperichil,'
it is a far cry from the kind that John Charles Thomas, for
example, sings on the concert stage.

The vast difference between this ring-shout (with per-

spiring dancers shuffling in a circle while chanting back
and forth) and the concert spiritual illustrates the full
range of American Negro religious music. How did the
blending of European and African music produce two
such different forms? One is, of course, a dance and the
other is a song. Thus the ring-shout, unlike the spiritual,
has a driving rhythm but lacks the sustained melody as
well as the harmony.

One general trend seems clear. If we start with a more-
or-less African example such as the ring-shout, we can see
that as the rhythm dwindled, the melody lengthened and
harmony developed. This process is enormously complicated by the West African tradition of improvisation, augmented by the free style of the folk hymn—no one melody
is sacred; it can always be changed by spontaneous embellishments. Thus, although many spirituals are written
down and ring-shouts generally are not, it is conceivable
that the former's sustained melody could have emerged
momentarily from a ring-shout. The evolution is fluid,
proceeding at different speeds in different mixtures, with
much depending upon the performer.

Take the evolution of melody. The song-sermon used
at camp meetings is only a short step from the ring-shout.
The fiery preaching supplies the call; the shouting of the
congregation adds the response. The preacher may use the
'zooning' style (field-holler and cry) or the 'gravy' style
(work-song grunt) or a combination of both. It is no longer
a dance but a singing sermon. The melody assumes added
importance because it carries the words, the immediate
message. In this transition, the flowing rhythm and the blue
tonality might remain unchanged but the melody tends
to crystallize. The preacher improvises the melody, within
traditional limits, but now it carries a new meaning for
which the congregation listens. (There may be dancing,
although less commonly so.) Soon the preacher finds cer-

tain melodic phrases that he likes and repeats them. (The parallel to a jazzman playing the same tune over and over again and settling upon certain figures is precise.) The song-sermon is on its way toward a set and probably longer melody. The increased length leads to overlapping and incidental harmony, while the entire process is hastened by the powerful and all-pervasive influence of European music, leading to further complexity in almost everything but rhythm.

The song-sermon is flourishing mightily today. The evangelical religions—white following Negro examples—perform it regularly. It can also be heard at the services of the various Sanctified sects in any good-sized American town. In big cities, it can be heard on the radio. Recordings of song-sermons have been selling to the colored trade since the mid-'twenties and were selling better than ever in the 'fifties. The connection with jazz is direct. 'Lots of people think I'm going to be a preacher when I quit this business, because of the way I sing the blues,' says T-Bone Walker. 'They say it sounds like a sermon.' Again, explaining why vibra-harpist Milt Jackson has such a fine sense of rhythm, Dizzy Gillespie observed seriously: 'Why, man, he's sanctified!' Jackson grew up (as did Gillespie) near a Sanctified Church in Detroit.

The same process applies to secular songs of the American Negro. On the trail of the spiritual and its origins, J. M. McKim noted in 1862: [8]

I asked one of these blacks—one of the most intelligent of them . . . where they got these songs. 'Dey make 'em, sah.' 'How do they make them?' After a pause, evidently casting about for an explanation, he said: 'I'll tell you, it's dis way. My master call me up, and order me a short peck of corn and a hundred lash. My friends see it, and is sorry for me. When dey come to de praise-meeting dat night dey sing about it. Some's very good singers and know how; and dey work it in—work it in, you know, till they get it right; and dat's de way.'

This is still the ring-shout—to be a 'good singer and know how' means, in part, a mastery of the call-and-response form—but now the words have become very important and, along with them, the melody. This is the birth of a topical song.

Colonel Higginson, who was puzzled by 'the mode of composition' of the spiritual, had a similar experience which he described in the *Atlantic Monthly:* [9]

. . . we . . . know nothing of the mode of composition. Allen Ramsay says of the Scotch songs, that, no matter who made them, they were soon attributed to the minister of the parish whence they sprang. And I always wondered, about these, whether they had always a conscious and definite origin in some leading mind or whether they grew by gradual accretion, in an almost unconscious way. On this point I could get no information, though I asked many questions, until at last one day when I was being rowed across from Beaufort to Ladies' Island, I found myself, with delight, on the actual trail of a song. One of the oarsmen, a brisk young fellow, not a soldier, on being asked for his theory of the matter, dropped out a coy confession. 'Some good sperituals,' he said, 'are start jess out o' curiosity. I bin a-raise a sing, myself once.'

My dream was fulfilled, and I had traced out, not the poem alone, but the poet. I implored him to proceed.

'Once we boys,' he said, 'went for tote some rice, and de nigger driver, he keep a-callin' on us: and I say, "O, de ole nigger driver!" Den anudder said, "Fust t'ing my mammy tole me was, not'in' so bad as nigger-driver." Den I made a sing, just puttin' a word and den anudder word.' Then he began singing, and the men, after listening a moment, joined in the chorus as if it were an old acqaintance, though they evidently had never heard it before.

I saw how easily a new 'sing' took root among them.

Again we have the creation of a topical song in a tradition which assumes an easy familiarity with the call-and-response pattern. The only really new element is the words, which were improvised to fit the old form. At the same time, the melody is probably beginning to lengthen and crystallize, a tendency strongly reinforced by contact with European tunes.

The next step in this blending, which produced both ring-shout and spiritual, is the jubilee. Jubilees are both cheerful and rhythmic, usually announcing some sort of good news. Perhaps the best-known example today is 'When the Saints Go Marching In.' It has a definite melody but, at the same time, it lends itself admirably to the call-and-response form. In fact, most people would probably prefer it chanted back and forth—the tune clearly has more life when sung this way. It can, however, be sung either way and still be readily recognized.

As the melody lengthens and establishes itself, the call-and-response form must be modified. In the case of certain spirituals, such as 'Swing Low, Sweet Chariot' and 'Nobody Knows the Trouble I've Seen,' this form is usually dropped altogether because the melody itself is featured at a slower tempo. The step from jubilee to spiritual, therefore, is quite short and frequently seems to be created by the thoughtful mood of the interpreter. For the spiritual is traditionally a music of sadness and deep conviction, a mood that would be destroyed by the call-and-response form and its exciting rhythms.

In semi-improvised music (the form is set), the feeling of the performer is all-important; everything depends upon his interpretation. This makes for an incredible fluidity in the evolutionary process. Thus, we have cultural feedbacks—the melodies of jubilees and spirituals, for example, are still used in the deep South as musical points of departure for ring-shouts. Everything that might interfere with the rhythm disappears: the melody is whittled away, the harmony is disregarded, the words become almost unintelligible. The whole performance moves 'back' in the direction of the West African circle dance, which it closely resembles. On the other hand, the same jubilee or spiritual on the concert stage has a set melody and careful harmony. At this point it is almost wholly European.

Searching for the origin of 'fixed' melodies leads inevitably to the 'spontaneous combustion' theory. In some cases they may have been improvised on the spur of the moment, although this improvisation takes place along traditional lines within a set form. Early researchers were astounded by the number and variety of melodies that might crop up during the singing of any one song. Laboring to write them all down while admitting 'our system of notation is inadequate,' these pioneers managed to capture a few tunes—jubilees perhaps, parts of song-sermons, and even snatches from ring-shouts—that, in spite of an added arrangement by the notator, were fine melodies in their own right and retained a hint of the original, blue-tinged magic. In this way spirituals were born.

The spiritual has been defined in R. W. Gordon's *The Carolina Low Country* as 'a tune—never twice the same—accompanied by not over two standard verses—not the same—followed by as many other verses as the singer happens to remember.' This is a vague but realistic definition. Before the Fisk Jubilee Singers went on the road in 1871, for example, there were two or three separate melodies that employed the words of 'Swing Low Sweet Chariot.' The director of the choir selected the particular melody that we all know today. Denominational schools, founded by wealthy and cultured Northerners for poor, uneducated Negroes, played a key role in the spread of the spiritual. The choir director of a Negro college has a strong and natural impulse to master the subtleties of European music and adopt them wholesale. Unfortunately, if a ring-shout is made to sound like a Northern version of 'Rock of Ages,' a great deal of vitality is lost. But students fresh from the plantation fields were members of the various jubilee groups so a bit of the blueness and rhythm was bound to survive.

The growth of harmony is as uncertain as that of the melody. Until the latter is pretty well established, no set harmony is likely to accompany it. The first appearance of regular harmony in the religious music of the Negro probably occurred in the touched-up transcriptions of early white collectors or the out-and-out arrangements of various choir conductors in Southern schools. The example of European music was, of course, overpowering, and the harmony of the Protestant hymn was superimposed upon everything.

Living on a Georgia plantation in 1839, the actress and musician Fanny Kemble wrote in her diary: [10]

My daily voyages up and down the river have introduced me to a great variety of new musical performances of our boatmen, who invariably, when the rowing is not too hard, moving up or down with the tide, accompany the stroke of their oars with the sound of their voices. I told you formerly that I thought I could trace distinctly some popular national melody with which I was familiar in almost all their songs; but I have been quite at a loss to discover any such foundation for many that I have heard lately, and which have appeared to me extraordinarily wild and unaccountable. The way in which the chorus strikes in with the burden, between each phrase of the melody chanted by a single voice, is very curious and effective, especially with the rhythm of the rowlocks for accompaniment. The high voices all in unison, and the admirable time and true accent with which their responses are made, always make me wish that some great musical composer could hear these semisavage performances.

This emphasis upon the 'time and true accent' (or rhythm), and the mention of 'responses' make it clear that she heard music in the call-and-response form. Notice, however, that the slaves are singing 'all in unison.' In other words, there is no harmony; everybody is singing his own version of the melody, in the manner of a folk hymn.

And yet Fanny Kemble found the music thrilling: 'extraordinarily wild and unaccountable'! Why? Because each individual is singing his own version of the melody—blue notes and all—with 'admirable time' or a fine sense of rhythm. The result is a free but rhythmically complicated heterophony, or combination of voices setting up different melodic lines at the same time. Add to this the exotic flavoring of the cry and the result is an unintentional but occasional harmony that might well fascinate (or repel) a person reared in the conventional European tradition.

This kind of unison singing was considered 'the true plantation style' even by the Virginia Minstrels, organized in 1843. (The first four-part harmonizations of minstrel songs did not appear until 1848.) Unison singing of religious music is carefully described by the editors of *Slave Songs* (1867), who found it puzzling but thrilling: [11]

There is no singing in *parts*, as we understand it, and yet no two appear to be singing the same thing—the leading singer starts the words of each verse, often improvising, and the others, who 'base' him, as it is called, strike in with the refrain, or even join in the solo, when the words are familiar.

When the 'base' begins, the leader often stops, leaving the rest of his words to be guessed at, or it may be that they are taken up by one of the other singers. And the 'basers' themselves seem to follow their own whims, beginning when they please and leaving off when they please, striking an octave above or below (in case they have pitched the tune too low or too high), or hitting some other note that chords, so as to produce the effect of a marvelous complication and variety, and yet with the most perfect time, and rarely with any discord . . . they seem not infrequently to strike sounds that cannot be precisely represented . . . slides from one note to another, and turns and cadences not in articulated notes.

Apart from the apparent use of rhythm, this kind of singing is not unlike the folk style of psalm singing. The 'effect of a marvelous complication and variety' combined with 'the most perfect time,' or sense of rhythm, is partly produced by the unison singing in the call-and-response form. The references to 'slides,' 'turns,' and 'cadences' are clues to the blue tonality that must have pervaded the whole performance.

Spirituals are still being sung in this fashion today. In 1951, on a field trip to Bluffton, South Carolina (a small village about 30 miles north of Savannah), Mr. Arthur Alberts and I recorded a dozen or so religious songs in this style. The singers themselves were quite aware that they were singing in the 'old-time' style, and took pride in it, a pride fostered by the work of Mrs. Lydia Parrish in and around the same area. This style of singing made a comeback in the early 'thirties, when contests were held, but it began to die out soon after.

In the Bluffton group of eight singers, headed by the Reverend L. E. Graham, each singer took his or her turn at leading the song. 'We sing not like it's written—everybody sing melody.' This meant that each had a chance to sing the call while the rest of the group responded. By far the most exciting of the songs was led by a farmer named George Bush who had just joined the group and whose fiery improvisations—savoring of the cry—embarrassed some of the other singers. They all disclaimed any connection with the Sanctified Church and the popular gospel song, which they associated with more worldly and less stable people. 'I've got to be satisfied,' Miss Geneva Mitchell remarked, 'before I'm sanctified.'

Again, an identical style of unison singing was recorded by Anthony Schwartz in the 'forties: a religious tune, 'The Drinking of the Wine' (privately issued), sung by the menhaden fishermen off Barnegat Light. These fishermen, recruited from the entire East coast and especially Florida, were using the tune as a work song as they hauled in fish nets. The call of the leader is answered by a unison roar of the crew as they tug at the nets together, and the sound of the incidental harmony is weird and wonderful.

In the recordings of a quartet known as Mitchell's Christian Singers, made in the 'twenties and later, we can hear a fascinating transitional stage in the evolution of harmony. Whether or not the legend that they never heard a piano is true, the group sings 'Swing Low, Sweet Chariot' (Melotone 6-04-64) as if they had just discovered the three simplest chords in our music. Here is European harmony —the harmony of the hymn—with the dew still on it. The transitions to the final chord, with what Fanny Kemble would have described as their 'extraordinarily wild and unaccountable' slurs, dips, slides, and loops, bring exclamations of delight from modern academic musicians who have tried—and failed—to notate them.

Searching for the origin of the harmony of the spiritual (and sometimes its melody) *as written down* can lead to the conviction that all spirituals were taken from the Protestant hymn. But the truth is that only the harmony of the spiritual could have come directly from the Protestant hymn, and even that was transformed at once by the cry into an over-all blue tonality that is unknown in the Old World. (This transformation was explained, not very long ago, by the theory that the Negro was unable to copy the Protestant hymn correctly—which may well be true in a sense not intended.) The transformation to a bittersweet blue tonality, shifting in and out of a mood and mode that is at once sad and gay, gives the spiritual one of its most appealing qualities.

The use of harmony, like the use of melody and rhythm, in Negro religious music varies infinitely according to time, place, and performer. The spiritual, as we know it on the concert stage, has the most European and the fewest African qualities of all American Negro music. At the same time, melodies of equal beauty are still being improvised at Negro religious services all over the country today. (They can be recorded, but not written down *as sung*.) 'In spite of indifference and resentment from many educated and middle class Negroes,' writes Sterling Brown of Howard University, 'the spirituals are still sung, circulated, altered and created by folk Negroes.' [12] And Alan Lomax writes: [13]

... there can be no question in the minds and hearts of those who have heard them that in the Negro spirituals American folk art reaches its highest point. Indeed, we assert that these songs form the most impressive body of music so far produced by America, ranking with the best music anywhere on this earth.

The religious music of the Negro continues to furnish a reservoir of inspiration to the entire jazz tradition.

13 | Ragtime

Ragtime flourished for about twenty years—from 1896 to 1917. Unlike the spiritual and the blues, the mood of ragtime is unfailingly cheerful, which may help to explain its sudden popularity toward the end of the long depression of the 1890's. The general public first heard ragtime near the turn of the century at a series of World's Fairs in Chicago, Omaha, Buffalo, and St. Louis, where itinerant pianists from the South and Midwest found employment along the midways.

By 1900, Tin-Pan Alley took over and ragtime became the coast-to-coast craze, along with a dance called the 'cake-walk,' circling the globe and taking London and Paris by storm. Inevitably, the character of the music was softened but its essentially 'raggy' or rhythmic nature could not be concealed. Ragtime became an indestructible part of the American musical scene, associated in the popular mind with the mechanical sound of the player piano. To this day, when the movies, radio, or television wish to evoke the proper mood for a barroom scene or its equivalent, they turn to ragtime.

Ragtime represents a deeper and more complete blending of West African and European musical elements, with a greater borrowing from the European, than anything that had gone before. It is no accident that ragtime originated in the Midwest and not in New Orleans, and that there were first-class white as well as Negro composers and performers. The greatest of them all, Scott Joplin, who happened to be a Negro, studied classical music long and well, as the form of ragtime attests. (After a while, Tin-Pan Alley learned to set some of it down on sheet music in a simplified form.)

Ragtime is largely notated piano music in the European tradition of written composition. Anyone who can read music can play it. The better compositions, however, are very difficult and require a jazz-oriented sense of rhythm. But ragtime is such a balanced blending that it became an end in itself, an undeviating approach to all music (you can 'rag' any tune). In that sense it was limited and therefore gradually grew away from the mainstream of jazz.

As piano music, ragtime lacked the expressiveness that can be heard in the field-holler and cry. It was confined to the tempered scale. This was an advantage, of course, when it came to form and structure. From the first, ragtime had a pseudo-rondo pattern of its own, a pattern which more or less resembles the rondo form of the minuet and the scherzo. (The pattern also occurs in the march, a more likely source for ragtime.) This pattern constituted a large and well-assimilated borrowing from European music.

For example, Joplin's 'Maple Leaf Rag' consists of four different tunes or strains, each 16 bars long. If we give each of them a letter of the alphabet, they occur in this order: AABBACCDD. (In the classical rondo, the first strain returns regularly before each new strain.) The third strain (CC) or trio—a name taken from the march—is often the featured tune, frequently repeated. With this European form came the distinction between composer and performer. Joplin composed the best rags, for example, but others performed them more effectively.

Yet ragtime was decidedly new. It could be instantly recognized anywhere in the world because of its rhythm. Although in *They All Played Ragtime,* Rudi Blesh and Harriet Janis point out that ragtime melodies frequently come from folk tunes, these melodies are less obvious than the rhythm. W. C. Handy, a champion of the blues, defines ragtime as 'rhythm without much melody,' a definition that fits a great deal of the later, more commercial type. For, unlike European music, ragtime is syncopated from start to finish. Syncopation (i.e. accenting the normally weak beat) had been used in classical music to communicate a feeling of restlessness and revolt. It had to be employed sparingly, however, because it soon set up a new, unsyncopated beat as the memory of the original beat faded. Ragtime solved this problem for better or worse by maintaining both a syncopated and an unsyncopated beat at the same time.

In its simplest form, the rhythm of ragtime consists of a steady beat in the left hand and a syncopated beat in the right hand. Thus, the left hand plays a heavy 2/4 rhythm, much like the march from which it is probably borrowed. The right hand plays eight beats in the same interval, but accents every third beat, an effect that may well have been taken from the minstrel banjo. This has been called 'secondary rag,' and it sounds just like the beginning of 'Twelfth Street Rag,' or at a slower tempo, 'I Can't Give You Anything But Love.' It can be graphed as follows:

RIGHT	1 2 3 4 5 6 7 8	1 2 3 4 5 6 7 8	1 2 3 4 5 6 7 8	1
LEFT	1 2 3 4	1 2 3 4	1 2 3 4	1

Borneman describes this as 'splitting the bar metrically rather than accentually,' and adds that it is 'unmistakably African in origin and approach.' [1] The combination suggests—intermittently and out-of-phase—a component of regular *vodun* rhythm.

This continual syncopation, which was easily notated, is merely the foundation. On top of this a good pianist improvises an endless variety of rhythmic suspensions, unusual accents, and between-the-beat effects. In other words, the best ragtime incorporates the horizontal rhythmic flow of all good American Negro music. It also retains its European form. The blend is a rare and sophisticated piano music that can be well played only by a very few, highly gifted virtuosos. They were the fountainhead of the ragtime craze.

In so far as it borrowed from European music, ragtime could be watered down, notated, and sold from coast to coast. In the form of sheet music, it was hawked at every music counter. The inevitable result perhaps is the monotony that we associate with the player piano. Most piano-roll companies employed a hack who could 'rag' any tune for issue on a piano roll in an equally nondescript fashion (one, at least, was still at work in 1956). And ragtime made good money for at least twenty years.

During the reign of ragtime, the formal European elements seem to have decreased slightly while the African elements increased. On the one hand, the pseudo-rondo form was whittled down to two or three strains, instead of the customary four—and sometimes only one was actually performed. On the other hand, both the harmony and the rhythm evolved in a direction opposite to that of European models. Thus, the piano went as far as it could to simulate blue tonality by playing a major and minor third ('E' and 'E-flat' in the scale of 'C') either consecutively or simultaneously. (This is a device that George Gershwin used again and again in 'Rhapsody in Blue.') The resulting dissonance, although slight, is a flagrant violation of old-time classical harmony. It became the hallmark of ragtime. And bit by bit, the rhythm became more flowing.

Tracing the growth of rhythmic complexity in ragtime is difficult because, here again, everything depends upon the performer. If we took our cues from the sheet music of the time, the result would be complete confusion, for almost every rhythmic trick imaginable was tried at an early date—whether or not the purchaser of the music could play it. This state of affairs was soon rectified by simplifying the sheet music, and any resemblance to the original was purely coincidental. Nevertheless, we do have a few piano rolls, played probably by the pioneers themselves, and the occasional testimony of witnesses who heard these pioneers in person.

The development of this rhythmic complexity has become associated, whether correctly or not, with certain geographical areas in the United States. Actually, there is no reason to believe that the same evolutionary process was not taking place, for example, along the Eastern coast —at a slower or perhaps less apparent rate. In any case, the parent style has been labeled 'Sedalia,' since this Missouri town first witnessed the growing fame of Scott Joplin. Joplin specified that his rags should be played slowly, in march tempo, and the piano rolls that survive (if authentic) prove that he practiced what he preached. The effect is like plain secondary rag—a plodding, heavy syncopation with no particular flow. Yet the over-all structure and the melodic lines are splendid, a fact which accounts for the fame of these compositions especially when played by a more gifted performer.

The next step in the process is connected with St. Louis, which is frequently referred to as the birthplace of ragtime. Pioneer musicians—both white and Negro—such as Tom Turpin, Louis Chauvin, and later, Artie Mathews began to play Joplin's rags and rags of their own composing with new fire and life. The difference is electric. Perhaps one of the not-too-technical changes may be described as the gradual disappearance of the heavy march two-beat in the left hand. Instead, the left hand tended to play four beats in the same time interval, evenly accented—no more 'oom-pah.' This, in addition to a little more complicated accenting in the right hand, made for a better and more flowing rhythm. In essence, the music simply became more infectious and danceable. (A clear-cut illustration of this change occurs on the last chorus of pianist Ralph Sutton's recording of 'Grace and Beauty' (Down Home #10) where he departs from the score for a whirlwind finish.)

The third step toward the development of a more complex rhythm is associated with New Orleans and ably illustrated by Jelly Roll Morton. Morton, Tony Jackson, and other New Orleans pianists heard the rolling rhythms created by the popular marching bands, and they began to incorporate these rhythms into their improvisations. In his left hand, for example, Morton adds a 'walking' (i.e. with melodic figures) bass and a contrapuntal melody. In his right hand, he adds further between-the-beat accents. Although the tempo is slower, the music has a new and increased swing and flow. The difference is strikingly illustrated by his two versions of 'Maple Leaf Rag' in the Library of Congress recordings (Circle, Album III, Sides 21-22).

The fourth and last step is best represented by the music played in New York City, during the late 'teens and early 'twenties. It was a big step, involving a new and deeper fusion of European harmony and African rhythms, and its ancestry was long obscured by labels such as 'house-party,' 'rent-party,' 'parlor social,' or simply 'Harlem' piano style. Ragtime reached its peak as a balanced blend in the compositions and performances of Luckeyth Roberts, James P. Johnson, Willie Smith, Fats Waller, and a host of lesser names. The music ranged from the revival-meeting rhythms of Johnson's 'Carolina Shout' (Okeh 4495) to the Debussyesque impressionism of Smith's 'Morning Air' (Decca 2269). For while assimilating other European elements, these musicians played with an increasingly forceful rhythm.

Meanwhile, the success of ragtime and its diluted and derivative forms was overwhelming. It became a featured part of latter-day minstrelsy, vaudeville, cabaret, and café. It became a syncopated way of life—and the light classics were ragged over and over again. On his European tours, beginning in 1900, John Philip Sousa featured such ragtime numbers as 'At a Georgia Camp Meeting' (Victor 315—a later version), 'Smokey Mokes,' and 'Hunky Dory.' It was a far cry from the real thing and yet old recordings lend support to the legend that Sousa preferred 'jazzy' drummers. Debussy's 'Golliwog's Cakewalk' and 'Stravinsky's 'Ragtime for Eleven Instruments' document the deep impression that ragtime made abroad, before Milhaud and other European composers became interested in jazz in the 'twenties.

Eventually, ragtime seems to have fallen apart under its own weight. At least development ceased, perhaps because of the difficulty of the music itself. The public could not play the real thing and the publishers could not make money issuing it. A few brave publishers such as John Stark, who enjoyed the music, refused to give up. Scott Joplin had indicated the ultimate goal, however, when he composed a ragtime opera, *Treemonisha*, which was performed once only (1915). Similarly, the late James P. Johnson composed choral works, concertos, and symphonies in the same idiom. The inner drive of ragtime composers—like that of most jazzmen—was toward musical respectability, which means one thing: European concepts. But the time was not ripe.

In the early 'fifties, James P. Johnson, old and sick, often

Earl Leaf

A sense of rhythm is acquired

Muriel and Malcolm Bell, Jr.

African influence—Gravemarkers, Georgia

Frederic Ramsey, Jr.

Minstrelsy Today

James Chapelle

Leadbelly

With Success
Ferd (Jelly Roll) Mor...

Jelly Roll Morton

Louis Armstrong

Sheldon Brody

Revival Meeting

Bessie Smith

Bix Beiderbecke

The Diffusion of Jazz

Robert Parent

Duke Ellington

Lester Young

Charlie Parker accompanied by Thelonious Monk

Hugh Bell

Dizzy Gillespie

Allan Grant, LIFE Magazine, © Time Inc.

Chano Pozo

From Jazz West Coast by William Claxton, Linear Publications, Hollywood, 1955.

Max Roach

wondered what could have happened to his beloved ragtime. For a brief moment, it seemed that the large compositions upon which he had been working were about to
be accepted and played, along with the time-honored
classics of Mozart and Beethoven. Johnson's concertos
were quite as complex and, in a sense, twice as difficult to
play as Mozart's. Perhaps his Afro-American folk origins
betrayed him, for the average classical musician is utterly
incapable of the rhythmic sensitivity that is necessary to
play Johnson's pieces. Only an orchestra composed of
Smiths, Wallers, and Johnsons could have done it. James
P. Johnson died in 1955.

The less complex part of ragtime did find a place to go.
It was incorporated into orchestral jazz. This transition
from piano to jazzband is emphatically demonstrated, once
more, by the talented Jelly Roll Morton and his Red Hot
Peppers. The trend was in the air and fast becoming a
reality, but Morton gave it outstanding form and sub-
stance. He simply orchestrated his own piano compositions for a seven-piece jazzband. Here, the orchestral
qualities of his piano style, formed by listening to marching bands, help to explain his unqualified success. The
solo and band versions of 'Kansas City Stomps' (Gennett
5218; Bluebird 5109), for example, offer startling proof.

Morton left little to chance on his Red Hot Pepper recordings of the mid-'twenties. On 'Doctor Jazz,' 'Black
Bottom Stomp,' and 'The Chant,' he frequently wrote out
ensemble parts for both clarinet and cornet—an unheard
of bit of interference with the New Orleans tradition. He
also left ample space for his own contrasting piano solos.
Wholly dominated by Morton's forceful personality, these
recordings have a rare cohesion. Their ragtime origins
make them sound over-arranged today—they start and stop
on the button, according to the four original strains and
Morton's notions of abrupt contrast. But they also have a

fiery pulse of their own, and the listener cannot help wondering what might have happened if the band had been given its head.

Ragtime faded out around 1917 as the blues began to come in. A list of song titles and dates of publication bear this out. Actually, ragtime continued to be played under the new name of 'jazz,' and is played to this day as a prominent part of a repertory associated with the Dixieland style. Above and beyond actual piano rags such as 'Maple Leaf,' 'Eccentric,' and 'That's A Plenty,' which are standard in the Dixieland repertory, this style is noted for its repeated renditions of such ragtime-flavored tunes as 'Sensation,' 'Original Dixieland One Step,' 'Ostrich Walk,' 'Muskrat Ramble,' and many others. With the exception of an occasional blues, Dixieland is largely orchestral ragtime, formally simplified and rhythmically complicated.

By the 'twenties, blues were popular, the phonograph made orchestral music available, and the radio made music itself inexpensive and common. Piano ragtime passed into the popular but comparatively uninspired hands of Rube Bloom, Ohman and Arden, and Zez Confrey ('Kitten on the Keys'), among others. Later, the swing bands of the later 'thirties—Chick Webb, Tommy Dorsey, Benny Goodman, and Earl Hines—recorded ragtime tunes such as 'Maple Leaf' and 'Down Home,' re-arranged and almost unrecognizable after the first chorus. During the 'forties, only a revival of ragtime on the West Coast kept many tunes recorded and available.

Ragtime developed a wider and more influential fusion of European and African musical elements than ever before. It began with such a large component of formal European characteristics that (although it absorbed more and more of the African rhythmic complexity during its twenty-year popularity) it was never able to go the rest of the way and incorporate the bittersweet mood of the blues. Ragtime remained cheerful, pianistic in concept, and predominantly European. But just because of this, ragtime spread farther—and thinner—than any preceding wave of Afro-American music, carrying with it an elementary but basic introduction to new rhythms.

PART FOUR : THE JAZZ AGE

14 | The Jazz Age Begins

When the novelist F. Scott Fitzgerald labeled the nineteen-twenties 'The Jazz Age,' he was not particularly interested in the music. He was trying to describe a state of mind. But it made musical sense, too, for during the 'twenties, jazz developed from an infrequent 'hokum' music in a few vaudeville acts to a household commodity. It spread swiftly, this time under its own name, and established itself by sheer penetration and quantity (aside from questions of aesthetics) as a powerful force in our civilization. After the Jazz Age, the music might be—and frequently was—criticized adversely, but it could be ignored only at the peril of losing touch with a pervasive element in American culture.

During the 'twenties, the channels through which jazz, near-jazz, and non-jazz-called-jazz reached the public multiplied rapidly. The phonograph, the radio, and talking pictures came into their own. A world war, Prohibition, and the boom before the bust of the Depression shaped and hastened the process. Jazz spread in many directions, on various levels, and at different speeds. No one man—even among musicians—heard it all. Almost everything depended upon who you were, where you were, and when you happened to be listening. For an incredibly important and complicated musical revolution was taking place—something of a cultural 'clambake.'

At the same time, the whole process was made more complicated by such crucial factors as the continual migrations of Negroes from country to town and from the South to the North where better jobs and living conditions sometimes existed; the crazy-quilt pattern of distributing and selling phonograph recordings; and the cultural lag between the performances of Negro and white musicians on the one hand and between the attitudes of Negro and white audiences on the other. And yet out of it all emerge four distinct peaks of jazz intensity—New Orleans, Chicago, New York, and Kansas City—places where the vanguard of jazz existed before and during the 'twenties.

Ludicrous misunderstandings resulted—as they still do. Langston Hughes, for example, saw this happen during the 'twenties: [1]

Once when Mr. Van Vechten gave a bon voyage party in the Prince of Wales suite aboard the Cunarder on which he was sailing, as the champagne flowed, Nora Holt, the scintillating Negro blonde entertainer de luxe from Nevada, sang a ribald ditty called, 'My Daddy Rocks Me With One Steady Roll.' As she ceased, a well-known New York matron cried ecstatically, with tears in her eyes: 'My dear! Oh, my dear! How beautifully you sing Negro spirituals!'

Today, many more people know the difference between a spiritual and a blues.

The general public first began to hear about jazz in 1917, perhaps the best date for the beginning of the Jazz Age. (The word 'jass'—later 'jazz'—turned up first in Chicago in the middle 'teens with an unprintable meaning.) On the evening of 26 January of that year the Original Dixieland Jass (*sic*) Band made its debut in New York at Reisenweber's Cabaret on Columbus Circle. This band consisted of five white pioneers, fresh from the Negro music of New Orleans, playing jazz by ear and just as 'hot' as they could. (According to trombonist Preston Jackson, the band was imitating the music of Joe Oliver in New Orleans; a year later in Memphis, clarinetist Buster Bailey was imitating the recordings of the Original Dixieland Jazz Band.) To ears accustomed to ragtime, the music was so new and strange that the guests had to be told to dance. When I asked him about it, drummer Tony Sbarbaro said:

We had a good press agent—he squeezed us in on the 2nd floor—Gus Edwards and a big revue on the 1st and Emil Coleman and high society on the 3rd—we sweated it out for two weeks and then we hit solid, the place was jammed.

Reporting the big news with such haste that a clarinet was referred to as a piccolo, *Variety* commented: [2]

There is one thing that is certain, and that is that the melodies as played by the Jazz organization at Reisenweber's are quite conducive to making the dancers on the floor loosen up and go the limit in their stepping.

And Jimmy Durante, who was just beginning his career as a ragtime-playing entertainer, added, 'It wasn't only an innovation; it was a revolution!' From then on, all the cabarets featured jazzbands of varying—and usually lesser —competence.

Still other bands, both white and Negro, had preceded the Original Dixieland Jazz Band, but this band played the right spot at the right time and hit the headlines from coast to coast. More important, the band made the first out-and-out jazz recordings, which were issued on Victor's popular lists and sold in the millions. (They were reissued in 1954.) Almost overnight, the word 'jazz' entered the American vocabulary to describe a rackety musical novelty with barnyard—or worse—antecedents. Thus—the same year that Storyville was closed by the Navy in New Orleans—New York, then Chicago, and then most of the cities of the North opened their doors to the new music.

The original impact was quickly diluted by a host of

imitators. Indeed, this process is standard in the spread of jazz. The earlier minstrel-concert-vaudeville orchestras of Wilbur Sweatman, Will Marion Cook, and James Reese Europe (the favorite of dancers Vernon and Irene Castle) were gradually supplanted by Vincent Lopez, Ben Selvin, Earl Fuller (with Ted Lewis), and Paul Whiteman, who supplied the 'new' jazz music, polished up for dancing. The Benson orchestra was doing the same for Chicago, Paul Specht for Detroit, and Art Hickman for San Francisco. By 1922, the Original Dixieland Jazz Band was playing commercial fox trots like the rest, simply because there was more money in it.

At the same time, there were people who played a very important part in the growth of jazz who never heard of any of these jazz bands. A year or so earlier one of them, for example, had jumped jail and fled to New Orleans. He was a guitar picker, born in Louisiana and raised in Texas, named Huddie Ledbetter, or Leadbelly. Professor George Herzog, Africanist and musicologist at Indiana University, feels that Leadbelly had serious claims as a composer and writes that his holler 'sounds most different from all occidental music (that is, European and British)—even more than the blues.' [3] In other words, it sounds African.

At the age of sixteen, Leadbelly had run away to Shreveport and begun his ramblings throughout the South. He was a part of the group of Negroes who earned a living by music—a tradition that grew up after the Civil War as the newly freed Negro learned to take care of himself. Around 1905, Leadbelly wandered into a saloon in Dallas and came face to face with the great blues singer, Blind Lemon Jefferson. They worked together for a time and Leadbelly learned much about the blues. (Later, in the 'twenties, Blind Lemon made some recordings that were sold in Negro neighborhoods and became prosperous for a short time before dying in poverty somewhere in Ohio.)

That was the year that sheet-music sales went over a million, but neither Blind Lemon nor his disciple could read a note.

New Orleans jazz—in contrast to the blues—didn't interest Leadbelly particularly. He had heard it in Texas back in 1910 and only the left-hand figures of the piano player intrigued him. (They didn't call it boogie-woogie then.) He could copy it on his guitar. And he hated New Orleans: [4]

You go down Rampart Street an' you liable to see anything. You see a man without no legs an' a woman doesn't have a nose. Nex' come a man wid his mouf jes' a hole in he face. Yassuh, you gonna see ev'y diffunt kind o' thing down yonder on Rampart Street in New Orleans.

He didn't even get a chance to team up with washboard beaters, jug blowers, kazoo players, tub thumpers, or alley fiddlers to serenade white folks for pennies on street corners. The town was too organized.

In fact, Leadbelly had been by-passed by the rapid urbanization of his own music. The brass bands and the sporting-house pianists were so well established that there was little chance for an old-fashioned guitar picker. His jigs, reels, ballads, and blues were all right on the rural circuit where a dance-song with a bit of a story filled the bill, but they didn't make much of an impression in the big towns. So he worked alone, making a living among his own people by playing and singing for square dances or 'breakdowns.'

The members of the Original Dixieland Jazz Band never heard of Leadbelly, either, and if they had, they wouldn't have been very interested. Leadbelly's contact with jazz per se was early and tangential, and yet he and a host of guitar pickers like him kept alive an enormous reservoir of music to which jazz and near-jazz returned again and again. For a good part of Leadbelly's music, with its powerful elements of the work song, the ring-shout, and the field-holler, provides a dynamic blend in which many of the qualities of West African music are fully represented. Without this original mixture, jazz could never have developed.

At the same time, there were other people who played an important part in the history of jazz and who might well have been astonished by all the fuss over the Original Dixieland Jazz Band. To them jazz was an old, old story in 1917. William Christopher Handy, for example, was almost forty-five years old and had published 'Memphis Blues,' 'Yellow Dog Blues,' 'St. Louis Blues,' and 'Beale Street Blues' by that time. In fact, Columbia called him to New York to make some recordings to compete with the Original Dixieland Jazz Band's records. His own band couldn't make the trip from Memphis, so Handy had to pick up unknown musicians in New York. The results were terrible. And nobody could deny that the Original Dixieland Jazz Band played with more drive and fire.

Handy was a composer and music publisher who be-came established before the young-man-with-a-horn legend even began. He was five years older than Buddy Bolden, and he came from a fine family of shouting Methodists who hated jazz—or any other secular music—before it had a name: [5]

But I'd say it was the way the Reverend Cordie White sang 'Train's A-Comin'' that set the tom-toms beating in my blood. Then when Brother Tobe Rice chanted 'Tell All the World, John' and Uncle Job Kirkman raised 'The Bridegroom Has Done Come,' my course was fixed.

It made no difference that, except for the words, the re-ligious and secular music were about the same. When Handy said that he wanted to be a musician, his father cried that he would rather see his son dead.

In the late 'eighties, Handy heard Terrell's band substitute an iron pipe for a string bass in Huntsville, Alabama; he played cornet with 'Lard-Can Charlie' in Bessemer in the early 'nineties; he heard barnyard imitations by Jim Turner on the fiddle and Billy Nichols on the crackerbox; and in 1896, at the age of twenty-three, Handy joined Mahara's Minstrel Troupe. He worked day and night to master his instrument, the cornet, studying the only available instruction books. This meant that he became a 'legitimate' musician, and he landed the job of bandmaster on his own merits.

At the same time, Handy was aware of guitar pickers such as Leadbelly. Around the turn of the century, he heard one near the railroad station in Tutwiler, Mississippi, and he never forgot it: [6]

A lean, loose-jointed Negro had commenced plunking a guitar beside me while I slept. His clothes were rags; his feet peeped out of his shoes. His face had on it some of the sadness of the ages. As he played, he pressed a knife on the strings of the guitar in a manner popularized by Hawaiian guitarists who used steel bars. The effect was unforgettable. His song, too, struck me instantly.

'Goin' where the Southern cross' the Dog.' The singer repeated the line three times, accompanying himself on the guitar with the weirdest music I had ever heard. The tune stayed in my mind.

The Great Southern and the Yazoo Delta (Yellow Dog) Railroads cross each other near the Moorhead Penitentiary in Alabama, and this colleague of Leadbelly's may have been singing about something he knew at first hand.

The event that turned Handy into an American composer occurred in Cleveland, Mississippi, in 1903. He was conducting a nine-piece dance band and reading the latest sheet-music from New York, when a guest requested that a local trio—bass, guitar, and mandolin—be allowed to play a few numbers: [7]

The music they made was pretty well in keeping with their looks. They struck up one of those over-and-over strains that seem to have no very clear beginning and certainly no ending at all. The strumming attained a disturbing monotony, but on and on it went, a kind of stuff that has long been associated with cane rows and levee camps. Thump-thump-thump went their feet on the floor. Their eyes rolled. Their shoulders swayed. And through it all that little agonizing strain persisted. It was not really annoying or unpleasant. Perhaps 'haunting' is a better word, but I commenced to wonder if anybody besides small town rounders and their running mates would go for it.

The answer was not long in coming. A rain of silver dollars began to fall around the outlandish stomping feet. The dancers went wild. Dollars, quarters, halves—the shower grew heavier and continued so long I strained my neck to get a better look. There before the boys lay more money than my nine musicians were being paid for the entire engagement. Then I saw the beauty of primitive music. They had the stuff the people wanted. It touched the spot. Their music wanted polishing, but it contained the essence. Folks would pay money for it. The old conventional music was well and good and had its place, no denying that, but there was no virtue in being blind when you had good eyes.

That night a composer was born, an *American* composer.

There was money in it—eventually—but nobody had the interest, or the skill, or the foresight to write it down until Handy came along.

The effect of Handy's work was far-reaching. He proved that jazz could make money. Or perhaps it would be more accurate to say that Handy showed how something of this jazz music could be written down and sold—'St. Louis Blues,' for example. And when tunes even remotely derived from jazz make a lot of money, jazz itself commands immediate attention. The growth and spread of jazz is speeded up. And a progressive pattern is established willy-nilly: non-jazz-called-jazz gives way to near-jazz, and near-jazz gives way to jazz. The music gets a chance to sell itself.

Many of Handy's blues were published and played—rather badly, to be sure—long before the public heard of jazz. These tunes made many musicians and some of the public conscious of blues before the Original Dixieland Jazz Band recorded in 1917, before the radio, and before the talkies. The early bands of Paul Whiteman, Art Hickman, Wilbur Sweatman, Earl Fuller, and many others (including the military bands) featured blues by Handy with considerable success, and Lt. James Reese Europe, who might have been the Negro Paul Whiteman if he had lived, made a hit with Handy's tunes in Europe during World War I.

There are other important people and events which cluster around the year 1917 when the Original Dixieland Jazz Band made the first jazz recordings and the Jazz Age may be said to have begun. There was a first-rate Negro band—Freddie Keppard and the Original Creoles—which had turned down an invitation to record a few months previously. The reason is still in doubt. One legend says that Keppard didn't want his style copied; another legend insists that the record executives decided that Keppard played too 'hot and dirty' for the family trade. Both could be true.

Jelly Roll Morton points out that Keppard and his Creoles, with the same instrumentation as the Original Dixieland Jazz Band, were playing more powerful jazz in New Orleans in 1908. 'I wish you could have heard those boys ramble on,' says Morton. The Keppard band left New Orleans in 1912, turned up in Los Angeles in 1914, and played Coney Island in 1915—an itinerary that shows the inadequacy of the New Orleans-to-Chicago-by-riverboat cliché of jazz history. Musicians traveled by trains and private automobiles, too.

There was another early white band from New Orleans that opened at the Lambs Café in Chicago in 1915. Billed as Tom Brown's Band from Dixieland, they played the Century Theatre in New York for eleven weeks and then went into vaudeville billed as the Five Rubes. (Their 'discoverer,' Joe Frisco, who brought them up from New Orleans, called himself thereafter the 'Creator of the Jazz Dance.') The Brown band, however, was a hokum band, an off-shoot of the 'spasm' bands which were highly popular novelties in vaudeville. Morton calls them 'bad bands . . . who played any job they could get in the streets,' but actually they were following a well-worn path pioneered by Negroes.

Sometime before 1920, the hypothetical peak of jazz intensity shifted from New Orleans to Chicago. Not long after the opening of the Original Dixieland Jazz Band at Reisenweber's, a young lady from Memphis on vacation from Fisk University got a job demonstrating sheet music at Jones' Music Store on South State Street in Chicago. She was paid three dollars a week. Her big chance arrived when trumpeter Sugar Johnny and his New Orleans band, which had been in and out of Chicago since 1915, advertised for a pianist. (The great soloists, Tony Jackson and Jelly Roll Morton, had been making big money since 1910 at Pony Moore's and the Everleigh Club—no band work for them.)

So Lillian Hardin, who later became Mrs. Louis Armstrong, tried out for her first job playing jazz: [8]

When I sat down to play I asked for the music and were they surprised! They politely told me they didn't have any music and furthermore never used any. I then asked what key would the first number be in. I must have been speaking another language because the leader said, 'When you hear two knocks, just start playing.'

It all seemed very strange to me, but I got all set, and when I heard those two knocks I hit the piano so loud and hard they all turned around to look at me. It took only a second for me to feel what they were playing and I was off. The New Orleans Creole Jazz Band hired me, and I never got back to the music store . . .

It was a case of sink or swing, and 'Miss Lil' never went back to Fisk, either.

Louis Armstrong was in the midst of a similar educational process—but on the teaching end. In 1920, disembarking from the 'Dixie Belle' at St. Louis, Armstrong visited a local dance: [9]

We watched close to see what their music would be like, because we knew they had a big reputation in St. Louis, and naturally we were interested to see how our New Orleans bands, like Kid Ory's and the rest, would stack up against them. Well, we were surprised. In no time at all we could tell they were doing things that had been done down home years before. The leader would try to swing them away from the score but they didn't seem to know how. I thought I could see he knew what we were thinking, because every once in a while he would look over to us and smile, but not as if he were sure we were liking it. After several numbers he had his trumpeter do a call to attention. When the room was quiet, he stepped out in front and announced: 'We are honored to have with us tonight three of New Orleans' most distinguished performers. They come from a town where they even have jazz music with their breakfast . . .'

We cut loose with one of the very newest hot songs that had just been getting around home when we left—and we let it swing, plenty. Every one of us three was a natural swing player and didn't need any scoring at all. We almost split that room open—man, did we play! . . .

Well, they all liked it fine. They stood up and yelled out

for more and the band boys were all on their feet, too, and the leader came over and shook our hands . . . It was the first time I had had an ovation like that in a really big city away from New Orleans.

The St. Louis jazzmen were not long in assimilating the newer and hotter style.

By 1920, according to Frederic Ramsey, Jr., there were over forty outstanding jazzmen from New Orleans in Chicago. Looking back, it now seems almost like a family affair. And in a sense, it was; for the general public and even white jazzmen knew almost nothing about it. There was considerable rivalry with Chicago musicians who controlled the musicians' union, making it difficult for the New Orleans jazzmen to get jobs.

The Jazz Age, however, was off to a flying start. While the public was raving about Al Jolson singing 'Swanee' in *Sinbad,* Bessie Smith was singing in a show called 'Liberty Belles' in Atlanta. On 14 September 1920, the first radio broadcast anywhere took place. Kid Ory, Reb Spikes, and Mutt Carey missed it; they had just left New Orleans for Los Angeles ('There was no place in town where one could purchase recordings by Negro artists'). The real, undiluted music was in the process of spreading from coast to coast.

15 | The Jazz Age Flourishes

If the Original Dixieland Jazz Band made jazz a household word in 1917, Paul Whiteman made it semi-respectable in 1924. That is, jazz became as respectable as high-powered publicity from coast to coast could make it. And the general public began to hear a lot about jazz and to like what it heard. Rudy Vallee described the 'new' music as 'symphonized syncopation,' a reasonably accurate label for the light classics played by Whiteman with a businessman's bounce. As we hear it now on recordings, the music sounds diluted past recognition. In 1924, however, it sold well.

Whiteman left San Francisco in 1919 for Atlantic City. In the following year, he was brought to the fashionable Palais Royale in New York City, while his first recording, 'Whispering' and 'Japanese Sandman,' made in November 1920, had a phenomenally large sale. (He remade the same tunes the same way in 1954.) To the music lovers of the day, Whiteman's orchestra sounded fuller and smoother and richer—and with reason, since he put together the largest band yet and played carefully rehearsed arrangements which featured as many semi-classical devices as possible. By 1922, he controlled twenty-eight bands playing on the East Coast, received $7,500 a week at the Hippodrome, and grossed over a million dollars annually.[1]

The big event, however, took place on 12 February 1924. That evening Whiteman presented a jazz concert at Aeolian Hall, the stronghold of academic music. There had been other concerts where jazz of sorts had been played, but this was the first jazz concert that captured the imagination of an influential part of the American public. Whiteman's aim was to get the approval of 'recognized authorities,' and he succeeded.[2]

My idea for the concert was to show these skeptical people the advance which had been made in popular music from the day of discordant early jazz to the melodious form of the present.

Among the patrons were Damrosch, Heifetz, Stokowski, Kreisler, McCormack, and Rachmaninoff. Victor Herbert composed a special suite for the occasion.

The first selection on the program was an intentionally old-fashioned version of 'Livery Stable Blues,' with all the wah-wahs, whinnies, and hokum of vaudeville jazz, intended to illustrate how crude this music had been *before* Whiteman. It was a hit: [3]

When they laughed and seemed pleased with 'Livery Stable Blues,' the crude jazz of the past, I had for a moment the panicky feeling that they hadn't realized the attempt at burlesque—that they were ignorantly applauding the thing on its merits.

Critic Olin Downes made just that mistake. He felt that 'Livery Stable Blues' was 'much better . . . than other and more polite compositions that came later.' It is easy to see now that he was right.

The band, flanked by an incredible array of instruments —Flügelhorn, euphonium, celesta, heckelphone, basset horn, octavina, and so on—performed twenty-six selections; compositions by Elgar, Friml, and MacDowell 'adapted to dance music' were presented. The sensation of the concert, however, was George Gershwin playing his own 'Rhapsody in Blue.' The only critic who didn't exactly cheer was Lawrence Gilman: [4]

. . . this music is only half alive . . . How trite and feeble and conventional the tunes are, how sentimental and vapid the harmonic treatment . . . Old stuff it is . . . Recall the most ambitious piece . . . the 'Rhapsody in Blue' . . . and weep over the lifelessness of its melody and harmony, so derivative, so stale, so inexpressive.

Gilman praised the 'rich inventiveness of the rhythms, the saliency and vividness of the orchestral color.' And judging by European as well as jazz standards, Gilman had reason.

Whiteman advanced the cause of jazz immeasurably. After the concert, jazzbands—good and bad—had an easier time finding jobs, and the evolution within the music was speeded up. Whiteman's own tendency was toward adopting European concert devices and blending them with jazz. The result was striking, easily intelligible, and profitable. He lost $7,000 on the concert by his own account, but the publicity was worth many times the amount. It was simple for his own publicity men to crown him 'King of Jazz,' while a few of the intelligentsia began to discuss jazz with some seriousness.

Meanwhile, an amazing number of apparently unconnected events—crucial in the history of jazz—were taking place all over the country in 1924. As we have seen, the big companies had discovered that there was a great market for blues among Negroes and started putting out more and more blues on their 'race' lists. (This meant that you could buy the records in stores in the Negro neighborhood but not in a white neighborhood, unless you knew enough to put in a special order.) The pianist and composer, Clarence Williams, told me that around 1924 when he opened a store on Chicago's South Side:

Colored people would form a line twice around the block when the latest record of Bessie or Ma or Clara or Mamie come in . . . sometimes these records they was bootlegged, sold in the alley for four or five dollars apiece . . . nobody never asked for Paul Whiteman; I doubt if they ever knew about him.

Similarly, when Leadbelly, who had been deep in the heart of a Texas penitentiary, was released in 1925, he didn't hear about Paul Whiteman but he marveled at the new blues records and he listened to and copied Bessie Smith.

When Bessie Smith played the Avenue Theatre on the South Side in May 1924, there was a near riot. Lonesome migrants from the deep South, who had trekked north during World War I in search of better jobs, jammed the theater to warm themselves in the music of their childhood:

Backwater blues done cause me to pack my things an' go,
Backwater blues done cause me to pack my things an' go,
Cause my house fall down and I cain't live there no mo.'

There is a persistent rumor that the sale of Bessie Smith's records kept the early Columbia company from bankruptcy, for in the first half of the 'twenties, record sales were off about 85 per cent, due perhaps to the fast-growing popularity of radio.

Bessie Smith's appearance, however, was a rare treat. Most of the time, the best that could be managed was a house-rent party, an unstable social phenomenon that was stimulated by Prohibition and made necessary by the Depression. The object of such a party is to raise the rent, and anybody who can pay a quarter admission is cordially invited. The core of the party usually centers around a pianist whose style was shaped by many similar situations: he plays very loud and very rhythmically. Elements of this style became known later as boogie-woogie, but much of it must have existed from the first time that a Negro, without orthodox instruction, worked out his own thoughts on the piano.

Legendary pianists known as 'Cat-Eye Harry,' 'Jack the Bear,' 'Tippling Tom,' 'The Beetle,' 'Speckled Red,' 'The Toothpick,' and many others were famous during the early 'twenties from Chicago all the way down the East coast to Florida. (There were a dozen or more separate regional styles—you could often tell where a man came from by the way he played—and thousands of bass figures for the left hand.) Cow Cow Davenport came from Alabama, Montana Taylor from Indianapolis, Doug Suggs from St. Louis, and Pete Johnson from Kansas City, but most of them flocked to Chicago in the early 'twenties, where they constituted a basic but largely unnoticed school of jazz.

In their way, the house-rent-party pianists are just as important to jazz as the guitar-picking colleagues of Huddie Ledbetter. Some of them left an indelible mark. Jimmy Yancey, who quit vaudeville in 1913 to work as grounds keeper for the White Sox, is closely identified with a boogie-woogie bass figure that is still frequently played. Pine Top Smith, who roomed with Albert Ammons and Mead Lux Lewis in Chicago, used a left-hand figure that has become standard for boogie-woogie. And when Mead Lux Lewis improvised his 'Honky Tonk Train Blues,' an impressionistic interpretation of the railroad trains passing back and forth on the South Side—which has been favorably compared to Honegger's 'Pacific 231'—he was creating an urban version of the guitar picker's 'Goin' where the Southern cross' the Dog.' (Later, Duke Ellington's 'Daybreak Express' and 'Happy Go Lucky Local' furnished more complex samples of the same tradition.)

The early boogie-woogie, honky-tonk, barrelhouse, house-rent-party pianists worked out their style without the slightest notion of how the European concert tradition ruled that a piano should be played. (Ragtime was different and incorporated more European influences.) Like Leadbelly, but with a piano instead of a guitar, they kept as much of the field-holler, the work song, and the ring-shout as they could, and the effect was highly percussive. The harmony might be non-existent, the melody completely lost, but the rhythm was usually a miracle of surging power. It was also highly complex and sophisticated.

On the night of Paul Whiteman's concert at Aeolian Hall, Louis Armstrong was probably playing close to his all-time best a few blocks away at the Roseland Ballroom on Broadway. He had left New Orleans in 1922 for Oliver's band in Chicago and in 1924 came east to join Fletcher Henderson. The splash that Armstrong made in Negro jazz circles in New York indicates that the New York musicians hadn't quite caught up. Drummer Kaiser Marshall says: [5]

I remember the day that Louis showed up for rehearsal . . . He had on big thick-soled shoes, the kind that policemen wear, and he came walking across the floor, clump-clump, and grinned and said hello . . . Louis played mighty well.

Trumpeter Rex Stewart tells me that Armstrong wore an old-fashioned box-back jacket. 'But man, after he started playin', box-back coats was the latest style!'

With the aid of arranger Don Redman, Fletcher Henderson was learning how to make a big band swing. (For a while, the alternate band at Roseland was the orchestra of Vincent Lopez.) The standard number of musicians in a dance band was nine: two trumpets, two saxes, one trombone, and four rhythm (banjo, piano, drums, and tuba). Henderson added an extra sax or trumpet for recordings, and he felt that Armstrong would make it a fine ten-piece band. It was a good band before Louis arrived but his arrival only created more problems. 'I changed my style of arranging,' says Don Redman, 'after I heard Armstrong.' Armstrong set the group on fire, as recordings testify, and then stood out above all the rest.

Fletcher Henderson was playing for white dancers and a few alert white musicians at the Roseland Ballroom on Broadway. He knew all about Paul Whiteman, as his early recordings show, and tried to imitate the plush arrangements. It made money. But Henderson was betrayed by his admiration for hot jazz soloists such as Louis Armstrong. Henderson insisted upon hiring Armstrong and, then and there, his band couldn't sound like Paul Whiteman's. It was too hot and rhythmic. After Armstrong left, Henderson's arranger Don Redman worked out the swing formula—a decade before the public heard the word. Meanwhile, Paul Whiteman purchased twenty arrangements from Don Redman, paying $2,000 for them in advance and knowing that his band would have trouble learning to play them. It was understood, of course, that Redman would help rehearse the band. 'That thirty-piece band could read the notes,' recalls Redman, 'but they couldn't seem to get the real feeling.' (Recordings by Henderson and Whiteman of Redman's arrangement of 'Whiteman Stomp' illustrate this fact.)

As far as the general public was concerned in 1924, Fletcher Henderson didn't exist. The public nevertheless heard about jazz from sources other than Paul Whiteman. Exactly nine days after Whiteman's concert, for example, three noisy white amateurs from St. Louis—two soda-jerks and an overweight ex-jockey—made a recording in Chicago at the suggestion of Isham Jones, the popular band leader. Jack Bland, Dick Sleven, and Red McKenzie played a banjo, a comb wrapped in tissue paper, and a kazoo (a toy horn with tissue paper that vibrates with humming). Billed as the Mound City Blue Blowers, this trio was in the ancient tradition of Negro street-corner outfits by way of the 'spasm' bands, whom they imitated loudly and well.

Their first recording, 'Blue Blues' and 'Arkansas Blues,' was released on the Brunswick popular series—which meant distribution wherever records were sold—and became a tremendous hit. So many copies were purchased that junk shops are still full of them to this day. Like the Original Dixieland Jazz Band in 1917, the Mound City Blue Blowers in 1924 played just as hot as they knew how —which was quite unusual and very impressive at the time. They were sold to the public, however, as a novelty, and high society found them amusing. At the wedding of Alice Busch of the Anheuser-Busch family, Jack Bland recalls: [6]

Some fellow came over and wanted to know if we could play *The Merry Widow* waltz . . . and he held up twenty dollars to Sliven. Sliven said 'Sure!' and we went right into *Rose of the Rio Grande* and kept playing [it] all night for more twenties [dollar bills] . . .

The Blue Blowers played the Palace, toured Europe, and became the darlings of society people who didn't know one tune from another but were thrilled by 'those freak instruments.'

As we look back at the history of jazz, we can now see that the Mound City Blue Blowers were playing—and quite competently—the sort of rough-and-ready music on improvised instruments that Leadbelly played as a youngster around 1900 and that W. C. Handy heard in Cleveland, Mississippi, in 1903 (although, in Handy's case, with stringed instruments). It was a sort of amateur tradition in which anyone who could hum a tune could—and frequently did—participate.

The 'spasm' band tradition depended upon participation. It exists today in rural areas and, significantly, among fanatic jazz aficionados. The first known band of this sort consisted of Emile 'Stale Bread' Lacoume with 'Cajun,' 'Whiskey,' 'Warm Gravy,' and 'Slew-Foot Pete,' and it played New Orleans street corners in 1896. The instruments, as well as the music, were improvised. (In 1902, Kid Ory was playing 'a homemade violin, bass viol, guitar, banjo—played on a chair for drums.') Some of them became professional musicians. The question of whether or not they played jazz is a matter of definition, but it seems narrow-minded to exclude them.

Parenthetically, a kind of feed-back occurs in jazz whereby white amateurs perform in the humble tradition of Negro song-and-dance bands on street corners. The parallel to blackface minstrelsy is close. These amateurs, cheerfully mistaking the melodic liberty of the field-holler for license, express themselves loudly but rhythmically. And they find a public. As time passes, the best of them turn professional, joining other professionals who enjoy old-time jazz. The element of participation is particularly clear in this approach. Something of this process helps to explain the New Orleans and Dixieland revivals which have been taking place since 1940 and which have been a powerful factor in the diffusion of jazz.

In 1924, hotter recordings than those of the Mound City Blue Blowers were being made by King Oliver, Fletcher Henderson, Bennie Moten, and Clarence Williams (with Armstrong and Bechet), but the Blue Blowers had the distribution and the attention of the public. Their influence, accordingly, was everywhere. Out in Spokane, twenty-year-old Bing Crosby was spellbound and set to work to copy them: [7]

At times I used a kazoo, sticking it into a tin can and moving it in and out to get a trombone effect in a trick I lifted from the Mound City Blues Blowers.

Like thousands of youngsters all over the country in the middle 'twenties, Crosby taught himself by means of phonograph records. The classroom in this case was Bailey's Music Company, a long-suffering store where Crosby and his friends went merely to listen, not to buy.

To Crosby and many others like him, a short-cut to fame and fortune had suddenly opened up. All you had to do was to master the trick of playing 'hot.' They didn't teach it at school and even the music teachers couldn't do it. You didn't even have to learn to read music—you played by ear: [8]

We'd take a couple of records in and play them, and Al would memorize the piano chords while I remembered the soloist's style and vocal tricks . . . The other musicians could read notes but they couldn't play the stuff the way we played it.

Thus, you became a sort of pioneering genius over night —even among musicians, most of whom couldn't 'jazz' it. You were a young man with a horn and, best of all, you made good money.

A few years later, another group of youngsters, at Austin High School in Chicago, were copying recordings together. As trumpeter Jimmy McPartland tells it: [9]

What we used to do was put the record on—one of the Rhythm Kings', naturally—play a few bars, and then all get our notes. We'd have to tune our instruments up to the record machine, to the pitch, and go ahead with a few notes. Then stop! A few more bars of the record, each guy would pick out his notes and boom! we would go on and play it. Two bars, or four bars, or eight—we would get in on each phrase and then all play it . . . in three or four weeks we could finally play one tune all the way through—*Farewell Blues.*

Here, a group of white Northerners were busy copying an older group of white musicians from New Orleans who, as their trumpeter Paul Mares reports, did their best 'to copy the colored music we'd heard at home.'

Phonograph records were probably the most effective single vehicle for the spread of jazz. Of course, hearing a jazzband in person could lead to equal or even stronger impressions. Around 1917, when the Original Dixieland Jazz Band made their recordings, a high-school boy in Bloomington, Indiana, named Hoagy Carmichael heard them and made an exciting discovery. His mother played ragtime, but here was something new. He called it 'sock' style and associated it with the great clarinetist Leon Rappolo and the New Orleans Rhythm Kings, the third white band to arrive from the Crescent City. 'Dood-dood-doodle, La-de-a-de-addle-la-da, sock that beat with your fist in your hand,' he explained to his friends.[10] To the heavy accent on the first and third beat—à la Sousa—a secondary accent on the second and fourth beat was added. The 'sock' style used an off-beat accent that became standard in the 'twenties—it was more complex and flowing—and made ragtime sound old-fashioned.

But in 1924, Carmichael heard the Wolverines with Bix Beiderbecke. They were the first hot jazz band of white and northern Midwesterners. The shock of recognition was instantaneous, the exaltation limitless.[11]

I could feel my hands trying to shake and getting cold when I saw Bix get out his horn. Boy, he took it! . . .

Just four notes . . . But he didn't blow them—he hit 'em like a mallet hits a chime—and his tone, the richness . . .

I got up from the piano and staggered over and fell on the davenport.

The pure, round tones from Beiderbecke's horn hit Carmichael at the right psychological moment, as they are still hitting the ears of people who were not yet born at that

time. From then on, Bix and jazz were synonymous to Carmichael.

The year before, Carmichael, Bix, and Bob Gillette had
heard Louis Armstrong playing second cornet with King
Oliver: [12]

The King featured two trumpets, a piano, a bass fiddle and
a clarinet . . . a big black fellow [then] . . . slashed into *Bugle
Call Rag*.

I dropped my cigarette and gulped my drink. Bix was on his
feet, his eyes popping. For taking the first chorus was that
second trumpet, Louis Armstrong.

Louis was taking it fast. Bob Gillette slid off his chair and
under the table . . . Every note that Louis hit was perfection.

Writing over twenty years later, Carmichael still prefers
Bix to Louis: 'Bix's breaks were not as wild as Armstrong's,
but they were hot and he selected each note with musical
care.'

Another youngster named Francis Spanier had been listening to Armstrong and Oliver in the early 'twenties. He
was white and fourteen years old—too young to be admitted to a public dance hall—and he sat on the curbstone and
listened: [13]

. . . I would go down to the South Side and listen hour after
hour to those two great trumpeters, Joe King Oliver and Louis.
That's when they were at the old Lincoln Gardens. It got so
that I knew every phrase and intonation they played, just from
listening, so that, in spite of myself, I was doing the same
things.

Spanier, later christened 'Muggsy,' never heard much of
Bix because he didn't travel often in college circles, but
he clearly preferred the Armstrong of 1924 anyway, as his
trumpet playing testifies to this day.

Beiderbecke's style grew out of the 'sock' style of Nick
LaRocca of the Original Dixieland Jazz Band, perfected

and refined, and it was set before he heard Armstrong, whom he greatly admired. (Although he tried, Bix couldn't play the New Orleans Negro style with any conviction—listen to *Flock o' Blues*, Gennett 5569.) The contrast between the lyrical and precise cornet of Bix and the wild and dramatic trumpet of Louis reflects the middle-class Davenport, Iowa, background of Beiderbecke and the uptown New Orleans of Armstrong's childhood. Later horns would be even more wild and dramatic than Armstrong's, but none could be more controlled and tasteful than Beiderbecke's. (To this day, a group of former jazzmen turned businessmen, who call themselves 'Sons of Bixes,' meet and play in the Beiderbecke tradition in Chicago.) In times to come, Bunny Berigan, Bobby Hackett, and Ruby Braff drew upon both styles.

Bix and the Wolverines were attended by an important complementary factor: an enthusiastic and understanding audience. George Johnson, the saxophone player in the band, recalls: [14]

Enthusiastic dancers to play to, dancers who understood our music as well as we did, whole days spent playing golf, and a full purse to supply anything we wanted . . . Those were merry days, with no end of gin to drink, horses to ride, and a grand lake to swim in.

In such surroundings, a serious jazzman had the incentive and the opportunity to study, practice, and develop his style. A few years later, Beiderbecke would go East to join Paul Whiteman, just as Armstrong went East to join Fletcher Henderson.

It was the start of 'white' jazz in the Midwest. The Wolverines were followed by the Austin High School gang, with which Joe Sullivan, Jimmy McPartland, Krupa, Mezzrow, Teschemacher, Bud Freeman, Eddie Condon, Dave Tough, Peewee Russell, and others were associated. Unlike

New Orleans, the style of these musicians—often and confusingly labeled 'Chicago'—sacrificed ease and relaxation for tension and drive, perhaps because they were mastering a new idiom in a more hectic environment. They had read some of the literature of the 'twenties—drummer Dave Tough loved Mencken and the *American Mercury*—and their revolt against their own middle-class background tended to be conscious. The role of the improvising—and usually non-reading—musician became almost heroic. 'I wonder,' Teschemacher said, 'if we'll ever get a chance to play hot for a living.' And that was before the Depression, which hit these and all jazz musicians hard.

In 1926, with the newspapers running stories on the death of Rudolph Valentino, movies were first billed above the jazzbands on the South Side of Chicago. The handwriting was on the marquee. In addition to early Depression tremors, Chicago was failing because New York had grabbed up most of the music business. (The tug of war with Hollywood came later.) By the middle 'twenties, most dance bands were booked out of New York, network radio programs emanated from New York, most recordings were made in New York, and Tin-Pan Alley was the acknowledged center of the music-publishing business. Singly or in bands, jazzmen migrated east. Meanwhile, Paul Whiteman and his orchestra were playing in a lagoon under Florida sunshine, helping to promote a real-estate boom that blew up in September 1926.

16 | The Jazz Age Ends

In a sense, after the great publicity attending the Paul Whiteman concert in 1924, the general public never heard of jazz again. Instead, everyone heard about 'swing music' in 1935, as played by Benny Goodman and others. Yet jazz continued its steady infiltration into every nook and corner of American life during these years. Some of the events that cluster around the year 1927, the year of Charles Lindbergh's flight, give us an idea of the extent and complexity of this process. For two years later, the Depression forced jazz underground again.

During the boom before the bust, the jazz scene was wildly confusing. On the surface, both Rudy Vallee and Guy Lombardo had just started and were doing well. The first successful talkie, 'The Jazz Singer,' with Al Jolson, opened on 6 October 1927. Warner Brothers made over three million dollars and all the movie stars began to take elocution lessons. Any connection between this talking picture and jazz was purely coincidental, in spite of the title, although Jolson had been a top-notch minstrel man and had learned a great deal from Negro artists.

Back in 1925, 563 radio stations had been licensed and a horde of dance bands soon discovered a new way to fame and fortune. 'Heigh-ho, everybody, this is Rudy Vallee,' said the reassuringly timid voice over the air waves, while the muffled band made polite noises in the background. Vincent Lopez, Ben Bernie, George Olsen, Abe Lyman, Isham Jones, Ted Lewis, Ray Miller, Paul Ash, Hal Kemp, Jan Garber, Paul Tremaine, Coon-Sanders, Ted Weems, Paul Specht, and hundreds more graduated from radio to theaters, ballrooms, and recordings.

The number of prosperous dance bands at the popular level multiplied, while the jazz content remained slight. At the same time, dancing the Charleston, the Black Bottom, and the Lindy was highly popular and the bands tried to oblige by playing a little hot jazz. Paul Specht, for example, had a small group from his band called the 'Georgians,' with Frank Guarente on trumpet, who were doing a good job of playing hot in the early 'twenties. Later, Abe Lyman's 'Sharps and Flats' worked at playing jazz, while by 1929 Ted Lewis featured two hot soloists, Muggsy Spanier and George Brunies. Most of these bands recorded a novelty now and then that might be called 'peppy.'

None of these large dance bands, however, could swing as a whole. The formula consisted of importing one or two 'hot' soloists, or 'get-off' men, letting them take a chorus once in a while surrounded by acres of uninspired fellow musicians. 'Society band leaders like Meyer Davis and Joe Moss always wanted to have at least one good jazzman in their bands,' says clarinetist Tony Parenti.[1] Bix Beiderbecke was doing exactly this for Paul Whiteman in 1927. Beiderbecke was very well paid and his colleagues all looked up to him—the 'hot' soloists were always the elite—but the frustration of being allowed to play so little, when he was hired because he could play so much, led to all kinds of personal problems and, indirectly, to the after-hours 'jam session,' where a musician could play his heart out.

Meanwhile, the peak of jazz intensity moved from Chicago to New York in the mid-'twenties. The vanguard of jazz (and, indeed, almost every stage in the history of its growth) seems to have materialized in Harlem. At the base of the structure—as in Chicago—was the parlor social or house-rent party. 'Almost every Saturday night when I was in Harlem,' writes Langston Hughes, 'I went to a house-rent party,' [2]

. . . in small apartments where God knows who lived—because the guests seldom did—but where the piano would often be augmented by a guitar, or an odd cornet, or somebody with a pair of drums walking in off the street.

This was the urban circuit for guitar pickers like Leadbelly and boogie-woogie pianists like Yancey, Lewis, and Smith.

On another level, New York was evolving a piano style of its own, greatly influenced by the Scott Joplin ragtime tradition. These were schooled musicians, composers, who tended to look down on boogie-woogie, such as Luckey Roberts, James P. Johnson, Fats Waller, Willie 'The Lion' Smith, and others, including young Edward Kennedy El-lington, just up from Washington, D.C., and tagging along. They had magic names that opened many a door in Harlem. In his biography of Duke Ellington, Barry Ulanov describes a character named 'Lippy,' who according to Duke Ellington 'had heard so much piano that he couldn't play any more. He only thought piano': [3]

Lippy knew where every piano, pianist and player piano in town was located. He and James P., Fats, the Lion and Duke . . . would cruise together. Lippy would walk up to any house at any hour of the night. He'd ring the doorbell. Somebody would wake up after a half-hour's inescapable ring-ing and shout out the window, 'Who the hell is making all that noise?' 'It's me,' said Lippy, 'and James P. is here with me.' It was magic, open sesame.

And another party was on, sparked by piano-playing giants who had both phenomenal technique and incredible fire.

On still another level, the big Negro swing band was

coming into existence. Fletcher Henderson had been building his band since 1923; Sam Wooding's band was playing
the Club Alabam on Broadway in 1925; Cecil Scott's band
opened in Harlem in 1926; Chick Webb and his band were
playing the Savoy Ballroom in 1927; and the bands of
Don Redman, Charlie Johnson, William McKinney, Elmer
Snowden, Luis Russell, The Missourians, and others were
forming or already formed. The audience was there and
Harlem was honeycombed with hot spots: The 101 Ranch,
Small's Paradise, The Band Box, Dicky Wells', The Lenox
Club, The Yeah Man, and, of course, the Cotton Club
where Duke Ellington became famous. The clubs were continually opening and closing like camera shutters but they
always featured hot jazz.

Developments in Harlem were complicated. The popular
idol of the day, Rudy Vallee, was genuinely puzzled: [4]

Truly I have no definite conception of what 'jazz' is, but I
believe that the term should be applied . . . to the weird
orchestral efforts of various colored bands up in Harlem . . .
These bands have a style all their own, and at times it seems
as though pandemonium had broken loose. Most of the time
there is no distinguishable melody . . . it is absolutely impossible for even a musical ear to tell the name of the piece.

Vallee was being humorously honest, and his attitude is
typical of most white musicians of the day.

The music wasn't the only thing that seemed complicated.
This was the period known as 'Manhattan's Black Renaissance,' when the white intelligentsia discovered that all
Negroes were untutored geniuses, or at least delightfully
talented. So Ethel Barrymore played 'Scarlet Sister Mary'
in blackface; Bessie Smith appeared and sang at downtown
literary teas (her comments were unprintable); and white
slumming parties kept hard-working Negroes awake all
night in Harlem. The phony side of the age is summarized

musically by a genuinely undistinguished recording of the Mills Blue Rhythm Band entitled: 'Futuristic Jungleism.'

In Harlem, at the Lincoln Theatre on 135th Street—the old stamping grounds of Ethel Waters, Butterbeans and Susie, Snake Hips Tucker, and Louis Armstrong—the dignified Negro actor, Jules Bledsoe, appeared in Eugene O'Neill's *The Emperor Jones*. Langston Hughes was in the audience: [5]

The audience didn't know what to make of *The Emperor Jones* on a stage where 'Shake That Thing' was formerly the rage. And when the Emperor started running naked through the forest, hearing the Little Frightened Fears, naturally they howled with laughter.

'Them ain't no ghosts, fool!' the spectators cried from the orchestra. 'Why don't you come on out o' that jungle—back to Harlem where you belong?

The citizens of Harlem neither knew nor cared about any jungle, and they didn't identify themselves with Africa, either. A little hot jazz would have made more sense.

The biggest jazz event of 1927 was probably Duke Ellington's opening at the Cotton Club in Harlem. The general public didn't hear about it but, sooner or later, the entire jazz world was influenced by it. The opening almost didn't take place because the Ellington band had a conflicting engagement, signed and sealed, at a Philadelphia theater. The gangsters who ran the Cotton Club knew what to do: they sent an emissary with bulging pockets to the employer in Philadelphia, requesting him to tear up the contract. 'Be big,' the emissary explained, 'or you'll be dead.' Ellington opened on schedule without any trouble.

The floor shows at the Cotton Club, which admitted only gangsters, whites, and Negro celebrities, were an incredible mishmash of talent and nonsense which might well fascinate both sociologists and psychiatrists. I recall one where

a light-skinned and magnificently muscled Negro burst
through a papier-mâché jungle onto the dance floor, clad
in an aviator's helmet, goggles, and shorts. He had obviously been 'forced down in darkest Africa,' and in the center of the floor he came upon a 'white' goddess clad in long
golden tresses and being worshipped by a circle of cringing
'blacks.' Producing a bull whip from heaven knows where,
he aviator rescued the blonde and they did an erotic dance.
In the background, Bubber Miley, Tricky Sam Nanton, and
other members of the Ellington band growled, wheezed,
and snorted obscenely.

The miracle, of course, is that the Ellington band kept
playing jazz. Actually, the band blossomed. If the floor show
needed some new 'jungle' sounds, Duke came up with a
number such as 'Black and Tan Fantasy' which had archaic
and reasonably authentic jazz effects that startled and
pleased everybody. The cry and the field-holler did yeoman
service. The tune was really based on the traditional 12-bar
blues and Miley's trumpet solo echoed an Easter church
cantata, 'Holy City,' played in a minor key, a tune his
mother used to sing. Duke Ellington, who had never been
south of Washington, D.C., his birthplace, became the
musical master of jungle sounds, from 'the heart of Africa.'

For Ellington's great and continuing contribution to jazz
is the broad musical palette which creates an unsurpassed
range of mood. Ellington works with the individual style
of each musician in mind. 'I have often seen him exchange
parts in the middle of a piece,' says his arranger Billy
Strayhorn, 'because the man and the part weren't the same
character.'[6] In a very real sense, the entire Ellington band
composes a tune. The rhythms of Chick Webb at the Savoy
Ballroom in Harlem might have more lift and, later, the
Count Basie band from Kansas City might have more drive,
but Duke Ellington continued to create musical pictures,

impressionistic studies in the jazz tradition, that were years ahead of the times.

Manager Ned Williams remembers when 'Paul Whiteman and his arranger, Ferde Grofé, visited the Cotton Club nightly for more than a week, and finally admitted that they couldn't steal even two bars of the amazing music.' [7] Meanwhile, for five years preceding the Depression, Ellington played stage shows on the Paramount circuit where he was an unfailing top attraction in thirty cities. In general, he played for white audiences, a policy which manager Irving Mills favored because it was more profitable. It also made his influence more widely felt among imitative white musicians.

In the Midwest in 1927, jazz was drying up. The stars of the smaller, pioneering white bands were leaving to join a series of more prosperous bands: Ben Pollack, Roger Wolfe Kahn, Jean Goldkette, and—always—Paul Whiteman. These bands were big, and Goldkette and Pollack were really hot now and then. The biggest hit on records was Gene Austin's 'My Blue Heaven,' which was made about the same time as Meade Lux Lewis's 'Honky Tonk Train Blues.' (In 1954, 'Honky Tonk Train Blues' brought around seventy-five dollars at auction while 'My Blue Heaven' couldn't be given away.)

Big bands were the thing. Bing Crosby, for example, joined Paul Whiteman in 1927 and immediately gravitated toward the nucleus of hot jazzmen: [8]

I lapped up the opportunity to work with such masters of their trade as Bix Beiderbecke, Joe Venuti, the Dorsey boys, Max Farley, Harry Perella, Roy Bargy, Mike Pingatore . . .

To Crosby, as to a growing group of people, big bands were all right, but the hot jazzmen within them were the tops. It followed that hot jazz was good, any other kind bad. By 1928, Crosby was visiting Harlem to hear Ellington; by 1931, he was a hit in his own right; and by 1954, he admitted in print that he had lost touch: 'Bop . . . eludes me completely.'

Among collegians, jazz followers were springing up and the day of the record collector was beginning. The story goes that as late as 1928, a survey of collectors at Princeton indicated that only one possessed any recordings by Louis Armstrong, and this collector was considered a specialist in pretty rough stuff. Yet the over-all trend is suggested by the influential 'pick-up' recording bands of Red Nichols. From about 1926 to 1932, Nichols selected anyone he pleased for a series of recording dates on the Brunswick label, all of it hot jazz. In 1929, he switched from Miff Mole to Jack Teagarden, from Arthur Schutt to Joe Sullivan, and from Fud Livingston to Benny Goodman. White musicians objected at the time to a change from 'white' to 'colored' jazz styles, although today it sounds as if the Nichols bands began to swing a little more as a result.

Underneath it all, a great and unnoticed change was taking place. The real peak of jazz intensity was shifting to the Southwest toward the end of the 'twenties. It had been a long time a-comin'. From 1900 on, great migrations from South to North occurred, especially during the two World Wars. The ravages of the boll weevil and rumors of better living conditions hastened the process. According to F. L. Allen, in 1900 'nearly three-quarters of the Negroes in America had lived in the rural South; by 1950, *less than one-fifth of them did.*' [9]

The Southwest, opened up after the Civil War, was the last reservoir of cheap Negro labor—and music. After World War I, for example, migrations from South to North doubled and tripled as Negroes from Mississippi, Louisiana, and Texas arrived in Oklahoma, Arkansas, and Kansas. Sharecroppers became city-dwellers overnight. The effect on the spread of jazz was important, since both the performers and an audience for the performances arrived in an environment where dance music was big business. Slowly but surely the whole musical picture changed.

One of the focal points for this musical revolution was Kansas City, which gangsters and the Pendergast machine kept wide open from 1927 to 1938. 'There was no Depression for the gangsters,' says pianist Sammy Price, who was there from '29 to '33. The gangsters were doing well and the jazz bands got jobs. 'I know no place was the hotbed of music that Kansas City was . . .' says drummer Jo Jones. 'The Kansas City influence first spread within a radius from Texas to Oklahoma and into Missouri.' [10] A fairly regular circuit for Negro dance bands existed from Houston and Dallas to Kansas City and Oklahoma City, and a series of stomping bands swung along this circuit: the Terrence Holder band from Dallas; the Jap Allen band (with Ben Webster) from Tulsa; the Troy Floyd band from San Antonio; the Alphonse Trent band from Cleveland; the George Morrison band (with Jimmie Lunceford) from Denver; Bat Brown, Gene Coy, Pardee's Footwarmers, and many more. And a new, more powerful style was evolving, as old recordings demonstrate.

Soon after 1927, Walter Page and his Blue Devils were touring Arkansas, Oklahoma, Texas, and Missouri with Lester Young playing tenor sax and—later—Count Basie playing piano. Basie was from Red Bank, New Jersey, and Young was from Woodville, Mississippi, but, like many others, they were attracted to the Southwestern renaissance. By 1929, Andy Kirk and his Clouds of Joy came up to Kansas City from Dallas with a girl named Mary Lou Williams playing piano. 'It was the first time,' recounts bandleader Harlan Leonard, 'we had ever seen a girl cat who could carve the local boys.' Mary Lou became a legend.

Ben Webster, a soloist with the Kirk band which at the

time could be hired for $45 a night, describes how the organization operated on a shoe-string: [11]

> We'd drive into a town and ask a filling station man where the ballroom was where we were to play. Then Mouse would drive up to within a block of the spot. We'd all get out, comb our hair and straighten our clothes, and walk casually over to the spot as if we were going from our hotel. About the time we got there Mouse would drive up in the truck, saluting to us, and unloading the horns. Mouse would always put on a taxi driver's cap after he let us out so he would look like a big time chauffeur when he drove up. Man, those were the days.

Webster still looks back on those Depression days with great pleasure because, like the Wolverines at Indiana in 1924, the band was playing for an audience that understood and loved the music.

As far as the general public was concerned, however, the popular bands of the Southwest were white. Coon-Sanders, Ted Weems, Bernie Cummins, and Henry Halstead broadcasted over the radio and played for dancing at the Hotel Muehlebach in Kansas City. They were also famous from coast to coast on popular recordings. Most of the recordings of the evolving Southwestern style by the Negro bands of Alphonse Trent, Jesse Stone, George E. Lee, and Bennie Moten were not on the popular lists. Instead of the off-beat bounce that Hoagy Carmichael discovered in 1924, the new style had four even beats. 'I don't dig that two-beat jive the New Orleans cats play,' Count Basie is quoted as saying, ' 'cause my boys and I got to have four heavy beats to a bar and no cheating.' [12] The accents actually came evenly in and around the four beats, for the Southwestern style was more complex and smoother-flowing. Later, one of its notable characteristics was the fluid and regular pulse of Freddie Greene's guitar.

It seems likely that this style would have developed in

the East sooner or later. It hadn't, however, in 1928. In that year, the novelist Ralph Ellison remembers hurrying to hear the great Fletcher Henderson band in Oklahoma City. The Eastern band was on a highly publicized tour with the famous jazzmen Benny Carter, Rex Stewart, Buster Bailey, Jimmy Harrison, and Coleman Hawkins. Arriving at the ballroom, the band unpacked their instruments and proceeded to play their best-selling recorded hits. Perhaps it was the trip or the climate, but the Southwestern audience was not moved. To them the music that rocked New York seemed to lack vigor.

The Southwestern style grew up in direct response to the everyday needs of an audience of dancers from the countryside of the deep South. They wanted their music hot and strong. As for the musicians, 'nobody got tired,' says drummer Jo Jones. The folk dance rhythms of the deep South influenced and were influenced by the fashionable big-band format. In the process, the problem of playing hot jazz with a big band was solved, à la Henderson, by harmonizing the solo line, adopting the call-and-response pattern, and developing the 'riff.' It was this style, made famous by Benny Goodman and brought to a peak by the Count Basie Band, that characterized the Swing Era.

Meanwhile, in December 1929, Herbert Hoover announced that 'conditions are fundamentally sound.' To jazz and the jazzman this was not entirely true. With a few notable exceptions, jazz was not heard from until 1935, six years later. The Austin High gang from Chicago, which had trekked to New York, lived on baked beans and salt and pepper sandwiches in a midtown hotel, taking whatever one-night jobs they could get. Jack Teagarden's vocal on a recording entitled 'Makin' Friends' expressed their real feelings:

'I'd rather drink muddy water, sleep in a hollow log,
Rather drink muddy water, Lord, sleep in a hollow log,
Than be up here in New York treated like a dirty dog.'

The mood of the 'twenties had evaporated and the public seemed to want only quiet, soothing dance music.

Some of the bands—Duke Ellington, Noble Sissle, and Louis Armstrong—escaped for a while to Europe. The 'sweet' commercial bands—Guy Lombardo, Wayne King, Fred Waring, Rudy Vallee—survived and prospered. Jan Garber hit the same snag twice—in 1929 and 1939 he switched to hot jazz and back each time. He learned, against his will, that sweet music paid off. Some of the white jazzmen joined commercial bands or got jobs in radio. Muggsy Spanier and George Brunies joined Ted Lewis; Gene Krupa went with Mal Hallett and then Charles 'Buddy' Rogers; Wingy Manone joined Charlie Straight's orchestra. Benny Goodman played radio jobs with B. A. Rolfe's Lucky Strike Orchestra. Colored musicians fared worse. Sidney Bechet opened a shoeshine stand, Tommy Ladnier a tailor shop, and Charlie 'Big' Green of Henderson fame died of cirrhosis of the liver and malnutrition, they say, on a Harlem door-step. The Jazz Age was over.

In retrospect, the 'twenties were the crucial years in which jazz established itself for better or worse. Certain patterns emerged during these years, patterns which help explain how jazz grew and spread, and hence the nature of the music. Of all the technological advances—the phonograph, radio, microphone, talking picture, juke-box, and television—which hastened and shaped the spread of jazz, the phonograph is by far the most important single factor. Again and again, developments in certain areas of the United States—and even in small districts such as Chicago's South Side and Harlem—can be traced in good part to the type and availability of music on recordings. (This was still true in the mid-'forties and clarinetist Tony Scott could truthfully say: [13]

When Bird and Diz hit The Street [i.e when Charlie Parker and Dizzy Gillespie played 52nd Street in New York] regularly . . . everybody was astounded and nobody could get near their way of playing music. Finally, Bird and Diz made records, and then guys could imitate it and go from there.

Jazz musicians are still going to school by way of recordings.)

Again, the vanguard of jazz seems to have flourished best where it had an appreciative and a dancing audience to support it. This is as true for the Wolverines on the Indiana University campus as it is for the Andy Kirk band in Kansas City and the Benny Goodman band of the late 'thirties. This sort of moral and practical support seems to begin among the relatively poor, and progress through the collegians among the middle classes, before reaching the intelligentsia. (The intellectuals, as Nat Hentoff points out, never quite came to grips with jazz as an American art form.) [14] Finally, the very well-to-do seem to be able to enjoy jazz only as a novelty—at its noisiest and crudest by way, for example, of the spasm bands. Only the solid middle classes seem to remain permanently unmoved—at least until the music has been accepted by everybody else.

The cultural lag between the jazz played by Negro and that by white musicians was still a prominent factor in the 'twenties. This is not to say that Negroes did not influence Negroes and whites influence whites—sometimes overwhelmingly—but rather that the over-all direction was from Negro to white. The style of just about all jazz trumpeters, for example, owes a great deal to Louis Armstrong. The Negro supplied the fire and feeling, the white supplied the polish and packaging. In a sense, the commercial success of the white bands paved the way for the employment of the better Negro bands, but the role of the Negro was highly unsatisfying. During the 'twenties, he was seldom rewarded for his own pioneering innovations.

Gradually, the cultural lag diminished, beginning within jazz itself where a musician is judged by his musical ability. When Jack Teagarden first appeared in a New York speakeasy 'wearing a horrible-looking cap and overcoat' (according to Jimmy McPartland), which he no doubt brought with him all the way from Texas, he played one chorus, solo, on trombone and all was forgiven; he joined the Pollack band along with Glenn Miller. Gradually, the usual point of view was reversed: white musicians began to idolize Negro musicians. This attitude carried over to critics and authors. For example, the French critic, Hugues Panassié, in his second book (1942) had the insight and courage to apologize for his first book (1934): [15]

... I had the bad luck, in a sense, to become acquainted with jazz first through white musicians . . . I did not realise until some years after the publication of my first book that, from the point of view of jazz, most white musicians were inferior to black musicians.

M. Panassié's predicament was caused, in part, by the kind of jazz available in France on phonograph records. (When Panassié, who lived in the South of France, came to the United States to supervise recordings of neglected musicians, Eddie Condon pretended to be insulted by his pronouncements. 'Do I tell him,' demanded Condon, 'how to jump on a grape?')

In a larger sense, the gradual change of attitude toward jazz was due, in essence, to the appeal of the music itself. A process of trial and error was taking place in which various elements of Afro-American music, with an increasing amount of harmonic, melodic, and rhythmic complexity, were being offered to and accepted by the public. The blending proceeded rapidly. A series of waves occurred, traveling from country to city, from South to North, and from Negro to white. These waves reached tidal proportions during and after the two world wars, especially in the large cities and during periods of prosperity. Thus, jazz penetrated more and more deeply into many areas of American culture.

PART FIVE : **JAZZ YESTERDAY**

AND TODAY

17 | The Swing Era and the Revivalists

During the decade of 1935 to 1945, a period known as the 'Swing Era,' the greatest mass conversion in the history of jazz took place. For swing music was sold —as a new kind of music—from coast to coast, with all the high-pressure tactics of modern publicity. It was brought to the attention of the public in the press and at the movies, on the stage and in the ballroom, on the juke-box and over the radio. And it made converts for whom new words such as 'jitterbugs' and 'bobby-soxers' were coined. And again, because most of them were young and liked to dance, swing music lasted quite a while. In many ways, it is still with us, although the fans are older.

During the 'twenties, the expressions 'sweet' and 'hot' were in use among musicians to distinguish between the music, for example, of Guy Lombardo and Duke Ellington. Both were generally thought of as jazz. The word 'swing' was only a verb employed to describe the basic jazz quality: good jazz should 'swing.' The story goes that the British Broadcasting Company, facing up to the penetration of American jazz, found something immoral about the expression 'hot jazz.' They were probably right, but they were fifty years too late. So they decreed that announcers must substitute the phrase 'swing music.' The phrase caught on and soon the promoters were using it to sell a 'new' music. Actually, the music was a logical consolidation of what had gone before.

Generally speaking, swing music was the answer to the American—and very human—love of bigness, for the formula of the big Harlem bands which had solved the difficult problem of how to assemble a large orchestra and still play hot jazz was adopted. At the same time, there was a real demand. With the repeal of Prohibition in 1933, jazz was brought out of the speak-easy. There was room to expand. The Depression was fading out as far as middle-class America was concerned, and a vociferous market sprang up among the college kids. They liked their music hot and their bands big. And they could pay for it.

What was the difference between swing music and the jazz that had preceded it? A comparison of the recordings of the Original Dixieland Jazz Band (1917) and the Benny Goodman Orchestra (1935) is startling. The listener is immediately struck by the results of the difference in size. The number of musicians has swollen from around five to more than twelve—better than double—and the music sounds smoother, fuller, more flowing, and paradoxically, simpler.

In his autobiography, *The Kingdom of Swing* (1939), Benny Goodman recalls: [1]

It was about this time [1934], or maybe just a little earlier, that large bands became standardized with five brass, four saxes, and four rhythm ... Ten men ... used to be considered the limit of even a large dance orchestra.

The thirteen musicians of the standard white swing band are divided into teams or sections: brass (5), reeds (4), and rhythm (4). The rhythm section backs up all the others with a steady—and what now seems a little heavy—pulse. The four saxophones play together as one voice, and the five brass (with exceptions where the three trumpets and two trombones follow different lines) play together as a second voice.

Given these two powerful voices, the brass and the reeds, the trick of making a big band swing had been amazingly simple. With the help of arranger Don Redman, Fletcher Henderson had figured it out in the early 'twenties. First a hot solo line was harmonized and written out for the whole section, swinging together. Then arrangers returned to the West African pattern of call-and-response, keeping the two sections answering each other in an endless variety of ways. There were still hot solos on top, with one or both sections playing a suitably arranged background, but that was not new. The repeated phrases which the brass and reed sections threw back and forth became known as 'riffs,' and 'riffing' developed into a fine art which built up each number, chorus after chorus, in the manner of a *bolero*.

At the same time, arrangers borrowed from European harmony to dress up each riff. The four saxophones would repeat a complicated phrase in four-part harmony, and the five brass would reply with a phrase in five-part harmony —all of it tinged with blue tonality. The individual musician had to work harder than ever before. He had to be able to 'swing' separately as well as with his section. And then the sections had to swing together, too. It meant endless rehearsals, a comparative loss of identity (except for the solo stars), and high-level teamwork.

Of course, much of it had to be written down first, for the arrangement made the band. In his autobiography, Benny Goodman describes what a good arrangement can do: [2]

Up to that time [1934] the only kind of arrangements that the public had paid much attention to, so far as knowing who was responsible for them was concerned, were the elaborate ones such as Ferde Grofé's for Whiteman.

But the art of making an arrangement a band can play with swing—and I am convinced it is an art—one that really helps a solo player to get off, and gives him the right background to work against—that's something that very few musicians can do.

The whole idea is that the ensemble passages where the whole band is playing together or one section has the lead, have to be written in more or less the same style that a soloist would use if he were improvising. That is, what Fletcher [Henderson] really could do so wonderfully was to take a tune like "Sometimes I'm Happy" and really improvise on it himself, with the exception of certain parts of the various choruses which would be marked solo trumpet or solo tenor or solo clarinet. Even here the background for the rest of the band would be in the same consistent vein, so that the whole thing really hung together and sounded unified.

Then, too, the arranger's choice of the different key changes is very important, and the order in which the solos are placed, so that the arrangement works up to a climax. In all these respects, Fletcher's ideas were far ahead of anybody else's at the time . . .

By late 1934, Goodman had some 36 Fletcher Henderson arrangements. Fletcher's ideas, however, were not 'far ahead'—he was writing fine arrangements that were new to the general public and even to white musicians, but they were at least ten years old to Harlem and to men like Don Redman, who led a band of fourteen men with similar arrangements at Connie's Inn in 1931.

The popularity of swing music was a long time in the making. Ever since the early 'twenties, when Paul Whiteman demonstrated that there was a lot of money in 'symphonic jazz' played by a huge band, bandleaders struggled to increase the size of their bands. It was particularly important if the band put on stage shows or played vaudeville. The 'sweet' dance bands succeeded in building themselves up to nine men and a violinist without much trouble. They used stock arrangements that offered no creative problems. With little improvising and less rhythm, these orchestras (referred to as 'mickey-mouse' bands by jazzmen) cheerfully churned out dance music that was melodious and did not interfere with the conversations of the patrons.

On the other hand, a great many of the highly gifted 'hot' jazzmen couldn't—or wouldn't—read music. Moreover, if more than half a dozen played together, the result was no better and they tended to get in each other's way. Collective improvisation with more than about eight men, with everybody off on his own extemporaneous creations, added up to a musical complexity which nobody enjoyed. For a while, a compromise was reached whereby a few hot jazzmen were hired by the big, sweet dance bands to take a solo once in a while during a heavy arrangement. They were the yeast in the musical dough.

Bix Beiderbecke, for example, was highly paid to stand up and swing all seven acres of Paul Whiteman's concert band (including George Gershwin) for perhaps twelve bars at a time. With the aid of a nucleus of jazzmen within the band, he succeeded with amazing frequency. At home jazz-loving record buyers wore out the grooves occupying a fraction of an inch on a Whiteman recording, concentrating on a few well-chosen notes by Bix. Their judgment appears sound today.

The big, sweet dance band was a profitable business. Where was the big, swinging dance band? As early as 1923, Fletcher Henderson had a band of ten musicians and ran head-on into the problem of making them play together as a team. With the aid of arrangers such as Don Redman, he gradually solved the problem. By 1926, Henderson led a truly swinging band of eleven jazzmen—a fact that can be documented by listening to 'The Stampede' (Col. 654). The band played regularly at the Roseland Ballroom on Broadway, where it became something of a legend among a few white musicians. White jazzmen in the 'twenties marveled at the fire and guts of the Henderson band and copied what they could, but they considered much of the music clumsy and crude. The band, they said quite sincerely, played out of tune and the individual musicians were always hitting 'clinkers' or wrong notes.

By European standards the white jazzmen were right. But the ears of most musicians are better educated today. What sounded rough and out-of-tune then sounds relaxed and swinging now. The jazzman's notion of the liberties that may be taken with the perfect pitch of European music has been steadily broadening toward a predictable goal—the freedom of the street-cry and the field-holler. Jazz that once sounded tortured has a habit of soon sounding tidy. Yet, in 1939, Benny Goodman still spoke of 'digging' the music out of a Henderson arrangement. This attitude was both typical and honest. A few years before, Isham Jones had enthusiastically purchased Don Redman's arrangement of 'Chant of the Weed,' only to discover that his band couldn't play it.

Fletcher Henderson and his big band were not alone. Before the 'twenties were over, Negro bands led by Chick Webb, Earl Hines, Cecil Scott, William McKinney, Charlie Johnson, Luis Russell, and, of course, Duke Ellington were all playing a style in which the whole band swung together. And before 1935 when Goodman arrived, these bands were joined by Cab Calloway, Jimmie Lunceford, Teddy Hill, Les Hite, Andy Kirk, Don Redman, and especially, Bennie Moten. This music was swinging, relaxed, powerful, but for the most part unheard.

The distinction between these colored bands and the Goodman band which started the swing craze is indicated by Goodman's own comment: [3]

... that's why I am such a bug on accuracy in performance, about playing in tune, and with just the proper note values ...

in the written parts, I wanted it to sound as exact as the band possibly could make it.

Goodman stressed precision and the accurate pitch essential to European harmony, and worked unceasingly toward that goal. At the same time, he says: 'Also a good drummer can do more in the way of giving swing to a band . . . than almost any other man in the outfit.' And he hired Gene Krupa. Add to this the arrangements of Fletcher Henderson, Jimmy Mundy, and Edgar Sampson, which lent themselves to rhythmic treatment, and Benny Goodman emerged with a refined and swinging blend that the general public at that precise moment was ready to enjoy.

There were at least two pioneering white bands preceding Goodman: The Dorsey Brothers and the Casa Loma band. (The Goldkette and Pollack bands were pre-swing orchestras—the Pollack band was small and played a kind of arranged Dixieland with tremendous effect; the Goldkette band was large, heavy, and impressive but did not swing in the Goodman sense.) Jimmy and Tommy Dorsey had been making records under their own names with a variety of musicians as early as 1928. By 1934, they had a fairly stable band of their own with twelve musicians—two trumpets, three trombones, three saxes, and four rhythm. This is one saxophone short of the standard swing instrumentation. 'We were trying to hit somewhere between Hal Kemp and the Casa Loma band,' Tommy Dorsey once told me. Unfortunately, the arrangements now sound heavy and cluttered and the rhythm was almost of the 'shuffle' variety.

The Casa Loma band from Detroit was a different story. With the same instrumentation as the Dorsey Brothers, but without the star soloists, the Casa Loma band adopted the arranged 'riff' almost too wholeheartedly. With the skill and foresight of such arrangers as Southern-born-and-bred Gene Gifford, the band learned to read harmonized solos and play riffs, the brass and reed sections calling and responding to each other in a variety of ways. What is more, they learned to roll along together, generating considerable swing as a whole. (In the early 'thirties, they recorded, first 'White Jazz,' then 'Black Jazz,' and Decca issued albums with the same titles, but not even the jazzmen saw anything unusual about it.) The Goldkette band and the Casa Loma band came from Detroit and played the same arrangements. 'The Casa Loma band could swing more,' Redman once told me, 'perhaps because they were a great team without so many highly paid and temperamental stars.'

How did the whole Casa Loma band learn to swing, using the call-and-response pattern between the sections? They must have had a collective ear that was relatively undisturbed by the so-called 'crudities' in the music of the Fletcher Henderson band and others. Above all, their arranger, Gene Gifford, was no stranger to the blues and gospel singing of the Southwest, which he toured in his 'teens with the Bob Foster and Lloyd Williams bands. In this territory, the call-and-response pattern was standard for practically all music, and the swing formula for big bands was no novelty. In 1932, moreover, they could have heard the first outstanding recordings of a big, swinging band with the 'five brass, four saxes, and four rhythm' that Benny Goodman later helped to standardize. These records were issued on Victor's popular series and stocked by record stores where white people traded: Bennie Moten's Kansas City band with Count Basie at the piano. And in the same year, this band played the Savoy Ballroom in New York and upset the jazz apple cart. 'The only time we were bothered,' says Count Basie, 'was when we played opposite a little guy named Chick Webb.' [4]

The Moten band raised the riff to a fine—and even improvised—art, while retaining the blazing solo work of top jazzmen, and frequently combined the best of both. The leaders of the brass and reed sections would invent a series of ascending riffs on the spur of the moment (i.e., a 'head' arrangement) which the entire section would forthwith play. And the riffs would build, bolero-like, back and forth between the sections, chorus after chorus, from simple to complex, into a swinging climax. For the over-all goal was always a more flowing, driving rhythm, with which even the riffs were never allowed to interfere. With the same goal in mind, the guitar was substituted for the banjo, and the string-bass began to 'walk,' or play melodic figures instead of pounding away at one or two notes. All of these innovations of the 1932 Moten band became standard five or six years later.

Meanwhile, the popularity of the Casa Loma band among the Eastern colleges was outstanding as early as 1931. And the Casa Loma band was Benny Goodman's model. Speaking of his booking agent and friend, Willard Alexander, who had just graduated from an Eastern college, Goodman writes: [5]

Since the Casa Loma was so popular with the college kids, it was tough trying to sell a sweet band against them, and he had the idea of building up some young band that would go into the same field, playing the kind of music that the youngsters liked.

In 1936, the Goodman band took the place of the Casa Loma band ('the one we had started out to buck') on the well-paid Camel Caravan radio show.

Interviewed in *Down Beat* in 1954, bandleader Les Brown extolled Pat Davis as his musical idol back in the early 'thirties. Who is Pat Davis? He played tenor saxophone, along with clarinetist Clarence Hutchenrider, trombonist Peewee Hunt, and trumpeter Sonny Dunham in the

Casa Loma band before it became known as Glen Gray's. In 1930 the average small-town white boy (especially on the East coast) who loved jazz heard only the Casa Loma band. Virtually alone, they played swinging jazz—mixed with a large amount of engaging sweet music such as 'Smoke Rings' and 'In the Still of the Night'—on phonograph records, in ballrooms, and on the air. As the first big white band to swing, they had an enormous influence in the East, where it counted heavily at that time.

The Benny Goodman story is the story of how many qualities suddenly jelled in one band to produce a blend of enormous appeal. Born in Chicago in 1908, Goodman was well known among musicians for his work with several groups before he came to New York with Ben Pollack's band in 1928. The Pollack band had both Goodman and Jack Teagarden as soloists but, like the Dorsey Brothers, had not as yet discovered swinging arrangements. Along with the Chicagoans, they became famous among white jazzmen on their own merits, nevertheless, playing at the Park Central Hotel in New York. 'In a way, those were the happiest days of our lives,' Bud Freeman recalls, 'only we didn't know it then, and maybe we don't even know it now.' [6] For a brief moment, the Pollack band with the white Chicago gang was the hottest thing in the jazz public's eye. (In those days, the burning question among hot jazz devotees was whether Benny Goodman or Jimmy Dorsey was the better clarinetist.) The Depression soon brought it to an end. 'A lot of people gave a lot of parties,' says Jimmy McPartland; 'you could get all you wanted to drink but nothing to eat.' [7]

While the Casa Loma band was building up its college following, Goodman made a living playing club dates (one-night local engagements) and radio programs in the studios with big, commercial orchestras led by B. A. Rolfe, Rubinoff, Al Goodman, or Johnny Green. Goodman had learned how to read music, swiftly and well, which meant more jobs. This did not endear him to his colleagues from Chicago who were inclined to sneer—and with some reason, considering the attitude of symphony men—at people who could read music. ('I can read them notes,' cried Wingy Manone indignantly, 'I just can't separate 'em—five flats look like a bunch of grapes to me.')

In 1933, Goodman met the resourceful critic, John Hammond. On a trip to England, Hammond had sold the idea of special hot-jazz recordings to a vice-president of the English Gramophone Company. Hammond promised to supervise the recordings himself and to feature the playing of Benny Goodman. At the time Hammond hadn't met Goodman, but he soon did and convinced him, too. What musicians should they hire? Hammond held out for Gene Krupa and Jack Teagarden, while insisting that a drummer who had played with Meyer Davis be dropped. Goodman insisted upon a heavy Arthur Schutt arrangement. They had to use a 'society' tenor saxophonist because he was the local contractor who got the musicians together according to union regulations.

In those days, if a musician wanted to record a popular tune, the music publishers insisted that he use a 'stock' arrangement, which would make the melody recognizable—and uninspired—wherever it was heard. He might be permitted to record a tune of his own, played hot, if he signed away the rights to the recording supervisor. Pressure was sometimes exerted to make him play in a 'corny,' or old-fashioned, style which would be sure to sell. Goodman recorded 'Shirt Tail Stomp' (Brun. 3975), for example, in a hillbilly style at the urging of record-company executives. When it was issued in 1928, Ted Lewis, whom Goodman burlesques on the record, liked it enough to offer him a job. The job helped pull Goodman through the Depression.

Hammond had insisted on special arrangements, however, and Goodman's first record for the English Gramophone Company—'I Gotta Right to Sing the Blues' and 'Ain'tcha Glad'—was a notable success in England. When the American record executives woke up and decided to issue it in the United States, only Hammond's violent objections kept them from coupling each side with a commercial number by Clyde McCoy or Harry Reser 'to insure the recording's success.' Goodman went on to make a series of recordings for Columbia at a new low of $100 a side, employing such musicians as Teddy Wilson and Coleman Hawkins and such singers as Billie Holiday, Jack Teagarden, and Mildred Bailey.

As the series progressed, Goodman began to appreciate and employ first-rate Negro musicians. On this point, he is quite frank about the importance of Hammond's influence: [8]

It was during these months, around the end of 1933 and the beginning of 1934, that I first began to make records with colored musicians. For this the responsibility must be given almost entirely to John Hammond, who really put me back in touch with the kind of music they could play . . . It just happened that in working along as I had during those seven or eight years, I had gotten out of touch with them . . .

Later on, Benny Goodman broke the precedent against bands of mixed color—not without some difficulty—by employing Teddy Wilson at the Hotel Congress in Chicago.

By 1934, Goodman had his own orchestra and a job which paid less than scale at Billy Rose's Music Hall. An air-shot over WMCA, however, made new friends. Three months later 'the mob found a cheaper band.' Then came the big break. The National Biscuit Company was ready to launch its new Ritz cracker, and an advertising firm sold them the idea of a 'Let's Dance' radio program with three bands: Xavier Cugat playing rhumbas, Kel Murray playing sweet dance music, and Benny Goodman playing a little more rhythmic jazz. The three bands alternated from eleven to two A.M. every Saturday night, and the program was carried by 53 stations from coast to coast.

The rumor of 'kick-backs' still survives, but the biscuit company financed eight new arrangements of Goodman's choosing during the first thirteen weeks. His choice is revealing. With the constant prodding of Hammond, Goodman hired better hot jazzmen and went to Fletcher Henderson for his new arrangements. At this stage in the development of swing music, we can pinpoint certain musical relationships. Henderson sold Goodman arrangements that Henderson had been using for three to five years. It was Goodman's precise style of playing the arrangements that hit the great American public as something new and exciting.

Thus, in December 1932, Fletcher Henderson recorded 'New King Porter Stomp' (Okeh 41565), using his own arrangement which he had worked out over a number of years. Later, he sold the arrangement to Goodman, and, in July 1935, Benny Goodman and his Orchestra recorded it as 'King Porter Stomp' (Victor 25090). The Goodman recording was two-and-a-half years later, but it must have out-sold the Henderson recording a thousand to one. Yet to all but die-hard Goodman fans, the Henderson recording now sounds better in just about every way, although this once-great band was falling apart at the time. The same pattern was pretty general throughout the swing era.

The 'Let's Dance' radio show, together with a series of recordings, began to build up a small but devoted following. 'I had to do what I thought I was best at,' says Goodman, 'and just then it was having a hot band.' From week to week, the band sounded better over the radio (at that, only every third number was played 'hot'). But the general public was as yet untouched. MCA, the Music Corporation of America, persuaded by a young collegian in their employ, Willard Alexander, decided to book the Goodman band, much to the annoyance of most of the people at the agency. At the time, MCA booked only sweet bands. They put Goodman into the Hotel Roosevelt in New York City, the home of Guy Lombardo. 'Every time I looked around, on the night we opened,' says Goodman, 'one of the waiters or the captain would be motioning to us not to play so loud.' The band was not a success.

In desperation, Alexander booked Goodman for a series of one-nighters, with a month stopover in Denver, to the West Coast where there seemed to be a little interest. The band worked its way out, playing in Pittsburgh, Columbus, Toledo, Lakeside (Michigan), Milwaukee, and then Denver—where Kay Kyser was pulling them in. The spot was called Elitch's Gardens and the owner phoned MCA at once, announcing that 'the music was lousy and the leader was a pain in the neck,' to quote Goodman himself. And business was terrible. By switching to stock arrangements, the band held the job but morale hit a new low.

The band's morale was still low after playing Salt Lake City and San Francisco. They recalled trumpeter Wingy Manone's observation: 'Man, good jazz just can't make it over them tall Rockies.' When they arrived at the Palomar Ballroom in Los Angeles, their new location for a month or so, the band became downright frightened. The ballroom had an enormous dance floor, plus a huge section with tables where food and liquor were noisily served. And they charged admission. For the first hour, the band played the sweeter tunes with the softer arrangements. Goodman was desperate: [9]

If we had to flop, at least I'd do it in my own way, playing the kind of music I wanted to. For all I knew this might be our last night together, and we might as well have a good time of it while we had the chance.

I called out some of our big Fletcher arrangements for the next set, and the boys seemed to get the idea. From the moment I kicked them off, they dug in with some of the best playing I'd heard since we left New York. . . .

The first big roar from the crowd was one of the sweetest sounds I ever heard in my life. . . .

The Swing Era was born on the night of 21 August 1935.

The immediate reason for the sudden success of the Goodman band, according to Benny himself, is that 'it was a dancing audience—that's why they went for it.' [10] Again, Goodman's phonograph records preceded the band's success, and disc jockeys had been playing some of the best of them. Further, the 'Let's Dance' program hit Los Angeles between the hours of 7 and 11 p.m.—the time of maximum listening and the time when the teen-agers could hear it. They were still dancing the Lindy and Goodman's music was just right for it. In a matter of months, the jitterbugs and bobby-soxers were dancing the Big Apple and the Shag—up and down the aisles of theaters, too—while the Goodman band played on. Above all, they were the first band to give the current hits of Tin-Pan Alley, such as 'Goody Goody,' for example, a jazz treatment which sold enormously.

If Benny Goodman became the 'King of Swing' in 1935, reaping all the publicity and profits, the man behind the throne was Count Basie. For it was the Basie band that gave depth and momentum to the whole swing era while planting the seeds that later gave birth to bop and the 'cool' school of jazz. In 1935, after the death of Bennie Moten, Bill Basie gradually built up his own band. He and his band were playing the Reno Club in Kansas City in 1936, when John Hammond heard them over experimental station W9XBY and alerted Benny Goodman and Willard Alexander of MCA.

The Basie band was scuffling. 'It was a cracker town but a happy time,' Basie recalls. At the Reno Club, imported Scotch was fifteen cents a shot, domestic ten cents, and a hot-dog stand was located next to the bar. 'We played from nine o'clock in the evening to five or six the next morning, including the floor shows,' says Basie, 'and the boys in the band got eighteen dollars a week and I got twenty-one.' When Buck Clayton joined on trumpet, the boys sacrificed twenty-five cents apiece and Clayton got two dollars a night. Down the street at the Sunset Club, boogie-woogie pianist Pete Johnson and blues-shouter Joe Turner (who made a great hit with rock and roll in 1954) were working for less. Actually, things weren't as bad as they seemed, because prices were low and tips from gangsters high.

MCA booked Basie for a trial run at the Grand Terrace Ballroom in Chicago. Nothing much happened. Then the band was brought to the Famous Door on New York's 52nd Street. The word got around fast. On the way to New York, Basie augmented his band from nine to fifteen men: [11]

—I wanted my fifteen-piece band to work together just like those nine pieces did. I wanted fifteen men to think and play the same way. I wanted those four trumpets and three trombones to bite with real guts. BUT I wanted that bite to be just as tasty and subtle as if it were the three brass . . . I said that the minute the brass got out of hand and blared and screeched . . . there'd be some changes made.

The Famous Door was about the size of a large closet and, once inside, patrons found themselves sitting under the guns. When the band started to play, some listeners felt as if they were inside a loudspeaker-enclosure with the volume up. You either loved it or hated it—there was no middle ground—but to New York musicians the power and swing of the Basie band was a revelation.

Aided by the ground-breaking success of Benny Goodman and the astute managing of Willard Alexander, the Basie band with its more relaxed and powerful beat became an immediate and lasting success. 'When we first came to New York we tried to experiment,' drummer Jo Jones recalls, 'so after a week of experimenting we found out that there was nothing old hat about what we had been doing.' [12] In a short time, Basie was influencing Goodman deeply. Goodman adopted Basie's numbers, such as 'One O'Clock Jump' (which was the first Goodman recording to sell over a million), and then began to use Basie and some of his musicians on recordings. Fortunately, Basie had recorded his own version of 'One O'Clock Jump' (in part, a riff taken from Redman's arrangement of *Six or Seven Times*) about seven months earlier and, although it did not sell nearly as well, the original had wide distribution and musicians could hear and appreciate it.

The very birthplaces of the musicians associated with Basie made a roll call of the Southwest: Herschel Evans, Denton, Texas; Jimmy Rushing, Oklahoma City, Oklahoma; Buck Clayton, Parsons, Kansas; Jack Washington, Kansas City, Kansas; Oran 'Hot Lips' Page, Dallas, Texas; Don Byas, Muskogee, Oklahoma; Joe Keyes, Houston, Texas; Joe Turner, Kansas City, Missouri; Walter Page, Gallatin, Missouri; Eddie Durham, San Marcos, Texas; and Lester Young, Woodville, Mississippi.

The Basie band accomplished a revolution in jazz that we are still trying to estimate. Specifically, the Basie piano style, with its frequent openings for the bass fiddle, led to the de-emphasis of the left hand in modern jazz piano. The style of drummer Jo Jones, who rode the high-hat cymbal, left its mark on bop drummers. And the relaxed style of tenor saxophonist Lester Young helped to produce the 'cool' school of jazz. A younger saxophonist, Dexter Gordon, says that he stopped playing after he heard Lester Young. 'It was too much . . . I threw my horn away and didn't touch it for two years.' [13] Benny Goodman reacted differently: 'This is the first time,' he told John Hammond, 'that I've ever heard a tenor sax played the way it should be and not overblown.' (He swapped his clarinet for Young's tenor saxophone and, they say, sounded like Young for a whole evening.) Above all, the Basie band developed the use of the 'head riff' (the improvised unison phrase, tossed back and forth by brass and reed sections) to the level of fine art. On a less evident but more important level than the Goodman band, the band of Count Basie underwrote the Swing Era.

For the next ten years, swing music made big money and bandleaders became as popular—and as unpredictable —as movie stars. Goodman's 'King Porter Stomp' was recorded in 1935, Bob Crosby's 'Dixieland Shuffle' in 1936, Tommy Dorsey's 'Marie' in 1937, Artie Shaw's 'Begin the Beguine' in 1938, and Glenn Miller's 'In the Mood' in 1939. (The importance of the disc jockey becomes evident.) The musical sources for many of these swing bands was documented, in part, by another band under the leadership of Charlie Barnet. He made a recording with 'The Duke's Idea' on one side and 'The Count's Idea' on the other (Bluebird 10453), paying homage to Duke Ellington and Count Basie.

Before the Swing Era of big bands ended, small-band jazz had begun to evolve in two diametrically opposed directions: the New Orleans revival and bop. Unlike bop, the New Orleans revival produced little that was new musically, but it made fanatical converts among the white middle classes—perhaps because, like New Orleans jazz, the style had an unembattled, relaxed, and outdoor quality—and it aided the diffusion of jazz all over the world.

The New Orleans revival presented jazz in one of its most cheerful and easily enjoyed aspects.

Although the New Orleans revival included a few old-time Negro musicians and, in fact, was based entirely upon earlier Negro jazz, the music was played largely by young white musicians for white audiences in a far different environment. In the background, the twenty-year-old recordings of Kid Ory, Jelly Roll Morton, and, especially, Joseph 'King' Oliver loomed large. Then, the living examples of Kid Ory, Kid Rena (rediscovered and recorded in 1940) and, above all, Bunk Johnson (1944) lent fuel to the flames. The story of Bunk's refurbishing—from new store-teeth to trumpet—made news in the Luce publications from coast to coast. At this point, several groups of young white musicians—many of them record collectors—burst into jazz.

In 1935 in Oakland, Lu Watters had a band that played a few Dixieland numbers. Around 1939, at the San Francisco World's Fair, he hired trumpeter Bob Scobey and trombonist Turk Murphy, and the band settled down to a careful reconstruction of the recordings of King Oliver, including the two-cornet precedent set when Louis Armstrong joined Oliver in 1922. They also went back to the tuba instead of the string bass, and the banjo in place of the guitar. By 1941, Lu Watters and his Yerba Buena band had made the first highly influential recordings of the New Orleans revival. In 1944 the dedicated jazz critic Bill Russell recorded some top-notch Bunk Johnson on the American Music label, while Kid Ory, along with Omer Simeon, Dink Johnson, and Mutt Carey recorded on Crescent.

The dam had burst and there was even a moment when to some it seemed desirable to run for the hills of bebop as Peewee Hunt, Art Mooney, and their diluted Dixieland versions of earnest imitations took over the Hit Parade.

It didn't last. Meanwhile, the Castle Band began to record Jelly Roll Morton's arrangements; the Frisco Jazz Band imitated Lu Watters; the early Bob Wilber band (associated with Scarsdale High School) copied King Oliver; the Tailgate Jazz Band played in what might best be called a Watters-Oliver style; and Turk Murphy, who left the Watters group and started his own band, began to compose and play new tunes in a reasonable facsimile of the old Oliver style.

This was just the beginning. Old-timers of the late 'twenties—bands led by Eddie Condon, Phil Napoleon, Jimmy McPartland, Peewee Irwin, Muggsy Spanier and their likes—found themselves playing a comparatively modern style which had absorbed much of the swing era. (To the record-collecting converts known as 'moldy figs,' however, this was not 'authentic' jazz.) Jazzbands of enthusiastic white youngsters sprang up all over the country, and the *Record Changer*, a magazine for record collectors, ran contests which were crowded with old-styled entrants. By 1956 bands of young collegians, who had never seen New Orleans and who sometimes played with more energy than skill, were selling out Carnegie Hall in New York City. At the very least, the enthusiasm was authentic and truly authentic New Orleans bands such as that of George Lewis gained a chance to be heard.

Perhaps the most striking result occurred outside the United States—bands of the New Orleans revival evolved swiftly in Holland, France, Japan, Australia, Uruguay, England, and many other countries. It was impossible to keep track of them all, but the French band of Claude Luter, for example, was generally conceded to have recaptured the King Oliver sound best—better, that is, than any of the young American bands.

In a sense, the New Orleans revival demonstrated that a good portion of the white world had caught up with and was enjoying—frequently to the point of active participation—an imitation of the music that the American Negro had played twenty to thirty years earlier. What is more, it showed again—as the sales of Benny Goodman's 1938 recordings in 1954 indicated—that there is practically no era in the history of jazz that does not have the range of appeal to make a revival possible. And many fine tunes were revived in the process. Swing music by big bands hit the public eye, made an incredible amount of money, and then faded out; but the music of the small-band New Orleans revival has been growing slowly and surely and seems to be here to stay.

Meanwhile, big bands were successful on three levels. Guy Lombardo, of course, continued to enlarge his band and make the steadiest income. For ten years, however, he had to move over and share a part of it with the swing bands. At the same time, some twenty or so big colored bands, with Ellington and Basie at their head, were probably playing better jazz than the white bands and, although earning about half as much, making a reasonably steady income. Another war, the record ban, a tax on dance floors, the microphone (which gave volume to any weak voice), a new style, and other imponderables brought the big-band boom to an end around 1945.

18 | Bop and After

By 1940 jazz had attained enough momentum and maturity to stage a revolution more or less within itself. No longer could the new developments be compared with reasonable accuracy to another wave from the South—although such waves continued and reinforced the boom in 'Rhythm and Blues' (formerly 'Race' and latterly 'Rock and Roll') recordings on juke-boxes in Negro neighborhoods. For 'bop' was a sudden eruption within jazz, a fast but logical complication of melody, harmony, and rhythm. European and non-European components merged according to what was increasingly a European pattern. The result was a broader, deeper blend.

The sounds of bop were literally unheard of and, accordingly, controversial. The very word seemed to give offense. At first, it was 'rebop,' then 'bebop,' and finally 'bop.' Musicians said the word was an imitation of a typical sound in the new idiom. (The word occurs in the 1928 'Four or Five Times' by McKinney's Cotton Pickers, at the end of Chick Webb's 1939 recording of 'Tain't Whatcha Do,' and in the title of Lionel Hampton's 1945 hit, 'Hey-Ba-Ba-Re-Bop'; but none of these recordings show any pronounced bop influence.) The likeliest source, suggested by Professor Maurice Crane, seems to be the Spanish expression 'Arriba!' or ''Riba!' (literally: 'up'), which is the Afro-Cuban musician's equivalent for 'Go!' Such an origin would fit the known facts of the wide influence of 'Latin' music on jazz and its direct influence on bop.

Although the beginnings of bop can be traced back quite a way, the new style evolved with terrifying suddenness. Topnotch jazzmen awoke to hear themselves sounding old-fashioned, a horrid predicament in a music where you are judged by your improvisations. Louis Armstrong, for example, broke his life-long rule of never criticizing jazz or jazzmen by calling bop 'that modern malice.' Referring to 'boppers,' Armstrong swung from the ground up: [1]

. . . they want to carve everyone else because they're full of malice, and all they want to do is show you up, and any old way will do as long as it's different from the way you played it before. So you get all them weird chords which don't mean nothing, and first people get curious about it just because it's new, but soon they get tired of it because it's really no good and you got no melody to remember and no beat to dance to. So they're all poor again and nobody is working, and that's what that modern malice done for you.

The advent of bop was not only sudden but also highly threatening to many established musicians.

Many economic factors were at work cutting down the cultural lag between Negro and white musicians and thus hastening the spread of new ideas. During World War II the old story of mass migrations from South to North repeated itself. The ban against Negro workers was broken down in many new areas and wartime jobs paid well. Once more the importance of the Negro market was discovered and, for the first time, a series of 52nd Street and Broadway nightclubs advertised for the Negro trade. Here was a highly receptive audience which in turn influenced the music and, by 1947–8, eager patrons formed queues around the block waiting to enter the Royal Roost, 'The Metropolitan Bopera House,' on Broadway.

Meanwhile, the color line in jazz bands was breaking down. Back in the early 'twenties, colored arrangers like Don Redman were writing for white bands such as Goldkette and Whiteman. By the 'thirties, mixed bands in the recording studio were no novelty. (Jelly Roll Morton appears to have been the first, back in 1923 with the New Orleans Rhythm Kings.) Then Benny Goodman featured Teddy Wilson at the Congress (not without difficulty) in 1936. Artie Shaw hired Billie Holiday in 1938. Jan Savitt had a singer billed as 'Bon Bon.' A little later, Tommy Dorsey hired Charlie Shavers, Charlie Barnet signed up Howard McGhee, Jimmy Dorsey featured June Richmond, and so on. In 1951, when the great colored trumpeter Roy Eldridge claimed 'he could distinguish a white musician from a Negro simply by listening to his style,' Leonard Feather gave him a blindfold test which proved him wrong.

The ice had been broken back in the 'thirties, and although the bands ran into difficulties touring the South, the practice of mixed bands became fairly common. The reason was simple: on the one hand, Negro musicians were outstanding additions to white bands; on the other hand, Negro bands—no matter how good—were paid about half as much as white bands. Hence, when Roy Eldridge was making $125 a week leading his own band and Gene Krupa offered him $150 a week as featured soloist, Eldridge joined Krupa. (Later he quit—the continuous and nerve-racking discrimination didn't help.) One of the results of these developments was that exciting innovations in jazz no longer trickled slowly from pioneering Negro bands to commercial white bands—the trickle was becoming a swift torrent and the new music spread rapidly.

Public interest in bop didn't last long—the musicians

themselves seemed to go out of their way to discourage it—and the threat in bop soon became more psychological than economic. But the young and formerly admiring bop musician did not hesitate to tell the old-timer: 'If you don't dig these new sounds, man, you're real square.' In fact, he made a point of doing so—in a variety of ways—and many older musicians felt this hostility keenly. The revolt in bop was frequently revolting.

There were several non-musical factors contributing to this antagonism within jazz. During World War II, Negroes in Harlem and elsewhere had been urged with more noise than understanding to fight the 'yellow-skinned Jap.' A few Negro leaders were arguing, with some logic, that the war was a white man's war and the fruits of victory would not go to the Negro. Simultaneously, a Mohammedan cult waxed strong in Harlem. Its members adopted Mohammedan names, dress, and sometimes studied Arabic. Many were both serious and sincere and there was historic precedent in Africa. Others toured the South in turbans and robes defying segregation. A few bop musicians joined these cults and *Life* made the worst of it, with tongue-in-cheek pictures of Dizzy Gillespie 'bowing to Mecca.'

The switch from 'hot' to 'cool' as the epithet of highest praise goes deeper. The prevalent greeting was 'Be cool, man,' and each musician sank into his own deep-freeze. There was reason in his madness: he refused to play the stereotype role of Negro entertainer, which he rightly associated with Uncle Tomism. He then proceeded to play the most revolutionary jazz with an appearance of utter boredom, rejecting his audience entirely. Again, there was a reason. The bop stance of hunched preoccupation, of somnambulistic concentration, was based—in part—on the desire to be judged on the merits of the music alone. But the bop musician overdid it, sometimes playing with his back to the audience and walking off the stand at the end of his particular solo.

They were just as hard on their fellow-musicians, too. 'The modulations we manufactured were the weirdest,' Dizzy Gillespie once told me, 'especially if some new cat walked in with his horn and tried to sit in with us.' (Jelly Roll had done the same thing long before.) This led, in part, to the composing of good new tunes by talented musicians such as Thelonious Monk, whose weird, wonderful, and pioneering modulations were referred to as 'Zombie music' by the musicians themselves, more in awe than anger. As late as 1955, at the Charlie Parker Memorial Concert with about twenty musicians waiting to play together, Monk selected a tune for the all-out finale that only Gillespie once knew—and he had forgotten it. It was a late but typical thrust of the Minton school of jazz, obscured by trumpeter Henry 'Red' Allen's fast switch to the blues.

A trifling shift in the musical amenities illustrates another detail of the rebellion. Usually, a musician nods his head as he nears the end of his series of solos to cue the next soloist. At Minton's, a musician launched upon a new chorus and then stopped short, leaving his successor to pick up the pieces. To an old-timer, this is sheer sabotage. After a while, even the big bands, such as Woody Herman's with drummer Dave Tough, copied another detail: the ragged coda. The men at Minton's were human, however, and the revolt had its limits. When the famous Benny Goodman came up to sit in, 'we used to just convert our style to coincide with his,' reports drummer Kenny Clarke, 'so Benny played just the things he wanted to play. We did that for others too.' [2]

Of all the phenomena associated with bop, the 'hipster' could be perhaps the least appetizing although he was often highly intelligent. The musicians themselves were fairly tolerant but, as a minority group within a minority which had fought its way to a kind of recognition, they had worked out their own code of conduct. The hipster, who played no instrument, fastened onto this code, enlarged it, and became more knowing than his model. A camp follower belonging to the fringe group following jazz, the hipster prided himself on his out-size musical integrity. He was desperately uncompromising. Armstrong, for example, with his success in entertaining 'white folks,' was anathema. Armstrong himself was puzzled and hurt by the cool sniping of the hipsters, who refused to see that Armstrong had already achieved a great victory over his own early environment.

The hipster was sophisticated in the sense that his emotions appeared to be anaesthetized. His face was a mask and few things moved him. The proper pose when listening to a Miles Davis recording was one of despair. Like frozen foods, he was on 'a Bird's-Eye kick.' And he could be casual to the point of dishonesty. 'Let's not haggle over the price of admission, man,' he would drawl to Bob Reisner, who was trying to run a successful concert at the Open Door, 'jazz is an art form, man, so let me in for free and don't be square.' And because he loved the music, Reisner would let him in free. The hipster was the jitterbug of the 'thirties in a Brooks Brothers suit and a crewcut. Perhaps narcotics were an inevitable part of such a pose, for the violent turmoil was there but it was inner. In one sense, he had come to desperate terms with a bewildering reality by rejecting everything.

As late as 1948, Oscar Pettiford was leading a bunch of 'wigs,' i.e., frantic characters, at the Clique on Broadway (the band included Fats Navarro, Miles Davis, Bud Powell, Dexter Gordon, and Lucky Thompson). 'While everybody was carving everybody and taking thirty-minute solos to prove it,' recalls Lucky, 'Pettiford kept on backing us up with his great bass.' The band played forty-five minute sets while one or two members soloed and the rest walked off the stand. 'Nobody bothered about the audience,' says Pettiford sadly.

Actually, bop was brewing long before the Swing Era stopped swinging. In 1940, when Andre Kostelanetz discovered swing music and announced: 'The only people who enjoy the terrible swing are those who play it,' a small gang of musical revolutionaries was experimenting after hours with sounds that might have congealed the blood of Kostelanetz. These pioneers, however, were triply concealed in big Negro dance bands. For the popularity of the big white swing band was undiminished at the time—Goodman, Shaw, Miller, and a dozen others were riding high.

Further, a new kind of big white band was emerging from the swing background: the groups of Boyd Raeburn, Earle Spencer, and, especially, Stan Kenton. These bands pioneered a style which became known as 'progressive,' a style which emphasized arrangements influenced by relatively modern classical composers. In a sense, they reversed Paul Whiteman's formula by adapting jazz to academic music, and they were a great force in the diffusion of jazz. Inevitably, but much later, bop ideas began to creep into this music. Only the Kenton band survived, however—testimony to its leader's flexibility and enterprise.

The big white band that absorbed elements of bop early and with success was the Woody Herman group. With a gang from the band, old-time drummer Dave Tough (one of the few who survived the change) dropped in on perhaps the first bop band, the Gillespie-Pettiford quintet on 52nd Street in 1944: [3]

As we walked in, see, these cats snatched up their horns and blew crazy stuff. One would stop all of a sudden and another would start for no reason at all. We never could tell when a solo was supposed to begin or end. Then they all quit at once and walked off the stand. It scared us.

And yet a year later, the Herman band was recording highly successful, bop-colored jazz—'Caldonia,' 'Apple Honey,' and so on—in an exciting blend of swing, progressive, and bop styles. To many youngsters in the army and navy this was the first hint of what was happening, for the Herman band was recorded and distributed on V-discs.

The two big colored bands of Earl Hines and Billy Eckstine—in that order—absorbed more of bop at an earlier date than any other big bands, simply because the two great pioneers of bop, among others, were members of the bands: Dizzy Gillespie and Charlie Parker. The Hines band also featured Sarah Vaughan and Billy Eckstine, who did much to popularize the new style, while the Eckstine band included such topnotch musicians as Fats Navarro, Leo Parker, Lucky Thompson, and J. J. Johnson—all of whom were to become famous later. These bands didn't exactly play bop—the radically experimental nature of bop necessitated a small group where new notions could be played, heard, and judged—but they were coming closer and closer.

Here, again, an economic factor helped to make the advent of bop seem more sudden than ever. The Hines and Eckstine bands were at their peak during the recording ban of 1942-4, and only the Eckstine band made any recordings. These recordings were few and poorly reproduced. Thus, only a handful of people in big cities who happened to hear the Hines or Eckstine bands in person had a chance to digest some of the new sounds. Followers of jazz from coast to coast, who were forced to depend entirely on recordings, heard no bop whatsoever until it wrung their ears full-blown in 1945. The cries of anguish were long and loud.

A good many of these cries were justified. For the technical demands of playing bop were great and masters of the new idiom few. Much that passed itself off as bop was worse than worthless, and the best-intentioned listener had a hard time separating the wheat from the chaff. But the two giants of bop stood out. In a general way, trumpeter Gillespie's style may be traced back to Louis Armstrong by way of Roy Eldridge (who also listened to Rex Stewart)—and the recordings exist to document it. The intermediate influence of trumpeter Roy Eldridge, however, is vastly important and as late as 1955 young trumpeters, growing up under the Gillespie influence, were still discovering Eldridge as a sort of missing link.

Gillespie's early idol was Roy Eldridge, whose place he took in the 1937 Teddy Hill band at the Savoy Ballroom in Harlem. At the time, Gillespie played a good imitation of Eldridge, but he gradually evolved a style of his own which made new departures—in the harmony, the melody, and the rhythm. In the early 'forties, when the soon-to-be-famous 'cool' trumpeter Miles Davis came to him humbly for help, Dizzy said, 'Learn to play the piano, man, and then you can figure out crazy solos of your own.' It was the turning point in the playing of Miles Davis. A little later, trombonist Benny Green learned the same lesson: 'Dizzy would take me to his house and show me on the piano the alternate chords and other things he was doing. It was like going to school.' [4]

Gillespie's harmonic understanding was advanced for his time, and he played notes that many of his contemporaries thought were mistakes. 'I don't want you playing that Chinese music in my band,' yelled Cab Calloway. So Diz clowned around in order to get away with it, and kidded about 'crazy chords'—the identical phrase that Jelly Roll Morton had used about twenty years earlier. (It was

Gillespie who, when asked by a heckler if his goatee was an affectation, replied, 'No, man, it's a fetish.')

At the same time, Gillespie incorporated his advanced harmonies in a complex melodic line, a melody played with dazzling technical facility. To the advanced harmony and complex melody, Gillespie added a sense of timing which indicated a clear comprehension of Afro-Cuban rhythms— one of his early interests. 'That Dizzy,' Cuban-born pianist Joe Loco told me, 'he makes these rhythms good.' It was Gillespie who hired the greatest of all Cuban drummers, Chano Pozo, for his big band in 1947. This was a direction that the later, cool school of jazz refused to follow. Gillespie blew the hot—not the cool—way, although it was some time before even the hipsters were aware of it.

The giant of giants was saxophonist Charlie Parker, known first as 'Yardbird' and then simply as 'Bird,' born in Kansas City in 1920. (There are rumors of an earlier date.) Parker told me that as a ten-year-old he had memorized the first eight bars of 'Swanee' on an old saxophone and joined a jam session where he tried to play the same melody on every tune. The laughter made him run away from home to Eldon, Missouri, a summer resort near the Lake of the Ozarks, where he practiced alone from 1932 to 1933 between odd jobs running errands. He was then thirteen years old. When he returned to Kansas City and graduated with his high-school class in 1936, they say that nobody could equal him on the alto saxophone.

By the time he was thirty years old, the jazz scene must have sounded to Parker like a musical hall of mirrors, for everyone who even pretended to be modern was copying some part of his style on every instrument in jazz. *'L'œuvre de ce genial improvisateur,'* writes the brilliant André Hodeir, *'est l'expression la plus parfaite du jazz moderne.'* [5] Like Louis Armstrong in 1930, Parker dominated the entire field in 1950. In fact, the range and wealth of his invention was so great that two more-or-less opposing styles evolved largely from his playing. No one musician has yet been able to absorb all of Parker, although some musicians are quite adept at certain aspects of his style.

For Parker had the harmonic understanding and the dazzling technique of Gillespie, plus a rhythmic sense which seems to be more sophisticated than the Afro-Cuban and yet remained four-square within the jazz tradition. Various melodic phrases improvised by Parker, as well as the more advanced harmonies on which they were based, have become clichés in the jazz of 1950, occurring even in the arrangements of commercial dance bands. (Listen, for example, to the background in the last chorus of Sinatra's 'Mood Indigo,' issued in 1955.)

Parker's 'hot' style, with its tortured, searing, blasting beauty, reminiscent of the shouting congregations of the South, fits well with the power and flash of Gillespie's playing. Parker's 'cool' style, with its oblique lyricism, gentle indirection, and almost apologetic nuances, helped to found a new 'cool' school of jazz. But no one could duplicate his sense of rhythm. The gifted West Coast pianist, Hampton Hawes, gives us a notion of what Parker's rhythms meant to him: [6]

It was Bird's conception . . . that influenced me most and made me realize how important meter and time is in jazz to make it swing. It was a foundation. I began experimenting, taking liberties with time, or letting a couple of beats go by to make the beat stand out, not just play on top of it all the time.

Jazzmen are still absorbing and assimilating this element of Parker's style.

What had happened since 1940? In terms of harmony, jazz developed along the same lines as classical music (by adopting the next note in the overtone series), but more recently and rapidly. It still lags behind. Bop represented a stage in the harmonic evolution of jazz roughly comparable to the period between Wagner and Debussy. Ninths and augmented fourths (flatted fifths) became the clichés of bop, although they continued to sound like mistakes to the average Dixieland musician whose ear could adjust no further. 'We really studied,' trumpeter Miles Davis informed me. 'If a door squeaked, we would call out the exact pitch. And every time I heard the chord of G, for example, my fingers automatically took the position for C sharp on the horn—the flatted fifth—whether I was playing or not.' To that legendary young man with a horn, Bix Beiderbecke, whose preoccupation with Debussy is echoed in his improvisation, bop might eventually have sounded fine. To Eddie Condon, wry spokesman for the Jazz Age, the new style was impossible. 'We don't flat our fifths,' he observed, 'we drink 'em.'

In terms of melody, bop seemed deliberately confusing. Unless you were an expert, there was nothing you could whistle, and if you were an expert, there wasn't much you'd want to whistle. Yet a great many bop numbers were based upon the chord progressions of standard jazz tunes such as 'I've Got Rhythm,' the 12-bar blues, 'Indiana,' and, of course, 'How High the Moon.' The piano, guitar, and bass would play the same accompaniment to 'Indiana' as they might ordinarily, for example, and the soloist would improvise as usual—but nobody would play the tune. It wasn't exactly new to jazz, but bop made a practice of featuring variations upon melodies that were never stated.

To take the place of the melody, bop evolved a framework of its own, a written or memorized unison chorus in bop style, played at the beginning and at the end of each number. It was generally quite complicated and, sometimes, even memorable. If you could manage to whistle the original tune at the same time, it would fit in a boppish way. In between, each musician took his solos in turn.

Charlie Parker, who, like Gillespie and other early boppers, had a high but unappreciated I.Q., knew exactly what he was doing. He dated the first occasion when he began to play bop in December 1939, at a chili house on Seventh Avenue between 139th and 140th streets: [7]

. . . I'd been getting bored with the stereotyped changes [i.e. chords] that were being used all the time at the time, and I kept thinking there's bound to be something else. I could hear it sometimes but I couldn't play it.

Well, that night, I was working over *Cherokee,* and, as I did, I found that by using the higher intervals of a chord as a melody line and backing them with appropriately related changes, I could play the thing I'd been hearing. I came alive.

This is an accurate and fairly technical description of what took place.

Since bop was played by small groups which permitted experimentation, the riffs or repeated phrases of the swing bands died out and a longer solo line became possible. The bop soloist now started and stopped at strange moments and places, reversing his breath pauses, and sometimes creating a long and unbalanced melodic line which cut across the usual rests. No more running up and down chords as in the Swing Era.

In terms of rhythm, bop made some radical changes. On first hearing, even a sympathetic listener might well have been dismayed. 'If that drummer would quit banging that cymbal,' the traditionalist objected, 'I might be able to hear the bass drum.' In point of fact, there wasn't any bass drum to hear—at least, not the heavy 'boom, boom, boom' of Gene Krupa's day. Instead, the hiss of the top cymbal dominated the music (once in a while, in the early days, the cymbal nearly drowned out the soloists), changing phase to fit the inventions of the soloist. The bass drum was reserved for explosions, or special accents, and the string bass—alone—played a steady, unaccented four-to-a-bar. The beat was there but it was light, flowing, and more subtle.

Many listeners were left painfully in the lurch and any resemblance in bop to the heavy march rhythm of Dixieland was entirely unintentional. To the soloist in bop, however, these changes were an enormous help. They gave him a new freedom and a new responsibility. The point is fervently made by pianist Lennie Tristano, an important transitional figure in the switch from hot to cool: [8]

Swing was hot, heavy, and loud. Bebop is cool, light, and soft. The former bumped and chugged along like a beat [worn-out] locomotive . . . the latter has a more subtle beat which becomes more pronounced by implication. At this low volume level, many interesting and complex accents may be introduced effectively . . .

Instead of a rhythm section pounding out each chord, four beats to a bar, so that three or four soloists can blow the same chord . . . the bebop rhythm section uses a system of chordal punctuation. By this means, the soloist is able to hear the chord without having it shoved down his throat. He can think as he plays . . .

The genius of Charlie Parker, like the genius of Louis Armstrong before him, had much to do with opening up new elbowroom for improvisation. For Parker made spectacular use of it.

Trumpeter Miles Davis, as quoted in *Down Beat*, remembers one trick of Parker's: [9]

Like we'd be playing the blues, and Bird would start on the 11th bar, and as the rhythm sections stayed where they were and Bird played where he was, it sounded as if the rhythm section was on one and three instead of two and four. Everytime that would happen, Max used to scream at Duke not to follow Bird but to stay where he was. Then eventually, it came around as Bird had planned and we were together again.

Davis called this 'turning the rhythm section around,' and adds that it so bewildered him at first that he 'used to quit every night.'

The harmonies in bop became so complicated—relatively—that the three instruments in the rhythm section that might carry a tune, the guitar, piano, and string-bass, could never agree on the same 'crazy' passing or substitute chord at the same time while improvising. There were too many choices in 'far-out' harmony; it was too easy to cross each other and, especially, the soloist up. So it became customary to play less when not soloing, 'comping' or punctuating with occasional chords, much like the bass drum. Again, only the string-bass kept a steady beat and that shifted from consecutive (diatonic) notes to intervals of a fourth or fifth which emphasized no particular sequence of chords. Dissonance (and key sense) was thus kept to a minimum and the soloist was given his head.

More specifically, two musicians in the customary rhythm section—the drummer and the pianist—evolved a new style of their own. It was a process, in part, of accommodation to new conceptions of a few great soloists, and there was usually some precedent to be found in the Count Basie band. Already, by the late 'thirties, Jimmy Blanton with Duke Ellington and Charlie Christian with Benny Goodman had made the string bass and the guitar, respectively, solo instruments of new force and flexibility. These two greatly gifted and short-lived musicians were not, strictly speaking, 'boppers' but they both blazed new trails that were essential to bop.

The new drum style is documented in a chance recording made by Jerry Newman at Minton's Playhouse in Harlem as early as May 1941 (Esoteric J-1). Christian, trumpeter

Joe Guy, pianist Thelonious Monk, and bassist Nick Fenton are playing very early bop, while drummer Kenny Clarke is playing fully matured bop drums. He uses his bass drum, but only 'to drop an occasional bomb,' that is, he 'boots' the soloist forward with an infrequent and unerringly timed explosion. The soloist writes the sentences and Clarke furnishes the paragraphing, giving the soloist a 'lift' and a feeling that he is being backed up solidly—down to the smallest melodic bit of improvisation.

Kenny Clarke's explanation of how he came to drum this way is simple enough to be true. He was working with Teddy Hill's big band at the Savoy Ballroom in 1937, playing for a knowing, dancing audience of boundless enthusiasm: [10]

We played so many flag-wavers, man, you know, fast, up-tempo numbers like 'The Harlem Twister' that my right foot got paralyzed—so I cut it all out except now and then.

In that era, the drummer was supposed to hit four beats to a bar with his right foot on the bass drum—a near impossibility on a fast number. So Clarke, aided and abetted by trumpeter Dizzy Gillespie who had just joined the band, concentrated on occasional bass-drum beats at what he felt were the psychologically right moments. He 'played' trumpet parts, too, assisting the soloists. In fact, he built in his drum beats with cymbal work and rim shots in a way that earned him the nickname, 'Klook-mop,' an attempt to imitate the sound.

Significantly enough, Clarke, like Gillespie, had played with 'Spanish' bands and was no stranger to Afro-Cuban rhythms. The predominant early influence, however, was probably the drumming of Jo Jones of the Count Basie band, who established a two hand-and-foot 'sock' style on the high-hat cymbal at the side of the drummer that became almost standard after 1936: 'ta-*TAAAH-tt*, ta-

TAAAH-tt, ta-*TAAAH*-tt, *TAAAH*-*TAAAH*, ta-*TAAAH*-*tt.*' (Jones was 'dropping bombs' in 1938, as air checks demonstrate, but he was not permitted to do so on recordings until much later.) Bit by bit, Clarke made the single right-hand 'ride' or 'top' or 'front' cymbal the rhythmic center of the performance—while the left hand added accents on the snare drum, the left foot played the high-hat, and the right foot exploded the bass drum; the top cymbal was the only regular and continuous sound made by the drummer, although it could vary to fit the notions of the soloist and it furnished an astonishingly light and flexible pulse for the entire band. For the drummer, the rhythmic center shifted from the right foot to the right hand—a switch that many 'swing' drummers have been unable to make. (Gene Krupa, for example, compromised in 1955 by adding accents to his regular four-four on the bass drum.) In a very real sense, the rhythm became more fragmented, more subtle and, above all, more flowing.

The new piano style was partly shaped by the growing flexibility of the string bass. While playing at the Spotlite Club on 52nd Street in 1945, pianist Clyde Hart decided to let bass-player Oscar Pettiford take care of the rhythm that a pianist was supposed to pump out with his left hand. 'That Pettiford,' Clyde told me, 'he has a big, fat, hairy beat.' So Hart concentrated on a fast and complicated line in his right hand with occasional punctuations in the left. No longer did the pianist need to use both hands in an attempt to imitate the range and sound of an entire orchestra. In fact, the pianist soon felt lost without a string bass to support him. Here, again, there was ample precedent in the Count Basie band. The Count had a long-time habit of playing a few brief and choice phrases with his right hand while his left hand remained silent in order to let the string bass be heard. 'I always enjoyed the bass,' said Basie, 'and we'd talk back and forth.' For Earl

Hines, Teddy Wilson, and, especially, Art Tatum had exhausted most other possibilities.

Later, George Shearing regulated the drums and bass carefully and returned to a full 'arranger's' keyboard to make the new harmonies more palatable, while others such as Chet Baker and Gerry Mulligan dispensed with the piano altogether. On the other hand, Dave Brubeck, aided by Paul Desmond, added a mind full of classical elements which he used extemporaneously with exhilarating effect—and without losing the beat—relying night after night upon improvisation.

The styles of the guitar and string-bass did not change very much—they simply became more flexible and prominent as soloists in the new idiom. Indeed, listening to the best of bop in 1945—the Gillespie album (Musicraft S-7)—one gets the impression that everyone in the rhythm section was very busy learning to assist the soloist: Dizzy Gillespie and, above all, Charlie Parker. Musicians began to talk about 'feeding' the soloist. In a sense, the musicians who survived were the jazzmen who learned to fill in behind Parker and lesser soloists with the correct beside-the-beat punctuations. A few, such as trumpeter Miles Davis, gradually evolved their own style. By 1955, bassist Charles Mingus was experimenting with fingering and chordal notions picked up while studying Segovia.

One of the by-products of the musical revolution called bop was the expression, 'cool.' At various times, the word was used to describe a sophisticated (if not arrogant) point of view, a particular school of musicians, part of a style of playing jazz, a different musical sound, and so on. In his *Encyclopedia of Jazz*, Leonard Feather dates the beginning of the era of 'cool jazz' by the recordings of a group led by Miles Davis in 1949–50.[11] If the cool style may be described as unexcited, quiet—almost dreamy—behind-the-beat yet striving for a feeling of relaxed swing (and many

modern musicians would agree with this), the cool manner of playing jazz had its first outstanding exponent in
Lester Young, the Cézanne of modern jazz, who played
tenor saxophone with Count Basie in 1936.

Among other things, a gradual evolution in jazz rhythms
had taken place. In the days of Dixieland, pioneering musicians pushed ahead the beat; during the swing era they
played right on top of it; then Lester Young began to lag-
along. (A little later, Erroll Garner made it part of his
piano style.) But back in October 1936 when Young made
his first recording, 'Lady Be Good' (Vocalion 3459), with
a quintet from the Basie band, his style of playing seemed
revolutionary. He sounded imperturbably un-frantic and
cool at a time when 'Get hot!' was the war cry and a new
generation of youngsters watched Gene Krupa adoringly
as he worked himself into a nightly lather. 'I play *swing*
tenor,' said Young, 'that lag-along style where you relax
instead of hitting everything on the nose.' He also
had a lighter, thinner sound—'Why don't you play alto,
man?' said Herschel Evans, his rival in the Basie band—
which contrasted with the full, lush vibrato of Coleman
Hawkins, the reigning tenor saxophonist.

Lester Young was a true original, whose influence was,
paradoxically, deep and lasting (he says he got some of his
style of playing from Bix and white saxophonist Frank
Trumbauer, an old-timer of the 'twenties). Slowly but
surely most of the modern tenor saxophonists began to
copy Young's style almost note for note, while other in-
strumentalists adopted the 'cool,' lag-along feeling and the
vibrato-less, sometimes flat, tone. Young had created a new
conception of jazz. In the words of the French musicologist, André Hodeir: [12]

On a cru longtemps que Young avait renouvelé le style du
tenor; c'est une nouvelle conception du jazz qu'il a fait naître.

And this was part of the jazz heritage that Charlie Parker also made his own—one of the elements in his wide-ranging style.

Meanwhile, the transitional figure of Lennie Tristano and his school of followers, which at one time included Lee Konitz, Warne Marsh, Billy Bauer, John LaPorta (but no Negro musicians), established another and less important meaning for the word 'cool,' especially among intellectually inclined white musicians. Arriving in New York City in 1946, after bop had reached its peak, Tristano carried jazz in the direction of further complexity. Describing his style in *Metronome,* Al Zeiger wrote: [13]

Chromatic passing tones form new chords; different voicings of chords produce dissonant sounds; intervals remain unresolved . . . added notes to chords produce block structures; bichordal structures are formed making for polytonality, and the tendency toward atonality becomes apparent. Lennie feeds his chords off the beat by use of irregular accents which result in short, chromatic, choppy phrases which are angular in nature. Wide leaping dissonant intervals also give this effect . . .

Dedicated and dogmatic, Tristano was ahead of his times in his attempt to employ extended forms and contrapuntal textures in his album of recordings in 1946 (Keynote 147), but his later 'Intuition' (1949) which Barry Ulanov described as 'free-swinging, free-thinking, free-feeling exploration of the collective subconscious . . .' seemed to many to lack rhythmic drive. The problem was to be cool without being cold-blooded.

Tristano's most famous disciple, alto saxophonist Lee Konitz, proved to be more influential than his master. A featured soloist in the Claude Thornhill band in 1947–8, Konitz was pulled out of the mainstream for a few years and returned with Stan Kenton in 1952 and his own band in 1954. 'I feel that it's possible to get the maximum in-

tensity in your playing and still relax,' says Konitz, un-
intentionally defining one of the goals of the cool school.
'Too many people have forgotten what Lester [Young] did
in the Basie days . . . he never sounded frantic . . . it was
very pretty and at the same time, it was very intense.' [14]

At the same time, Konitz—like every other modern jazzman—worshipped Charlie Parker, although this influence
was not as strong as that of Lester Young. 'Listen to Parker's "Yardbird Suite," ' Konitz once told me, 'that's the
Parker I like.' On 'Yardbird Suite' (Dial 1003), Charlie
Parker plays some of his most lyric, tender, almost shy
improvisations. One of Parker's many facets, his incredible
gentleness, had a profound influence on the 'cool' style of
playing—on the other hand, the searing, blasting beauty
of Parker in a church-revival mood had none.

By 1948, elements of the cool style popped up in the
pioneering big bands. Woody Herman's 'Early Autumn'
(Capitol 57-616) made tenor saxophonist Stan Getz famous
overnight. At the age of twenty-one, Getz at his best combined something of Lester Young's light sound and lag-
along rhythm with a touch of Parker's lyric sweetness.
Later, Getz announced that he was changing his style to
'stomping' tenor, which offers a hint of what he lacked—
the fire—but this was largely true of the entire cool school.
Some spoke of Getz as having a 'West Coast sound,' which
at that time meant about the same thing. (Wingy Manone
claimed that Getz had the sound 'that came with the horn.')
It is significant, for example, that the early followers of
the cool school would desert the stand if they saw a conga
drum in the vicinity.

The first big band to arrange and play the solos of Charlie
Parker was the band of Claude Thornhill. 'The arrangers
always caught on to our ideas first,' says Dizzy. Canadian-
born Gil Evans created versions of 'Anthropology' (Columbia 38224) and 'Yardbird Suite' (Columbia 39133)

which combined a swinging, danceable beat and Parker's melodic lines, as well as openings for solo work by Gerry Mulligan and Lee Konitz who were in the band. By his use of French horns and unusual voicings, Evans achieved a new blend which was immediately described as 'cool' and which became very popular among musicians. In retrospect, the music seems to belong to the swing era, but it still contained more than a hint of what was to come.

For a nucleus of musicians from the Claude Thornhill band—Lee Konitz, Bill Barber, Gerry Mulligan, Joe Shulman, and Gil Evans—participated in the historic Miles Davis recording dates in 1949 which included 'Move,' 'Budo,' 'Jeru,' 'Israel,' 'Boplicity' (Capitol LP H459) and set the tone for a new and highly influential approach. Artistically, the recordings were a broadly co-operative affair—not without considerable wrangling—which reached some constructive compromises. For the first time in modern jazz, serious and artistic use was made of the French horn and tuba. The contrapuntal and restrained blending of sounds in the writing of arrangers Gil Evans and Gerry Mulligan suddenly opened up new directions in jazz.

In one sense, the Davis recordings could be thought of as the end of cool jazz. The bored arrogance associated with cool 'cats' was entirely absent—these were hard-working, creative musicians who were both serious and earnest. And the sound itself was at least mellow. Of the melody instruments, both the French horn and the tuba have a warm tone and are low-pitched like the baritone saxophone, the string bass, and the trombone. Only the trumpet and alto saxophone are high pitched, and Miles Davis played in the low or middle register. Hence the musical texture was deeply voiced, closely woven, and almost 'hot.'

On the other hand, the blend was startlingly new, the harmonies were coolly modern, the rhythm had that lag-along feeling, and the tone of the solo instruments was

light and dry in the best cool style. Above all, these recordings demonstrated that European instruments, early
forms, and more modern harmonies could be introduced
into jazz without necessarily ruining the feeling of a light,
swinging rhythm. The floodgates were opened for a new—
but not always as successful—kind of jazz which could be
quite easily arranged and not so easily played by conserva-
tory-trained musicians with a real feeling for contrapuntal
jazz in an extended form.

Shortly after the Miles Davis recordings in 1949–50, the
so-called 'West Coast' school of jazz leaped into promi-
nence, sparked by Shorty Rogers from Massachusetts and
Gerry Mulligan from New York City, and showered the
market with palatable recordings. As French horn player
John Graas remembers it: [15]

Shorty brought a fairly complete knowledge of what was
happening all over the country with him when he settled on
the coast. Then there was the effect of his own studies with Dr.
Wesley La Violette which gave us a common language . . .
He's a composer and teacher and has a wonderful way of com-
municating the knowledge of form—especially counterpoint—
to a musician . . . Several of us studied with Shorty too . . . He
made us listen to Basie, Dizzy, Charlie Parker, Lester Young
. . . we listened in record store booths to everything . . .

To me, Shorty and Gerry are fundamentally alike, but
Mulligan's main contribution was to bring jazz dynamics down
to the dynamic range of a string bass—and then to use counterpoint in a natural, unschooled way . . .

I would agree with some who say those of us who can use
a wider range of emotion should do so . . .

When Pacific Jazz recorded the pianoless quartet of Chet
Baker and Gerry Mulligan, with disc jockey Gene Norman
plugging them on the radio, the dam broke. 'Soon we all
got a chance on records,' adds Graas.

At first, the West Coast group consisted entirely of white

musicians who played quietly, lyrically, close to the melody, contrapuntally, and with a broader range of tunes and instruments. Some people nicknamed it 'bopsieland' style. The Chet Baker-Gerry Mulligan 'My Funny Valentine' (Fantasy 525) was a runaway best seller. The public loved it, the tune became popular again, and Baker was compared favorably to Bix Beiderbecke. The so-called cool characteristics were the contrapuntal flavor and the feeling of understatement and restraint. Drummer Chico Hamilton and saxophonist Gerry Mulligan, however, could hardly be called cool. (Mulligan once wrote that he had been 'about equally' influenced by Lester Young, Dizzy Gillespie, and Charlie Parker.) And with the advent of several Negro musicians such as Hampton Hawes, Chuck Thompson, Buddy Collette, Frank Morgan, and others, West Coast jazz warmed up. The word 'cool' had lost its meaning except in the general sense of fine and mellow.

Perhaps the cool trend on the West Coast hit its last peak in late 1955, when the arranger and saxophonist Jimmy Giuffre eliminated the steady pulse of the drums and string-bass altogether. 'The beat is implicit but not explicit,' writes Giuffre. 'In other words, acknowledged but unsounded.' The listener is supposed to feel rather than hear the rhythm. At this point, Giuffre is duplicating the performance of classically trained musicians. Although the melody instruments are given new freedom—they don't have to fit in with the chords of the piano or 'fight' a pounding beat—they seem to have difficulty producing the kind and even the amount of swing that a well-trained classical group can produce.

By 1956, the term 'West Coast jazz' was as imprecise as 'cool.' Writing in *Playboy*, Bob Perlongo announced that there was no such thing and proceeded to try to define it: [16]

The melting pot of jazz . . . sizzling concoction of raucous jazz (McNeely), classical jazz (Brubeck), swing-thinking jazz (Charles, Gray) experimental jazz (Baker, Mulligan), and neo-Afro-Cuban jazz (Rogers).

In other words: everything. Meanwhile, back East the Count Basie band had been impressing musicians all over again with the importance of rhythmic propulsion. 'Swing,' in the sense of a relaxed but flowing pulse, was the common goal from the Modern Jazz Quartet to the experiments of Bud Powell, Billy Taylor, Horace Silver, Oscar Peterson, and Thelonious Monk.

In fact, along with such additions as trumpeter Donald Byrd from Detroit and altoist Julian 'Cannonball' Adderley from Florida, modern jazz in New York as played by Art Blakey and the Jazz Messengers, Sonny Rollins, Max Roach and Clifford Brown, Art Farmer and Gigi Gryce, Gillespie, Davis, and a host of others never lost its fire. The harmonies of cool jazz—and bop—were adopted, the detached attitude faded out, the light sound stayed on here and there, but the music always had an edge, a bite. In a word, it was changed but it was still fundamentally hot and swinging.

The advent of bop seemed like a revolution chiefly because it was devastatingly sudden. (In 1955, the *Times* crossword puzzle defined bop as 'music so-called.') At its best, bop was a logical complication of many things which had gone before. The more complex forms and harmonies were, of course, largely European, as well as the flat, vibrato-less tone (a loss in expressiveness). At the same time, more complex rhythms from Africa by way of Cuba added vitality to the whole. By the 'fifties, the clichés of bop were turning up in Tin-Pan Alley arrangements of pop songs.

19 | Afro-Cuban Music

The powerful and largely rhythmic influence of Afro-Cuban music on jazz and, especially, bop reached a peak in the winter of 1947 when bandleader Dizzy Gillespie hired the Cuban drummer, Chano Pozo, for a Town Hall concert. Backed by the acrid brass of a young and hungry band, Pozo crouched in the center of the stage and flailed a many-voiced conga drum with blistered hands. He held the audience in awestruck silence for thirty minutes, chanting in a West African dialect, while he built from a whisper to a shout and back again. 'The greatest drummer I ever heard,' said Gillespie.

Famous as a dancer, drummer, and composer, Luciano Pozo y Gonzales was born in Havana on 7 January 1915 and led a hectic life in the Cuban underworld of almost pure African rhythms. During the five-or-so weeks of Mardi Gras, when 'Los Nanigos'—a slighting term for what was originally the Abakwa religious cult from the region of the Niger River in Africa—were permitted to come out into the open, Pozo furnished the rhythmic spark. He also composed a few hit tunes, 'El Pin Pin' and 'Nague,' which made him relatively wealthy overnight. With the money, Pozo bought and wrecked a series of automobiles, escaping miraculously unhurt. When his music publisher in Havana refused him an advance of a thousand dollars, the story goes, Pozo assaulted him and landed in the hospital with four slugs from the guns of the publisher's bodyguards.

Then Pozo migrated to New York City, where his fame spread but his luck ran out. He was shot and killed in 1948 at the Rio Café, a bar in Harlem. His murderer was caught and brought to justice but the details of how and why Pozo was killed remained a secret. A rumor went the rounds that Pozo had refused to pay an 'illegal' debt, although thousands of dollars were found concealed in the sole of his left shoe as his body lay in the morgue.

As a boy, Chano had been fascinated by the West African music that survives practically intact in the slums of Havana and had made himself master of the rhythms, a virtuoso drummer. These were the rhythms that Chano Pozo brought directly to the United States and the pioneering Gillespie band. The influence of this Afro-Cuban drummer pinpointed a trend.

Modern jazz drummers still speak of Pozo with genuine admiration. The regular drummer with Dizzy Gillespie at the time of the Town Hall Concert was Teddy Stewart, who admits that taking a back seat while Chano Pozo 'broke it up' gave him an inferiority complex. 'But, man,' he adds earnestly, 'that Chano was way ahead of us all.' The bass player in the same band, Al McKibbon, took up the conga drum: 'Pozo used to parcel out rhythms to us while we were on the road and, man, we knocked out some terrific combinations on the backs of the seats.' Pioneering bop drummer Max Roach studied in Haiti while his colleague Art Blakey visited North Africa. After Pozo, the rhythmic ceiling was unlimited.

The example of Chano Pozo, however, is only one incident in the history of the influence on the United States of the music of West Africa by way of South America, the West Indies, and particularly Cuba. Actually, all the music involved was already blended to some degree. The blend of music 'South of the Border' simply had a much more powerful African element and its general effect on the blend of musics in the United States was to augment this element. Within the United States the final blending proceeded at different speeds, in different places.

From the earliest days of jazz, when Creole ('signifyin' ') songs in New Orleans used a rhumba rhythm and Jelly Roll Morton incorporated in his playing a tango rhythm which he called 'the Spanish tinge,' the influence of 'Latin' music on the music of the United States has been increasing. Nor was it limited to New Orleans; sooner or later it invaded most of the East Coast cities. Old-time composer and pianist Eubie Blake, for example, recalls an elaborate composition 'The Dream' played with a tango bass by an itinerant musician named Jessie Pickett in Baltimore around 1898.[1]

The same music, diluted in a thousand ways, soon reached Tin-Pan Alley. The tango, which borrowed its characteristic rhythm from Havana, according to Nicolas Slonimsky, was the craze on Broadway in 1914. Two years earlier, W. C. Handy had used a tango type rhythm in 'Memphis Blues,' a detail which he repeated in 'St. Louis Blues' (1914). 'Tango Palaces' became popular and *The Four Horsemen of the Apocalypse,* a hit movie starring Rudolph Valentino in 1921, made much of 'the lascivious tango.' Around 1929 the rhumba became popular in the United States (almost all Cuban popular music is referred to as 'rhumba' in the United States); the conga, a Cuban carnival dance associated with Desi Arnaz, was well known by 1937; Carmen Miranda and the Brazilian samba clicked in 1946, and the Cha Cha Cha and Pachanga followed in the 'fifties.

On the surface, genteel orchestras at expensive nightclubs were playing simplified tangos, rhumbas, congas, and sambas for society. Xavier Cugat, for example, who rates as the Guy Lombardo of Latin music, found that American dancers could not follow the real Cuban versions. So he chopped them up, putting the deep conga-drum accent on the fourth beat and making it sound almost like a march anyone could follow. Like Paul Whiteman many years before him, Cugat helped popularize Latin music by making it simpler and more palatable: he created one of the first and easiest of the new blends.

The real Latin music, however, found a home in the 'Spanish' sections of a few big cities—Miami, Los Angeles, New York—where a large Latin population lived. During the Depression in 1930, Noro Morales and a small group were playing true and fiery rhumbas at El Toreador, a Harlem nightclub which was owned by a Cuban, Frank Martini. Xavier Cugat was continually importing top-notch Cuban musicians such as Miguelito Valdes, Anselmo Sacaras, Desi Arnaz, and Luis del Campo, who soon left him and branched out for themselves with more dynamic music. Several of these musicians came from the Orquesta Casine de la Playa of Havana, an incubator of Cuban talent which later employed Perez Prado.

On the other hand, established jazzbands were beginning to experiment with Latin music. Cab Calloway recorded 'Doin' the Rhumba' in 1931 and, later, with the assistance of Cuban-born trumpeter and arranger Mario Bauza, produced a considerable amount of Cuban-flavored jazz on records under such titles as 'The Congo Conga,' 'Congo,' and 'Chili Con Conga.' At the same time, Duke Ellington, aided by the Puerto Rican-born trombonist Juan Tizol, who joined him in 1932, began recording such tunes as 'Caravan,' 'Conga Bravo,' and 'Bakiff,' which indicated a new and better assimilated blending with Caribbean music. Meanwhile, more or less unnoticed, jazz and

'Latin' musicians had been playing together on local 'gigs,' or one-night jobs, in the big cities of the United States.

In its own way, the jazz tradition had been well established for many years when, in the early 'forties, the Latin tradition suddenly boomed. Afro-Cuban bands became very popular in and around New York City and the mambo dance swiftly became a national fad. One peak in the advent of this dance in the East can be dated. On Easter Sunday 1946 a 'Tico Tico' dance was given at Manhattan Center. It was one of many typical affairs. Five Afro-Cuban bands furnished three hours of dance music apiece (after three hours, union rules decree higher pay): Hosé Budet, Alberto Iznaga, El Boy, Luis del Campo, and Machito. The dance lasted from one o'clock in the afternoon to one o'clock the next day. By three o'clock—two hours after opening—the Fire Department closed the doors on a shouting mob of 5000, each of whom paid $2.75 to get in. (The night before, Harry James and his band attracted 500.) Manhattan Center could hold no more.

By eight o'clock—seven hours after opening—the heavily stocked bar manned by ten bartenders was bone dry. 'Various parties on the balcony,' recalls Gabriel Oller of the Spanish Music Center who helped arrange the affair, 'were bouncing bottles down among the dancers, and service men in uniform were firing small arms at the ceiling.' [2] Keeping the music going was the only solution to these irregularities: 'When music stop, everyone punch everyone; when music start, everyone dance,' adds Oller. In spite of eight professional bouncers and fourteen policemen, four customers were hospitalized at St. Vincent's, and one police lieutenant had his scalp lifted by a flying chair.

The huge ballroom was gaily festooned with bunting from a previous auto show. Toward midnight, Oller noticed a stationary patron swiftly climbing a rope of bunting near the edge of the balcony. The patron appeared stationary because the bunting was unraveling as he climbed. When he reached for the balcony, another patron pushed him back toward a ten-foot drop on the crowded dance floor. The tableau continued unchanged until a policeman knocked out the second patron and pulled the first to safety. Licenses for Tico Tico dances were revoked the next day.

The Afro-Cuban bands that played for this dance used rhythms based upon the traditional 'off-center' accents of the clavés, or wooden sticks, that make a penetrating hollow sound when struck together. The Cuban musicologist Fernando Ortiz says that the clavé rhythm is 'the soul of Cuban music,' and it occurs in practically all Cuban music including the Afro, the Bolero, the Guaracha, the Mambo, the Cha Cha Cha, and so on. To reconstruct this rhythm, count to eight twice, accenting the first, fourth, and seventh, and then the third and fifth digits (*1*, 2, *3*, *4*, 5, 6, *7*, 8; 1, 2, *3*, 4, *5*, 6, 7, 8)—or repeat the jingle: '*Shave* and a *hair* cut, *bay rum*.'

On top of the clavé beat, Cuban music adds supplementary rhythms played by the conga drum, the bongoes, the cimbales, and even the string bass and piano. While each of these rhythms is comparatively simple by itself, the combination can swing remorselessly. The over-all effect, as clarinetist Tony Scott once remarked, is like a powerful locomotive with various sets of wheels rolling and a variety of pistons churning. On the other hand, the locomotive is on rails, traveling straight ahead, undeviating in its simple harmony. The *montuno*, or *ad lib* passage, which can be inserted in any rhumba if the soloists wish to take a chorus, is often based on just one, or sometimes two, chords. In other words, the rhythm is complex but the harmony is simple.

Cuban music poses problems to the jazzman as, indeed,

jazz poses problems to the Cuban musician. For jazz uses an apparently simpler rhythm, a 4/4 march beat upon which, however, an infinite number of off-beats and unusual accents may be superimposed. The jazz-oriented listener can tell more easily when the rhythms of jazz, as compared to the rhythms of Cuban music, are inspired—the difference seems to be far more obvious. Accordingly, the jazzman has some difficulty learning to improvise to the clavé beat—the accents are confusing—and staying on just one or two chords and improvising during a *montuno* seems unnecessarily limiting and monotonous.

In turn, the Cuban musician finds the basic jazz rhythm limiting while the jazz harmonies seem far too complicated. He has difficulty following the variety of passing notes, modulations, and substitutions from chord to chord. He learns, however, to 'jump the clavé,' that is, ignore the clavé accent for a few measures while the jazz rhythm dominates the music. The practical result is a transitional stage in which the soloists are jazzmen and the drummers are Cubans. In 1950, a musician who was at home in both jazz and Cuban music was rare and in demand.

There are many stages in the process of blending jazz and Cuban music which existed simultaneously. On one hand, after the triumph of Chano Pozo with the Gillespie band in Town Hall, many established orchestras—Stan Kenton, Jerry Wald, Gene Krupa, King Cole, Woody Herman—hired one or more Cuban drummers. In the words of Stan Kenton: [3]

Rhythmically, the Cubans play the most exciting stuff. We won't copy them exactly, but we will copy some of their devices and apply them to what we're trying to do. The guys in our rhythm section are doing just that. So are the guys in Woody's. And while we keep moving toward the Cubans rhythmically, they're moving toward us melodically. We both have a lot to learn.

With the possible exception of a solo specialty, the Cuban drummers with these bands had to fit into a jazz rhythm. On the other hand, many 'Latin' bands including Machito, Tito Puente, Miguelito Valdes, and others, hired jazzmen to do the solo work. These jazzmen had to improvise on top of the clavé beat. It was a two-way educational process.

The most dramatic stages in this process seem to have occurred in little-known 'Latin' bands where commercial success never interfered with experimentation. One unstable pattern consists of a Cuban bandleader and one or more energetic jazzmen. Cuban-born René Touzet, for example, who led a rhumba band from the piano at the Avedon Ballroom Sunday afternoons in Los Angeles, hired a drummer named Jackie Mills in 1946. Mills got the job because he happened to know his Cuban rhythms but his boss reckoned without Jackie's strong loyalty to jazz. Over a period of a year or so, Mills overhauled the entire band by persuading Touzet to hire various friends of his.

'It was a complete ball,' Mills recalls. 'One by one, I got Touzet to hire Bob Cooper, Art Pepper, Pete Candoli, Buddy Childers, Chico Alverez . . .' [4] These were topnotch jazzmen on vacation from the Stan Kenton band. Things began to hum when Touzet hired Johnny Mandel to play bass trumpet and write arrangements. Mandel experimented with jazz arrangements of 'Latin' numbers and the use of Cuban rhythms with jazz tunes. He even put the 12-bar blues to a mambo rhythm and called it 'Barbados.' (Charlie Parker recorded it later.) The jazzmen learned to improvise to the clavé beat and the Cubans learned to jump the clavé when necessary. The dancers loved it but Touzet did not. He felt like the tail to a foreign and swinging kite. When Kenton re-formed and called his musicians back, Touzet breathed a sigh of relief.

Another unstable pattern in this merging of musics occurs when a Cuban bandleader became enamored of jazz.

Luis del Campo, who was brought to New York by Xavier Cugat, developed into an enthusiastic jazz fan. He soon organized his own band and was something of an institution in the Yorkville section of Manhattan. Not that the local burghers of German descent went to hear the band—the Domino Ballroom was jammed with Puerto Ricans from Harlem. Late in 1949, Del Campo began to hire jazzmen, starting with saxophonist Frank Socolow, who had been playing with Boyd Raeburn's large experimental band. 'Luis really loved jazz,' says Socolow, 'and I suggested that he get an arranger like Mandel to pull the style together.'

The five-man rhythm section of the Del Campo band—three drummers, piano, and string bass—remained entirely Cuban and furnished the rhythmic foundation of the music. Dominating the rhythm in a fashion that suggested the original (Cuban) one-man band was a fabulous fat boy who distributed calling cards reading: 'Jimmy Santiago (La Vaca) DRUMMER'; in the upper left-hand corner was a picture of a cow. (In 1954, he was drumming with Chico O'Farrell.) On top of the rhythm, jazzmen Socolow and Mandel took the solos. The search for a trumpeter who would fit in—Red Rodney tried it for a while—was not successful. Meanwhile, Mandel got busy with his 'Cubop' (a phrase that was popular for a short while in the late 'forties, i.e. Cuban music combined with bop) arrangements.

By 1950 the Del Campo band was playing jazz numbers with a rolling rhumba rhythm that attracted large, dancing audiences. Del Campo himself, a very handsome gentleman, turned the band loose while he danced with the more attractive customers. The legend that he dropped dead because of the excitement produced by his own band is not entirely true. He knew he had a bad heart and only a few months to live. Del Campo died on the dance floor with a beautiful blonde in the act of executing some strenuous steps to some fine music. It was the end of one fascinating experiment.

Perhaps the most stable pattern in this blending of blends was established by Machito and his Afro-Cubans. Organized in 1940, this band slowly but surely assimilated the jazz idiom—they grew up in the Cuban idiom—and created a new blend of both. By 1950, even his competitors were putting Machito at the head of Afro-Cuban bands in the United States and he was in continual demand at a dozen or so ballrooms in and around New York City. The key to the pattern was Mario Bauza, Machito's brother-in-law, who organized the band, arranged the music, and played lead trumpet.

Born in Cuba, Mario Bauza came to New York as a boy and soon became interested in jazz. He learned to play trumpet by copying the recordings of Phil Napoleon and Red Nichols. By 1931, he was playing with Noble Sissle and the next year with Chick Webb, whose name became synonymous with the Savoy Ballroom in Harlem. After six years with Webb, Bauza joined Cab Calloway who, according to guitarist Danny Barker, had been watching Xavier Cugat at the Waldorf and had decided that the next step was to play Cuban music. 'He had society eyes, man!' Bauza was the man who persuaded Calloway to hire young Dizzy Gillespie, a trumpeter who knew his Cuban rhythms.

'Mario was doing a lot of arranging for Cab,' says Gillespie, 'and he gave me some fine ideas.' Sitting side by side in the Calloway band, Bauza and Gillespie traded musical notions and, with the aid of Cosy Cole, worked up a few of their own specialties. On his off days, Bauza had a little Cuban band of his own to play one-night jobs and Gillespie sat in with him now and then. (Gillespie was also perfecting his spitball-throwing technique while in the Calloway band, a skill that helped lead to a hassle with

Calloway and the parting of the ways after a fateful concert in Hartford.)

When Mario Bauza left Cab Calloway to organize the Machito band, he knew both Cuban music and jazz from the ground up. At first, he wrote and rehearsed arrangements for two trumpets, four saxes, and a four-man rhythm section of the jazz variety—trying to strike a balance between the two traditions. It worked out well. Soon, in 1946, he added a third trumpeter and a conga drummer and later, as prosperity permitted, another trombone and another conga drummer. The manner in which the instrumentation grew is significant: the added trumpets and trombones permitted fuller harmonies in the jazz tradition, while the added drums kept the Cuban rhythms complex and paramount. It was a double synthesis.

'We're playing Cuban music,' Bauza insisted in 1952, 'and we always will.' In terms of the dominant rhythm, this is quite true. But as competitor Tito Puente once said: 'Machito blows the most progressive sounds in Latin music.' In other words, the Machito band absorbed a lot of jazz, especially jazz harmonies. And it built up a large jazz following accompanying Flip Phillips and Charlie Parker on recordings and Howard McGhee and Brew Moore at the Royal Roost nightclub on Broadway. Later, the band was featured at Birdland. The music itself was new, exciting, and palatable. A clue to its essence is furnished by the fact that, whereas the drummers were all born in Cuba or Puerto Rico, two of the soloists were born in Baltimore and Boston.

Certain more or less mechanical mixings have proved unexpectedly successful. In 1948, Stan Kenton borrowed some of the drummers from Machito's band for a recording of 'The Peanut Vendor,' which was a well-deserved hit. Again, in February 1949, Machito's drummers walked into a radio studio at the suggestion of impresario Bob Bach and sat in on a broadcast with Will Bradley's Dixieland jazzband. The vocalist was Ella Fitzgerald. The combination of five or so Cuban and jazz drummers was electric and air shots of the session are now collector's items. 'We didn't know exactly what would happen,' says Bach, 'but it sure turned into a swinging thing.'

By 1955 the general popularity of the mambo dance obscured the accomplishment of the Machito band by highlighting dilutions of the mambo rather than blends of jazz and Cuban music. Quite a few people in the cities learned to take their mambo 'straight,' without the bop and without much Cuban influence. There were mambo bands, however, that did not compromise. Tito Puente was one of the best. Billed as 'The Mambo Kid,' he was born in New York City in 1925 of Puerto Rican parents and furnishes evidence for the musicians' belief that Puerto Ricans are the best rhythm men. Puente's band at the Palladium on Broadway consisted—with the exception of the piano and string-bass—of trumpets and drums, a combination known as a 'conjunto' or jam band.

The trials of bandleader Perez Prado, who did much to start the mambo craze, form a contrast to the steady climb of Tito Puente. Along with the pioneering Anselmo Sacaras, Prado was identified with the mambo in Cuba as early as 1943 when he was pianist with the Orquesta Casine de la Playa (in Havana). He then migrated to Mexico City —he had trouble obtaining admission to the United States —and proceeded to set the musical world of Latin America on fire with recordings of excellent fidelity (echo-chamber and all) made at RCA-Victor's pet studio south of the border. This music, because of its new and appealing blend, became widely popular.

Soon Decca executive and bandleader Sonny Burke heard Prado's 'Que Rico el Mambo' during a vacation in Mexico and returned to make 'his own version' which he called 'More Mambo.' Columbia Records lost no time in discovering several more 'authentic' mambo bands of their own, while Capitol Records had Dave Barbour make 'his own version' of the new hit. At this stage, RCA-Victor finally transferred a few of Prado's most popular recordings from the Spanish to the popular listings and they became available in most record stores.

The biggest single influence on Perez Prado—outside of Cuba—was Stan Kenton, and Prado entitled one of his recordings: 'Mambo à la Kenton.' The resemblance, however, is superficial. In Prado's arrangements, the six-man brass section performs prodigious feats with the rhythm, harmony, and melody, while the reeds stay more or less in the background—a reversal of the usual jazz procedure. Prado completes the performance with an occasional half yell, half grunt, in the manner of an excited mule driver. The combination is dramatic and precise but without the flowing pulse of Puente or the well-assimilated blend of Machito.

The gap between Afro-Cuban music and jazz is closing. By 1954, a West Coast group organized by Howard Rumsey and playing at the Lighthouse, Hermosa Beach, California, was putting together a pretty fair mambo, while a group of Cuban musicians recorded by Norman Granz (Mercury LP 515) were playing fine jazz of the post-bop variety. Meanwhile, Duke Ellington, Woody Herman, and Count Basie, among others, began to play an occasional mambo. The dancers at the Savoy Ballroom in Harlem insisted upon it, and the bands had to satisfy the demand.

On the other hand, musicians such as Joe Loco and Ed Bonnemere were making a great success of playing Tin-Pan Alley hits on the piano with an accompaniment of Cuban rhythms. In the process, the clavé beat was gradually being eliminated. 'I don't use the clavé beat,' says Bonnemere, 'except on regular Cuban numbers.' And, of course, American jazz bands don't use it, either. At the same time, the rhythm is much more complicated than it used to be in the swing era: certain combinations of Cuban rhythms have survived in jazz and assisted in the added complexity of bop rhythms. Jumping the clavé has become a standard procedure.

The latest wave of influence from West Africa by way of Cuba, Afro-Cuban music gave the dance back to the dancers in the form of the Mambo, the Cha Cha Cha, and later dances. People could participate. Compared to the mambo specialist, however, the jitterbugs of the late 'thirties seem like prim citizens, although the commercial dance studios were busily employed teaching a modest mambo step that anyone, but anyone, could master. Again, Afro-Cuban music brought a large and enthusiastic audience along with it in the process of blending with jazz, a new musical proletariat composed of people from the West Indies, Mexico, and South America, and it made many jazz converts to Latin music. The demand was genuine, the support consistent, and the combination self-propelled.

PART SIX : THE NATURE OF JAZZ

20 | The European Tradition: Harmony

I have an old friend who has devoted a lifetime to studying, teaching, and playing 'classical' music. He calls it 'serious' or 'art' music, with the not entirely unintentional implication that all other music is an artless pleasantry. But he is favorably disposed toward jazz, speaks of it kindly in the classroom, and cites it as an example of unpretentiousness in popular music. This attitude gives him the reputation of being liberal minded, and the students love it. I discovered by accident, however, that he really feels that jazz is immoral.

'Jazz,' he told me one evening, 'is unnatural, abnormal, and just plain unhealthy.' I know of no effective way to answer this sort of pronouncement on any human activity. When pressed for reasons, however, he fell back on more rational assertions: 'the harmonies of jazz are childish, the melodies are a series of clichés, and the rhythms are monotonously simple.' Here is something technical and specific. What is more, these criticisms are reasonably typical and comprehensive. Since my friend (and others like him) occupies an important position in the world of music on the strength of his own unquestioned merits, his comments should be taken seriously.

Let me say at once that I feel that these criticisms are not valid, and that they arise from a failure to realize that jazz is a separate and distinct art that should be judged by separate and distinct standards. Like any other dynamic art, however, the special qualities of jazz cannot be described in a few words. The history of jazz may be told, its technical characteristics may be grasped, and the response it evokes in various individuals may be analyzed. But a definition of jazz in the most complete sense—how and why it communicates satisfying human emotions—can never be fully formulated.

A beginning can be made, nevertheless, by examining jazz in a perspective of the musics of the world to show how it differs from other music. In this manner, we may arrive at an understanding of the musical objectives and the distinguishing characteristics of jazz. Any art form should be judged in terms of its own aims, and jazz has suffered particularly from criticism which condemns it for not doing what it isn't trying to do. This mistake originates in the application of standards of criticism that are not relevant.

Since we are all immersed in the classical tradition of Europe and, consciously or not, tend to accept its standards as universal, classical music must inevitably serve as a basis for comparison and contrast in defining jazz. Classical music and jazz have crucially different characteristics, although this fact is frequently ignored or forgotten, and an appreciation of these differences is the first step toward a real understanding of jazz.

In order to appreciate the cause of many of the fundamental differences between jazz and classical music, we must note the effect of equal 'temperament' (or tuning) in the history of European music. To oversimplify drastically, in the days before Bach (who died in 1750) most claviers—the ancestor of our piano—were tuned differently than the piano is today. In fact, each clavier was frequently tuned differently from the next. The keyboard, however, was more or less standardized as it is today.

There were several systems of tuning, but the best of the claviers sounded in tune only when the pieces were in simple keys such as 'C,' 'G,' and 'F'—keys that use a majority of white notes on the keyboard. If a composer or performer attempted a chord that employed many black notes, the resulting music sounded badly out of tune. Further, it was impossible to modulate from one key to another, except in a very limited sense.

Meanwhile, one of the neatest theories of how the clavier should be tuned was making converts. It was based, in part, upon the laws of acoustics and was known as 'pure' temperament. 'Pure' temperament was the favorite of mathematicians like Kepler and Descartes. Whether or not it was ever used in actual practice is highly doubtful since, for a number of reasons, it didn't work out. But the reasons it didn't work out are essential to an understanding of jazz, because the result was the eventual acceptance of a compromise method of tuning which, in turn, led to basic differences between classical music and all the other musics of the world.

Perhaps the easiest way to understand the theory of 'pure' temperament is to glance at the standard graph of a vibrating string (or column of air).

The interesting fact is that, while the string vibrates as a whole and sounds a note with a definite pitch, it also vibrates in halves, thirds, quarters, fifths, and so on. Each of these subdivisions has a faster vibration and sounds an increasingly higher pitch—although the sound may be relatively soft—according to a mathematical ratio. These sounds are known as the 'partials' in the 'harmonic series,' and, since their number and intensity vary with different instruments, they explain why different instruments sound different when playing the same note.

What attracted the mathematicians, however, was the interesting relation between these 'partials' and the scale on the piano. Suppose that this string, when plucked, sounds the note of C (256 vibrations-per-second, according to standard pitch). If you halve the string, the vibrations are exactly doubled and the pitch is precisely an octave higher. If the string is divided in thirds, the pitch is G (more than an octave higher); if it is divided into fifths, the resulting pitch will be E (over two octaves higher). And so on. Bring these partials down to the middle octave, and you have the 'major triad'—C, E, and G—the notes of a bugle-call.

Here, they thought, is the proof that this 'pure' scale or series of notes is scientific and 'instinctively natural.' The catch, of course, is that it won't work all the way. First, you have to follow the 'harmonic series' to a point where the 'partials' are as numerous and as obscure as the stars in the Milky Way in order to locate the last two of the seven notes in our octave. Then—in terms of the vibrations-per-second of each note—here's the scale you arrive at (with the differences between each note in parentheses):

256	288	320	341.3	384	426.6	480	512
C	D	E	F	G	A	B	C
(32)	(32)	(21.3)	(42.7)	(42.6)	(53.4)	(32)	

With this tuning, if you begin on C and play each note consecutively up the scale it sounds fine. The trouble begins when you take D (or any other note) as a starting point for another scale: it sounds out-of-tune because the distance between each note is not in the same ratio—the notes are not an equal number of vibrations apart. Further, these errors multiply when you try to play chords—and the 'black' notes on the keyboard have not even been considered.

One musicologist estimates that it would take seventy-two keyboards to an octave to make 'pure' tuning pure, that is, permitting modulation from key to key. Yet the neatness of the idea that our scale could be 'scientifically correct' and, at the same time, 'instinctively natural' still haunts musicians today (who also speak of 'perfect pitch' as if it were an innate characteristic), although it is utterly impractical and has been abandoned. Sir Hubert Parry explained it this way: [1]

The reason lies in the nature of numbers themselves . . . To state it mathematically, the expansion of the octave ratio is incommensurable with the expansions of the ratios of all other intervals . . . In other words, a twelve-tone division of the octave is necessarily imperfect because of the nature of the number series itself.

For this (and other) reasons, the dream of a perfect scale on the piano, scientifically based on the laws of acoustics, remains only a dream.

Accordingly, an all-important compromise was gradually adopted known as the 'tempered' scale. This method of tuning had been proposed as early as 1482, but it was not generally accepted in Europe until 1850. The idea of the 'tempered' scale (or 'equal temperament') is to tune each note on the keyboard the same number of vibrations apart. It is an arbitrary system whereby the 'pure' pitch of some notes is raised and the pitch of other notes lowered, so that the errors are more or less evenly distributed between octaves. Thus, the 'tempered' scale of today has no scientific basis; it is a practical compromise.

But it led to fabulous results. For the first time in the history of music, the possibilities of harmony began to appear. Bach composed his 'Well-Tempered Clavier,' which consists of a series of pieces running through each and every key. He demonstrated that a tune sounded equally good—or bad—in any key. Some of the notes may have sounded sour at first, but the human ear—that marvel of adaptability—made a readjustment and, by 1850, the new tuning was accepted as 'natural.'

The great discovery, however, was that a composer or performer could modulate freely from one key to another. The vast area of chord relationships was opened up and the harmonic scramble was on. As one pioneer composer, Jean-Philippe Rameau, announced as early as 1726: 'Melody stems from harmony.' In other words, chord progressions come first and the tune later. Thus, although melody and rhythm were still a part of the picture, the overwhelming emphasis was upon the exploitation of harmonic possibilities. (Around 1940, bop made some similar discoveries.)

In the process of specializing in harmony—a process necessarily dominated by the piano keyboard—classical music carried harmonic complexity to (and perhaps past) its peak. It also developed other important characteristics. Since the emphasis was upon harmony, everything that tended to spoil the purity of the harmony began to disappear. The chord was all-important, and in order to make it sound harmonious each note in the chord must be exactly right. Thus, the characteristic of 'true' or exact pitch became crucial.

Further, in order to maintain the purity of the harmony, the use of *glissandi,* or sliding tone, was restricted; *vibrato* was standardized or even eliminated; and *tone color* was often minimized. In singing, the goal was largely to imitate the 'perfection' of instruments and to conceal all the mechanics of vocalization. In a word, many of the natural qualities of the human voice—a rich source of expressiveness—were eliminated. (In the 'fifties, 'cool' jazz was headed in the same direction.)

'Classical' music is the youngest of the Fine Arts—there was great literature, theater, and plastic art in Greco-Roman days—the great and complicated structure of the symphony and other forms evolved in a little over two hundred years. The significant fact is that, thanks to the 'tempered' scale, this rapid evolution took place along formal, structural lines in terms of increasingly complex harmony, and the analogy of the symphony to musical architecture is well taken.

To be more technical, the methods by which the harmony of 'classical' music obtained variety became comparatively limited to changing the volume, the tempo, and key; contrasting major and minor modes; manipulating the melody within limits which have already been described; and varying the instrumentation. These methods did not interfere with the complication of the harmony although, as we shall see, they did interfere with the possible development of melody and rhythm.

In addition, as musicians lost their public and composed more and more complex pieces which had to be written down in elaborate scores, it became necessary (for a variety of reasons) to have the music performed by specialists; conducted by great personalities; and produced in large halls after intensive preparation for passive audiences. This inevitably led to the loss of such characteristics as spontaneous improvisation, group participation, and other qualities of direct and immediate communication.

The gains in the rapid evolution of harmony, however,

far exceed the losses. Classical music developed a hitherto unknown structural vocabulary, on a formal and intellectual level, which is able to communicate (to those who are conditioned to understand it) a tremendous and sustained range of emotion. But for certain technical reasons—the 'tempered' scale and the consequent exploitation of harmony—classical music developed to a point where it could no longer make use of certain of the elementary—and basic —means of expression. Important areas were left undeveloped.

21 | Melody and Rhythm

The characteristics that classical music did not develop to any great extent—and related characteristics are found in jazz—become fairly obvious when the musics from other parts of the world are examined. For the adoption of the 'tempered' scale and the consequent evolution of classical music occurred only in Europe. The music of the rest of the world was developing, or had already developed, along far different lines.

The highest development of melody, for example, which is the most simple and direct means of musical communication, has occurred in the Orient. Professor Curt Sachs says that there it has grown 'to a refinement unknown in the white continents.' Hindu music has been defined as 'the most elaborately articulate melody' in the entire world. In other words, the role of melody in Hindu music represents the peak of human achievement in that direction.

There are many diverse kinds of music in India, and there are as many rules of performance as there are varieties of music. The music of Uday Shankar, however, is reasonably accessible in the United States (Victor Album M-382). This music is the classical Hindu type, as contrasted to the popular and folk types, and the rules of its performance are comparatively well known. To most

Americans it sounds a little unpleasant and definitely out-of-tune.

Since Hindu music never adopted an 'equal-tempered' scale, it makes no use of harmony. Instead, every creative effort is devoted to making the melody as articulate as possible. In order to communicate all shades of human emotion, a complex melodic system was devised with a great many rules of performance.

To be specific, Hindu music employs a system of 'ragas,' that is, a set series of notes between octaves, which are very similar to our modes. But whereas we have the 'major' and 'minor' modes, Hindu music has some five hundred 'ragas' in practice and a thousand or so in theory. Just as European composers use major and minor, and the contrast between them, to communicate fairly definite moods, Hindu musicians utilize their five hundred 'ragas' to communicate a wider and more exact variety of emotions.

Shankar's 'Danse Indra,' for example, was composed in the 'Bhairava raga,' which means that it uses a scale of seven notes in which two are flatted, that the pitch should be low, and that the tempo should be medium. This 'raga' is identified with the sentiment of tranquillity, the time of morning, and the season of early autumn. It also has its own special color, animal cry, and Indian deity—among other specific attributes. In other words, it can communicate a complex combination of feelings. And this is one of the simplest 'ragas.'

A more important difference, however, between European and Hindu music is the scale. Our 'tempered' scale divides the octave into twelve notes—seven white and five black keys on the piano—but Hindu music divides the octave into twenty-two notes. In effect, their octave is divided into intervals a little larger than quarter-notes. Although no one melody employs all twenty-two intervals, various melodies employ all these intervals at one time or another, and the musician may raise or lower the pitch by one or two 'degrees.' One of the most obvious results is microtonal variations in pitch that sound like whining and are practically incomprehensible to the European ear.

Hindu music is performed entirely from memory and an unusual and unswerving devotion is needed to become a great musician. Karandikar, the drummer with Shankar during the 1949–50 season in New York, admits that his friends have tried to stop him from practicing his rhythms in his sleep, and cites the example of the master-drummer in Bombay who continued playing although he had just learned that his son was dying. He and his friends insist, however, that many better drummers exist in India.

Perhaps the most crucial difference between Hindu and European music, however, is the matter of pitch. To an academic musician who, because of the great importance of harmony in European music attaches crucial importance to correct pitch, the microtonal variations of pitch in Hindu music may be genuinely painful. But unlike jazz, Hindu music is accepted as different, its variations in pitch are known to be intentional, and no attempt is made to judge it by classical standards.

Turning to the subject of rhythm, which was briefly dealt with in the first chapter, we can say that the world's highest development of this fundamental element occurred in Africa. Nobody knows why. The 'tempered' scale was never adopted there and no system of notation grew up, so harmony remained comparatively undeveloped. Although there is some harmony and a lot of melody in West African music, the great emphasis is upon complex rhythms or polyrhythms. 'The syncope [off-beat], an African commonplace,' says the late Professor Hornbostel, 'is a European achievement.' [1]

In comparing and contrasting the musics of the world, Professor Herskovits describes African music: [2]

Music styles are found where polyrhythms are the counter-part of the polyphony of Euroamerican music, where drums are more important than singers; where voice quality is of little significance, but alertness to rhythmic details paramount; where the drummer, not the singer, is recognized as the vir-tuoso musician.

This music is also played by ear and from memory, with-out benefit of notation. Our system of time signatures with fixed measures, in which we count in two, three, four, six, and eight—there is no provision for five or seven—does not begin to utilize all the possibilities and often makes writ-ing down non-European music impossible. 'Western staff notation,' says Professor Curt Sachs, 'with its strictly set off lines and spaces, necessarily distorts the specific char-acter and flavor of primitive music.'

A West African drummer thinks nothing of matching an already established combination of 6/8, 4/4, and 3/4 rhythms with an additional 5/4 rhythm. Anthropologist Alan Merriam found an Afro-Brazilian song played in 12½/4 time, that is, twelve-and-a-half beats to every bar. (Professor Waterman double checked it.) African drum-mers have been reported who accented every fifteenth beat for reasons of their own. Significantly, African music —unlike our own—has no great body of theoretical litera-ture to accompany it, but African musicians—again unlike our own—know exactly what the music means to them.

Perhaps the clearest way to illustrate the West African rhythmic influence in the blend that is jazz would be to con-trast two piano recordings: José Iturbi's *Boogie Woogie Etude* composed by Morton Gould (Victor 10-1127) and Pine Top Smith's *Pine Top's Boogie Woogie* (Brunswick 80008). Since the music is in the tempered scale of the piano keyboard, the problems associated with blue tonality do not arise and we can reserve the problem of expressive-ness for the next chapter.

Here Iturbi, the highly trained academic musician, challenges comparison with the self-taught Pine Top on the latter's home grounds. It is immediately evident that Iturbi's playing has 'a' rhythm in the sense of a regularly recurring pulse. One could dance to it, if necessary, but it definitely does not set one's foot to tapping. On the other hand, Pine Top's playing certainly does. The listener is tempted not only to tap his foot but also to nod or sway in time with the music—perhaps even 'do a dance' —depending upon the listener's personality. We are all acquainted with this response, but how is it brought about?

The first distinction that should be made is the vast and basic differences in the aims and objectives of the two pianists. Iturbi is playing a novelty piece for the Concert Hall—an amusing encore—exactly as written. He is chiefly concerned with executing a dramatic and virtuoso interpretation of the composition for an audience that is diverted in advance by the notion of Iturbi playing 'boogie woogie.' He puts the piece across with the aid of all the time-honored devices of classical music at his command.

Pine Top, however, is improvising a musical background for a new dance-step, which he is attempting to popularize for commercial reasons, and he is chiefly concerned with making his listeners want to participate. Accordingly, he concentrates upon turning out the most infectious and compelling rhythms that he can create for an audience that contains many connoisseurs of what is danceable. It is highly specialized music, for rhythm is Pine Top's only business and his bread and butter depends on it.

The methods by which the two pianists achieve their separate goals are different, too. Iturbi emphasizes the melody, such as it is, bringing out the changing melodic figures—some of which owe their origin more to Tin-Pan Alley than to jazz—by means of the pedal and dynamic changes in volume. Pine Top has a melodic figure in the bass, but his use of it is primarily rhythmic. The same figure is repeated insistently and hypnotically, with no change in volume, while his right hand plays complementary rhythms.

Again, Iturbi takes pains to bring out the harmony, which is just complicated enough to suggest that the piece is a 'serious' composition and not entirely of jazz origin. This is also accomplished by the use of the pedal and sudden changes in volume. In fact, Iturbi goes further, utilizing a standard 'classical' device, and holds the foot-pedal down for the duration of several chords, thus forcing a blend. The result is vaguely 'modern' and dissonant—and rhythmically blurred.

Pine Top adheres strictly to a three-chord harmonic progression—the twelve-bar blues—and makes no attempt to complicate the harmony. The simple progression serves in a small way to support the rhythmic contrasts for, while the 'break' is based on the tonic chord, he picks up his rhythm as he switches to the sub-dominant chord, thus creating a double contrast.

Finally, as regards rhythm, Iturbi maintains a strict tempo which is frequently overshadowed by his melodic and harmonic effects. By way of redressing the balance, he plays the occasional and elementary syncopations very loudly. The effect is rather tense and unrelaxed. Iturbi realizes quite rightly that boogie woogie, even when played as more or less of a joke by a classical musician, should be rhythmic. But he can do no more than reproduce the score as written, employing a series of peaks in volume that tend to shatter the rhythm.

Pine Top, on the other hand, subordinates both melody and harmony, makes no use of the pedal, and indulges in no changes in volume for dramatic effect. The only peaks in his performance are rhythmic—his own personal twist

—where he changes the accent for four bars, by way of a contrasting 'break,' and then picks up the over-all rhythm again. The net result is a steady, continuous rhythm that flows along in an easy, relaxed, and yet compelling fashion. Technically speaking, Iturbi produces the feeling that he is playing straight (not dotted) eighths, while Pine Top creates the feeling of triplets (three accents to every quarter note). This may literally be true of Iturbi's playing but Pine Top's rhythms are too complex to be precisely notated in our system.

The crux of the matter is that Pine Top creates his easy, flowing style *by complicating the rhythm*. He does this by means of 'rhythmic suspensions,' that is, by subdividing the usual stresses into many unusual accents that carry over, around, and about the basic beat. The fundamental 4/4 march rhythm is not only unaccented, but it may never be stated explicitly, although it is strongly felt. The basic beat has become a pattern which Pine Top uses as a point of departure for his exploration of the intricacies of duple rhythm.

The analogy of stepping stones across a brook is helpful here—the more stepping stones there are, the easier it is to cross the brook in your own style. With his four undeviating accents to a bar, Iturbi permits only a 'regulation' march on his four rhythmic stepping stones. But Pine Top, with his accenting over, around, and about this march beat, not only permits but also persuades the listener to dance across the brook (on a variety of stepping stones) in any way that he may please.

The potential complexities of duple rhythm are infinite, but it is clear that Pine Top (and other jazz musicians) are limited to a complexity that is intelligible and appealing to the audience. It is no accident, for example, that the most rhythmically complex music played commercially in the United States is found in Harlem and is played by

Afro-Cuban bands for Latin-American dancers. Erroll Garner's lag-along piano style presents a more easily appreciated kind of rhythmic complexity. But the precise extent of this complexity awaits the invention of an instrument that can chart these rhythmic subtleties.

By comparison with Pine Top's rhythms, Iturbi's seem mechanical, heavy-handed, and undanceable. The distinction between the two styles may be simply stated: the European conception of rhythm is chordal, or *vertical;* the jazz conception is linear, or *horizontal.* By the same token, any jazz music worthy of the name is notable for the horizontal flow of its rhythms for, unlike classical music, the constant use of rhythmic suspensions by virtually every instrument is a central characteristic of jazz.

22 | Expressiveness in Jazz: A Definition

Working toward a tentative definition of jazz, we should add that, in addition to the differences in harmony, melody, and rhythm, jazz also differs from classical music in expressiveness. Jazz customarily employs improvisation, variations in pitch, a more flexible vibrato, unusual *glissandi,* and various other unorthodox elements which are seldom permitted in the academic tradition. One of the results of these differences is that jazz is played in an idiom which utilizes 'blue tonality,' a source of considerable misunderstanding.

For example, Natalie Curtis-Burlin writing about folk singing concludes: [1]

The mellow softness of pronunciation added to vocal peculiarities—the subtle embellishment of grace-notes, turns and quavers, and the . . . upward break of the voice—these can be but crudely indicated . . . A recorder realizes, perhaps better than another, how approximate only is any notation of music that was never conceived by the singers as a written thing.

The difficulties are greater in jazz, for each instrument tends to vocalize simultaneously along the lines of its own characteristics. Thus, a classical musician, who has been trained to approach music through the written score, would receive a very imperfect notion of what was taking place if he used this method to study jazz.

Further, conventional notation makes no allowance for the illusions to which the ear is susceptible. It would be quite natural for a musician trained in the equal-tempered scale of the piano—as all classical musicians are—to relate all deviations from it to the nearest half-step in this scale, and conclude that these deviations are childish blunders in pitch. (Sigmund Spaeth went further. He announced that the ears of all 'primitive' peoples are bad because they don't use the 'civilized' equal-tempered scale.)

This question of correct pitch bears directly on the contrasting means of expressiveness in classical music and jazz. Fortunately, we are on firm ground here because of the research of a psychologist, Dr. Milton Metfessel, who has written a pioneering book entitled *Phonophotography in Folk Music*.[2] By means of an apparatus consisting of an 'optical lever, a timing device, and a modified moving-picture camera,' Dr. Metfessel has been able to chart and analyze, with scientific accuracy, the voices of singers ranging from Melba to Bessie Smith.

Dr. Metfessel documented the fact that Negro folk singers, and especially blues singers, make use of a fabulous variety of unorthodox vocal devices ranging from what he terms 'intonation tones' (sounds that are continuously changing pitch within the compass of a tone), through 'falsetto twists' and 'interpolated notes,' to 'swoops,' 'glides,' 'wavers,' 'clips,' and many different patterns for attacking and releasing each note. He concludes that, unlike classical singing where the aim is to imitate an instrument, the goal of a blues singer is to make free use of his or her voice, that is, to employ every sound of which his or her voice is capable—including the mechanics of breathing—in order to attain expressiveness, especially *rhythmic* expressiveness.

Two points deserve special mention. In his analysis of blues singing—the archetype of jazz—Dr. Metfessel found numerous instances of what he calls 'interpolated-tone patterns,' that is, a sudden break in the voice (up or down, and to varying extents) within the duration of a single tone. The field-holler or cry furnishes many examples of this. The African musicologist Ballanta-Taylor suggested to Dr. Metfessel that 'the interpolated tone in American Negro singing . . . is the vowel pitch of African speech, while the other two tones in the complete pattern belong to the melody of the song.' [3] This suggestion is reinforced by the fact that in African speech pitch is of first importance and the meaning of a sound changes completely with a variation in pitch.

Again, it was discovered that Negro folk singers, and especially blues singers, have a consistent habit of hitting a note—frequently and with a great variety of approaches —that does not occur in the equal-tempered scale of classical music. They sing what is known as a 'neutral third,' that is, a note precisely between 'Do' and 'Sol' (the tonic and the fifth) which is a little more than five vibrations a second lower in pitch than the 'Me' on the piano. To a classical musician it sounds flat.

Actually, this neutral third is seldom sung by itself and precisely on pitch. What Dr. Metfessel located was the average pitch of the notes in this area, and they were all bunched around the neutral third. It is evident that, far from being a childish blunder in pitch, this characteristic of jazz is intentional and fundamental. And the most logical explanation is that this consistent gravitation toward a neutral third is due to a feeling for a non-European scale —a scale other than the equal-tempered scale of classical music—presumably a scale which is found in Africa.

Thus, Natalie Curtis-Burlin reports that when C. K. Simango, a native of Portuguese East Africa, first saw a piano, he tried it out for a while and then announced: 'This note is too high and the next one is too low and there is none in between!' [4] The British musicologist, A. H. Jones, who has spent most of his life in Africa studying African music, writes me that he has never heard an African sing the exact third or seventh of our tempered scale (i.e. as it sounds on the piano).

The evidence for such an assumption is difficult to obtain because of the real scarcity of information about African music. Nevertheless, certain conjectures may well be suggested. We have, for example, a reasonably exact knowledge of the jazz scale. Using the term, 'scale,' to mean 'a definite series of tones within an octave used as the basis of musical composition,' Winthrop Sargeant reconstructed a jazz scale based upon an analysis of a great many jazz records. Arranged in logical sequence, these are the notes that a jazzman tends to use when improvising: [5]

At two places in the jazz scale—the third and the seventh (E and B)—a square note linked to a regular note is employed in order to indicate that something extraordinary occurs to the melody in these areas. These are the so-called 'blue notes,' or areas where the pitch varies widely, and the unusual notation is an attempt to suggest what happens. As the research of Dr. Metfessel testifies, these two notes are sung in an almost infinite variety of ways with all the unorthodox vocal devices known to Negro folk singing. The result is blue tonality.

Although the variety of scales in Africa is extensive, we know that one type of scale frequently found there (and elsewhere outside of Europe) employs a neutral 'second' as well as a neutral third. The neutral second is so called because it falls two tones above the fifth, exactly halfway between the fifth and the eighth (or octave). In other words, the neutral second occurs just below the seventh (B) in the upper half of the jazz scale. And again, this is a pitch that does not occur on our piano keyboard.

In general, the musics of the world seem to have evolved in some such fashion: starting with the octave (discovered when men and women sing together), the fifth is hit upon next, then the neutral third, and then the neutral second—as the melody becomes more complex and more and more intervals are employed. Beyond this point, however, the similarity ceases and various musics evolved variously.

Turning to the 'diatonic' scale of classical music, a scale that may be loosely described as what you hear when you play the white notes on the piano keyboard from C to high C, we may observe that this scale consists of a whole step (a black key intervenes), a whole step, a *half* step, a whole step, a whole step, a whole step, and a *half* step. That is (keeping the black keys in mind), the white keys progress upward by two whole steps, a half step, three whole steps, and a half step. There are two places—after the third (E) and the seventh (B)—where there is no black key between the white keys and therefore the difference between the white keys is only half a step.

Understanding the nature of this diatonic scale is important, since it was the prevailing scale of the civilization into which the Negro was plunged when he was brought to the New World. In the course of three hundred years or so in the United States, the Negro adapted his own musical heritage to the prevailing tradition and a mixing took place.

Thus, the Negro would necessarily adopt the diatonic scale which he found around him but, at the same time, his own tradition of the neutral third and second might survive just long enough to influence the diatonic scale and cause a different treatment of these two areas. For the diatonic scale, it will be remembered, has *half* steps at these points in the scale which make the pitch noticeably sharp or higher. The impulse of the Negro, therefore, would be to flatten these two notes toward a conformity with African practice, and thus a compromise would result whereby varying pitch might be employed. In some such manner the jazz scale, with its distinctive characteristic of the two 'blue notes' and over-all blue tonality, may have evolved.

The jazz scale is a new and significant development in the history of music in general and American music in particular and, combined with the documentation by Dr. Metfessel of how it (and other elements) function in actual blues singing, affords an insight into the crucial distinction between jazz and classical music. It has penetrated a large share of our popular music. Above and beyond the basic difference in rhythm, the melody and even the harmony of jazz is slightly but distinctly different, and classical standards do not quite apply to either. What is more, the expressiveness which results from the sum of these differences belongs to jazz.

One of the results of this expressiveness is a unique immediacy, a direct communication here and now—from the living to the living—which jazz seems to provide. The common attitude toward jazz and folk arts in general is that they do not need to be studied—somehow, their virtues and defects may be fully understood without really looking or listening. But if you listen carefully to a jazzman's improvising, you can almost tell what he had for dinner. There is a legend that, during the late 'thirties when Louis Armstrong recorded a series of wonderful performances, he was starting on his fourth honeymoon. In any case, the communication is often direct and immediate, the contact clear and true.

To return to my friend who has devoted a lifetime to studying, teaching, and playing classical music and who really thinks that jazz is immoral, I feel that his specific criticisms that 'the harmonies of jazz are childish, the melodies are a series of clichés, and the rhythms are monotonously simple' may be flatly denied. It is true that, except for more modern experiments, the harmonies of jazz are relatively simple. The harmony of jazz was taken from European music and developed along the same lines as European music, but more recently and rapidly. It still lags behind.

But to say this and no more is to miss the point. The European harmony adopted by jazz simply forms the mold into which the jazz performance is poured. Further, in the course of performance this harmony is fundamentally altered. The melodic tendencies inherent in blue tonality develop a unique manner of handling cadences and of grouping European harmonies. Harmonic patterns unknown among the simpler folk accompaniments of Europe have evolved in the United States. (For example, the sounding of the major and minor third simultaneously on the piano, in order to imitate the blue note of the field-holler, is directly contrary to academic European concepts of harmony.)

For the same reason, the melodies of jazz differ from those of Europe. Some of it is no doubt due to the fact that improvisation plays such a large role in jazz. As the critic and composer, Eduard Hanslick, noted: improvisation creates a type of music that has to be judged by standards of its own. But the melodies of jazz also employ the blues scale and all the unorthodox techniques and devices that occur in American Negro folk singing. And slight but fully intended changes in pitch may prove downright irritating to a trained classical musician, who must value precise harmony above all else.

The criticism that the rhythms of jazz are monotonous is perhaps the most frequent and, at the same time, the most easily disproved. By his own criteria, the classical musician is quite right: he examines a jazz score, notes that the time signature is always 4/4, and concludes that the rhythms are simple. He probably does not realize that jazz cannot be accurately notated or that jazz is almost never played precisely on the beat or that duple rhythm lends itself to infinite complexities. The fact that academic musicians generally find it impossible to play jazz probably has something to do with the nature of jazz rhythms. For in spite of the rapid and continuing fusion of European and West African music, there is no musician in the year, say, of 1955, who can rightly be considered pre-eminent in both fields. That time, however, is sure to come.

Until then, jazz is a separate and distinct art that should be judged by separate and distinct standards. Putting together these and other comments which occur throughout the book, we may define jazz tentatively as *a semi-improvisational American music distinguished by an immediacy of communication, an expressiveness characteristic of the free use of the human voice, and a complex flowing rhythm; it is the result of a three-hundred-years' blending in the United States of the European and West African musical traditions; and its predominant components are European harmony, Euro-African melody, and African rhythm.*

PART SEVEN : **JAZZ TOMORROW**

23 | The Conquest of Jazz

The fanatical devotion which jazz kindles in the breasts of respectable citizens from Melbourne to Stockholm and from Buenos Aires to Iceland is difficult for an American to understand. The love of jazz, for example, has been known to short-circuit peace negotiations, armies of occupation, and even two nations at war. During the German occupation of France, Lieutenant Dietrich Schulz-Köhn, a member of the conquering army, spent all his spare time working on the 1943 edition of Charles Delaunay's *Hot Discographie,* a listing of jazz records. The fact that Delaunay was active in the French resistance movement or that his workshop was a way-station for the rescuing of Allied fliers bothered nobody.

In fact, Lieutenant Schulz-Köhn became something of an international legend. *Das Schwarze Korps,* the official publication of the Storm Troopers, had warned that the German army was infected by a passion for American swing music. Nevertheless, a lieutenant named Schulz upset negotiations for the surrender of German troops at St. Nazaire and Lorient by inquiring whether anyone collected the recordings of Benny Goodman. As Dr. Schulz-Köhn now recalls: [1]

I was taken prisoner in St. Nazaire . . . Charles Delaunay first sent me a pencil, writing paper . . . Later we got a phonograph from a Swede . . . Then I wrote for records to Stockholm, to Paris, to Borneman in London . . . Hampus Morner in New York.

The appeal was international and the response immediate. POW Schulz was soon listening to his beloved jazz.

On the other hand, the penetration and spread of jazz among nations that are not exactly friendly toward us is astonishing. Jazz was banned in Japan during the war. Mr. Tay Muraoka, president of the Hot Club of Japan, was bounced out of bed on a gray December dawn by the military police, hustled to headquarters, and relieved of his jazz recordings. Muraoka's most vivid recollection, during the eighteen-hour interrogation that followed, was the foul odor that permeated the place. Headquarters had been converted from a stable. 'To my surprise,' says Muraoka, 'they couldn't notice it, although I pointed it out.' [2] After his release, he listened secretly to Station Tokyo playing jazz fifteen minutes a day to make American soldiers homesick. He also consoled himself with a few salvaged recordings which he played under a quilt late at night in a closet.

Banned by Mussolini, jazz in Italy—as in France—became one of the distinctive features of the resistance movement. With the arrival of jazz-conscious American troops, the murmur of interest grew to a rhythmic roar. There were eighteen Hot Clubs in Rome and lesser towns such as Padua and Alessandria. Jam sessions took place every Friday night in Rome at the Conchiglia Club, across the street from the shrine of classical music, Santa Cecilia. Disc jockey Leone Piccioni, the son of the Minister of Justice, staged an hour-long session every fortnight over the state network.[3]

In Russia, jazz poses a problem. *Komsomolskaya Pravda*, the Communist youth organ, published a drawing of the Soviet zoot suiter—wide-shouldered, wasp-waisted, jacket drooping near the knees and commented: [4]

His stare is vacant . . . his hair is full of brilliantine, his walk is languid, his ideal is the divine Linda . . . [at class] . . . He sits holding one leg over the other, chewing American gum which somehow found its way into his hands. He smiles crookedly, his answers are made in a lazy voice, he is indifferent to everything except the possibility of getting a shirt from abroad . . .

The *Herald Tribune* headlined the item: 'Moscow Views the Zoot Suiter as Nothing but a Red Square.' The Russian editor was not particularly well-rounded, either, for he refers to the singer consistently billed as 'The Divine Sarah [Vaughan]' as 'the divine Linda.'

More recently, Mrs. Thomas Whitney, wife of a former Associated Press correspondent in Moscow, reports that 'dzhaz'—or jazz—is bootlegged all over Russia: [5]

American songs, too, continue to be sung by the Russian people, who manage to hear and learn them from foreign broadcasts and from records made from those broadcasts or smuggled into the country from abroad and sold 'from under the counter,' Mrs. Whitney said. 'One of their best sources . . . is from the musical backgrounds of anti-American movies and anti-American plays. American music is permitted for that, and Russian composers can write jazz for that. So the people, while they are supposedly learning to hate America, are really loving its music and learning it.'

The recurring denunciations by *Soviet Art,* the highest cultural authority in the Soviet Union, to the effect that jazz is 'crude, poverty-stricken, alien and superfluous' [6] prove that these attacks are ineffective.

For the Russian government has had to face the fact that many of their own people, as well as people in the satellite countries, know and love jazz so much that they are willing to risk their necks to hear or play it. The jazzband of Kurt Walter, according to journalist Richard Hanser, played in Chemitz in the Soviet zone until the local com-

missars became dangerously troublesome. Then the band
filtered across the border, one by one, into West Berlin: [7]

> In the course of this maneuver, the drummer performed
> what may be one of the great escape feats of modern times.
> He made it through the Iron Curtain with snare drum, sticks,
> brushes, wood blocks, cow bells, cymbals, maracas and bass
> drum.

The band became the main attraction at a dance casino
in Hamburg.

The iron curtain, it seems, is acoustically transparent.
Beginning in the early 'fifties, Radio Free Europe and the
Voice of America have been beaming jazz, near-jazz, and
just plain Hit Parade music to Bulgaria, Hungary, Czecho-
slovakia, Yugoslavia, Poland, Russia, and elsewhere with
amazing results. Denunciations of jazz boomeranged and
then ceased. Youngsters apparently identified with it, for
better or for worse, and they soon came to know the difference between good and bad jazz. In one sense, jazz became
the rallying point for the adolescent conflicts of one-
seventh or more of the earth's surface.

Hence the big switch. In September 1955, the Polish
government announced that 'the building of Socialism proceeds more lightly and more rhythmically to the accompaniment of jazz.' By December, the publication of the
Czechoslovakian Youth Front, *Mlada Fronta,* stated: 'Good
classical jazz is not only a beneficial aid in the fight against
racial discrimination but also a sign of friendship between
nations.' [8] (Another young Czech had just flown a stolen
plane out of the country with the comment: 'There is such
a thing as too much political talk . . . but everyone craves
good American jazz.') Russia capitulated in January 1956:
'Fruitless discussions about whether jazz is necessary . . .
already have lost any point.' [9]

Meanwhile, Moscow's only nightclub which featured

'jazz,' the Novy Yar, closed on the eleventh of January after three months of big business. According to a dispatch in the *New York Times:* [10]

Word got around that the nightclub was suitable for idle foreigners as window dressing for the New Look, but sober Soviet types should stay away.

The cover charge—before food or drink—was sixty rubles or about fifteen dollars, a month's rent in Moscow. Besides the band, the Novy Yar featured girl acrobats, a magician, Spanish dancers, a girl harpist, and a person described in a Reuters dispatch as a 'crooner, who breaks all precedent by donning white tie and tails.' [11] This was the only nightclub in all Russia that was permitted to stay open until 2 A.M.

The reason why the Novy Yar was shuttered is anybody's guess. The best reason probably never occurred to the management: the leader of the band was Leonid Utesov, the 'King of Russian Jazz,' whose music has been described as 'reminiscent of Fred Waring and his Pennsylvanians—with a touch of Kostalanetz.' [12] To any Russian who knew his jazz and had enough capital to get in, the jazz of the Novy Yar was a poor joke. To the Russian youngster who had become an *aficionado* through listening to the foreign radio, Utesov's jazz was terribly square and did more harm than good. In fact, because of their scorn for Utesov, Russian youth probably achieved hitherto unknown solidarity.

So jazz was a Russian problem which, by 1956, remained unsolved. V. Konen was put to work on the situation and came up with 'Legend and Truth about Jazz' in *Sovietskaya Muzyka.* [13] With the exception of occasional blunders of minor detail, Konen's article is highly intelligent, but his general attitude is what a modern jazzman would call that of a 'moldy fig,' that is, one who believes that no good jazz was created after 1926. He speaks of 'the bitter arguments being waged in our country about jazz,' but his own comments lead to further controversy of the kind that split France, for example, in two: the modernists versus the traditionalists. Only the rebellious youngsters seem to know much about modern jazz in Russia.

Among our allies, the popularity of jazz is even more pronounced. At the Australian Jazz Convention held in Melbourne in 1948, fifteen local bands competed and the Graeme Bell outfit went on to tour Europe for fourteen months. Admission to the convention was five shillings (about 45 cents), which did not include the 'Riverboat Trip' complete with jazzband, guaranteed to reproduce the true spirit of 'life on the Mississippi.'

The popularity of jazz in Sweden is almost unbelievable. Nearly every high school in Stockholm is reliably reported to have its own jazzband, and a poll revealed that about two out of every three youngsters play some sort of jazz instrument—usually the sax or clarinet. The National Palace, Stockholm's famous concert hall, is owned by jazz enthusiast 'Topsy' Lindblom who—quite logically—was once Olympic champion of the hop, skip, and jump. Even the Lapps compete in Lindblom's jazzband contests. In 1948, a group of high-school students led by Olle Grafstrom won all contests, toured Finland, and made several successful movie shorts.

Perhaps the peak of jazz idolatry has been reached in France. An elaborate festival was produced in Nice in 1949, and a more or less competing Salon du Jazz which turned away an overflow crowd of 5000 was presented in Paris in 1950. One hundred and thirty works of art—by Léger, Dali, Dubuffet, Severini, Baumeister, and Mondrian —were shown. Special jazz films were exhibited. Lectures were given by pundits Goffin, Radzitsky, and Hodier. Concerts were played by American jazzmen Sidney Bechet, Roy

Eldridge, Don Byas, and James Moody accompanied by French jazz musicians. The French Ministre de L'Education Nationale put in an official appearance and stayed over to see the films.

The experiences of American jazzmen abroad leaves them dazed and shaken. The iron curtain swung wide for trumpeter Rex Stewart—formerly with Duke Ellington—when he played a concert in Berlin. 'Man, I nearly got cheered to death,' he told me. The hall was filled with shouting Russians who crossed official boundary lines in unofficial droves.

When Louis Armstrong visited Europe in 1950, armed guards had to be called out to protect him in each of nine countries. His worshipers threatened to trample him down. 'My trip to Europe was something that I shall never forget,' he wrote later, and added, apprehensively, 'My Gawd, how could I!' He had an audience with the Pope, who inquired kindly about his children. Armstrong replied that he had no children but that this state of affairs was not due to lack of effort—a remark that was deleted from the version appearing in *Holiday Magazine*.[14] On his return, Armstrong received a thank-you note from the State Department.

In 1952, a jazz trio composed of Gene Krupa, Teddy Napoleon, and Charlie Ventura toured Japan. 'It was the most tremendous thing I've ever experienced,' exclaimed Krupa wonderingly, 'even greater than any of the big days with Goodman.' Saxophonist Ventura was stunned: [15]

The experience was just too much . . . There was nothing the people wouldn't do for us. And they'd wait for hours just to get an autograph, or take your picture, or shake your hand. We'd get off the stand, and waiting for us in the dressing room would be three little baskets of cold towels, three big bottles of beer, three stacks of sandwiches—everything in threes.

Weeks later, the three jazzmen were still unwrapping gifts that had been showered upon them.

There was some doubt among bookers whether Norman Granz's package of nine musicians and Ella Fitzgerald, billed as Jazz at the Philharmonic, would make a hit abroad. The first concert in Stockholm was sold out six hours after it had been announced, and the group proceeded upon a highly successful tour of Sweden, Denmark, France, Belgium, Holland, Switzerland, and Germany. Mr. Granz, a former philosophy major at the University of California, was hard hit by the attitude of the audiences: [16]

The wonderful thing about the people of Sweden . . . is their treatment of jazz artists. The moment we arrived, there was a press conference at which all of the newspapers took pictures and interviewed us . . . The European audiences . . . have a healthier respect for all art forms, whether it be dance, painting, or in this instance, jazz.

'Daddy-O,' reported Miss Fitzgerald happily, 'it was the most.'

After five furious weeks in Europe in 1953, Stan Kenton and his orchestra came home for a rest. The high point of the trip took place in Dublin, when the close of the concert was greeted by 'a solid wall of sound. You couldn't distinguish anything—cheers or whatever—it was just continuous sound.' The emotional impact was literally indescribable: [17]

A man came up to us in Germany and was very much carried away by the concert. He said: 'Jazz is not only music but also *a way of life,* and that's a thing we want to know more about.'

Then there were the kids who couldn't speak English. They'd grab me by the arm; I could feel them trembling. Tears came into their eyes and all they could say was 'Stan!'

Lionel Hampton's band, which plays a far different style, followed Kenton abroad with similar success. They returned with a solid half-year's booking for the following year. Hampton was struck by the seriousness with which jazz is discussed: [18]

Jazz there is like politics. It's the big sport of intellectual Europe, but it gets to be a serious one . . . They fight physically . . . Like at a concert we gave, Panassié clapped at the end of a number. The man behind him thought he clapped too long or something and slapped Panassié on the top of the head. Up came Panassié and his cane, but the cops stopped it. The people all around though were ready, they were grumbling and mumbling.

Hampton's main problem was the 'impresarios who wanted to give us the money for next year.'

Reports on the Hamburg riot during Armstrong's 1955 tour vary. According to Belair in the *New York Times*, the riot was caused by the crowds which were turned away. A French reporter blamed the promoter, terrible acoustics, and Armstrong's tardiness. But the *U.S. News & World Report* quotes Armstrong in a taped interview as saying: [19]

People just wanted us to play on some more. We played an encore. I took a bow with my shirt off [Armstrong had been changing his clothes in the dressing room], but they still wouldn't go. Nobody was hurt.

I was supposed to play two concerts that night, but they broke up the chairs—they got tired of applaudin' with their hands and started applaudin' with the chairs . . .

Then the police turned the fire hose on them. The hall was a mess. The same thing happened in Roubaix, France. And in Lyons, too . . . We played for three hours in Lyons and the people clapped from 1 to 1:30 in the morning.

A few days later and in another country, according to the *New York Times*, the 12,000 Frenchmen out of the 15,000 who were unable to get seats for clarinetist Sidney Bechet's concert in Paris 'wrecked the joint.'

Incidentally, anyone who wonders about Louis Armstrong's adequacy as an ambassador of good will might well glance at the taped interview. Asked if he is a religious man, Armstrong replies: 'Yeah. I'm a Baptist and a good friend of the Pope's and I always wear a Jewish star a friend gave me for luck.' Asked which is his favorite European country, Armstrong replies promptly: 'All of 'em.' Asked if the reason people insist on quiet while he is playing is because he's a famous artist, Armstrong replies: 'No, it's because I'm playin' something they want to hear.' And when some 'Berlin cats' wanted him to blow his horn at a Russian sentry guarding a Red Army statue, Armstrong excused himself: 'All I know is the horn, not politics . . . the Russians might have taken it wrong.'

The cause of the riot in Oslo seems clear. An impatient janitor turned a fire hose on a crowd waiting to buy tickets for an Armstrong concert. It was election day and the janitor was trying to keep the entrance to a newspaper building open. 'While those crazy mixed-up adults were voting in municipal elections today,' the New York *Post* reported, '2,000 kids fought for tickets to a concert by Louis Armstrong.' [20] If the ticket-buying crowd was anything like the crowds that have turned out for Armstrong elsewhere, however, adults formed a good part of the group.

A sparkling new idea was tried in 1956 and worked out famously. Dizzy Gillespie and his orchestra (with the author as lecturer) were sent on an eight-week tour of the Middle East by the United States government. They played in countries where no jazzband had ever appeared—because there was very little money in it—and they played for modest salaries. The idea, as Winchell put it, was 'to win over the people,' especially in those critical countries which Russia had been flooding with free talent. The friendly and free-wheeling band of sixteen musicians—four white and twelve colored—led many people to abandon their Communist-inspired notions of American democracy in the course of one concert. 'This music,' said the United States Ambassador to Lebanon, Mr. Donald Heath, 'makes our job much easier.'

Some of the implications of these incidents were brought home to many Americans by Belair's special to the *New York (Sunday) Times* which appeared on the front page: 'United States Has Secret Sonic Weapon—Jazz.' Commenting on another sold-out concert by Armstrong, this time at Victoria Hall in Geneva, Belair wrote,[21]

America's secret weapon is a blue note in a minor key. Right now its most effective ambassador is Louis (Satchmo) Armstrong . . . This is not a pipedream from a backroom jam session. It is the studied conclusion of a handful of thoughtful Americans from Moscow to Madrid . . .

The disappointed customers were not Swiss 'hep cats' but sober adults willing to pay almost $4 to hear musical individuality . . . they find in jazz a subject for serious study . . . A German Swiss of Zurich came closest to the explanation . . . 'Jazz is not just an art,' he said. 'It is a way of life.'

Belair suggests a reason for the appeal of jazz: 'the contest between musical discipline and individual expression it entails' symbolizes modern existence. Pointing out that jazz, unlike classical music, is best played by Americans, Belair concludes that it has a high propaganda value—for to be interested in jazz is to be interested in things American.

Indeed, jazz has come to represent a kind of international brotherhood. 'I know a lot of people here,' writes author and critic Nestor R. Ortiz Oderigo of Buenos Aires, 'who have studied the English language and American history because of their interest in jazz . . . For jazz is a wonderful music and a great force for drawing human creatures together.' [22] The president of the Frankfort Hot Club, Olaf Hudtwalker, observes: 'A jam session is a miniature democracy. Every instrument is on its own and equal. The binding element is toleration and consideration for the other players.'

The Swiss journalist, Arthur Goepfert, names names: 'We get an hour-and-a-half program from the Voice of America; a half-hour of talk, a half-hour of jazz, and a half-hour of Lombardo. If it were all jazz, you'd make a lot more real friends.' The British film editor, Peter Tanner, writes: 'I have many friends, some of whom I have never met, through jazz.' [23] And Lionel Hampton sums it up: 'People would say to us, jazz is the only true art form America can present to the world. We gave the symphonies and classics to music, but jazz is for you to give.' [24]

Meanwhile, the 'Record Exchange' of the French Hot (Jazz) Club—which once had to send to Rumania in order to get otherwise unobtainable recordings of American jazz —handles swaps by fans in Egypt, Uruguay, Java, Spain, India, Argentina, and North Africa, as well as all of Europe. And as far back as 1949, over one hundred and ten magazines devoted entirely to jazz had appeared in such cities as Reykjavik (Iceland), Dublin, Batavia, Gothenburg (Sweden), Barcelona, Sastra (Argentina), Antwerp, Columbo (Ceylon), Tokyo, Melbourne, and Zurich, while the number of Hot Clubs all over the world must run into the thousands. The world conquest of jazz seems to be virtually complete.

24 | The Appeal of Jazz

The only group of social scientists who have attempted a partial explanation of the appeal of jazz are the psychiatrists. In 1951, Dr. Aaron H. Esman outlined the basic theory and, in 1954, Dr. Norman M. Margolis enlarged upon it. Their hypothesis: 'Jazz is essentially a protest music,' and they support it with careful and lengthy arguments. Stripped of technical terms, the main point of their theory is that, just because jazz is looked down upon by the general public, people who love this music choose jazz—in part—as a way of expressing resentment toward the world in general.

To spell it out: why has the general public rejected jazz? People think of jazz in connection with the Negro and with the red-light districts of Storyville in New Orleans and, later, Chicago and other large cities; they think of jazz in connection with the gangster underworld and Prohibition ('Jazz is the music of the brothel and the speakeasy'); and they think of jazz in connection with the periods of 'moral laxity' that followed World War I and World War II. This is a heavy load for any music to bear. In fact, jazz came to symbolize moral and criminal anarchy —or worse—to many people, and it takes real courage and, according to this theory, a rebellious spirit to identify oneself with it.

Further, jazz ran counter—and perhaps intentionally—to the prevailing moral climate. As Dr. Margolis writes: [1]

As jazz progressed out of the specific areas of its birth, it ran into the American culture which places a high value on properness, control and restraint. In other words the general Puritan, Anglo-Saxon tradition, by this time solid in this country, dictated a rigid cultural conscience which required the repression of the objectionable impulses with which jazz had become associated and symbolized.

(Here, by the way, may be a reason why Europeans with their less Puritanical culture tend to accept jazz as it is, while Americans tend to blame it for practically everything from juvenile delinquency to the common cold.) These 'objectionable impulses' which jazz ignites in people—as well as the fact that the music itself is different—constitute a threat, build up anxieties, and thus lead to repression.

The psychiatrists say that people who identify with jazz choose to protest in this way, consciously or not, and that the three main groups in our society to which this applies are Negroes, intellectuals, and adolescents—although there are exceptions, of course. Of these groups, the adolescents are the most significant because 'the psychological fountainhead of jazz is the psychology of the adolescent.' For jazz, like no other art in our culture, involves conflicting attitudes that seem to be made-to-order for the adolescent.

Psychiatrists and others (including parents) agree that the adolescent is often a rebel. And for good reason. He is caught between childhood and adulthood. There are pressures on him to grow up, to leave his parents, to be an independent, creative adult. At the same time there are pressures on him not to grow up, not to express the 'objectionable impulses' which he is just beginning to experience, not to leave the protection of his parents. The adolescent is blocked both ways, however, and the result is first confusion, then conflict, resentment, and hostility.

But with jazz, the adolescent can have his cake and eat it. Becoming a fanatical jazz *aficionado* is a good—and often noisy—way to protest against his parents and society (he knows they hate the stuff). On the other hand, he now belongs to a tight little group of fellow sympathizers; he is one of a cult with ready-made and dogmatic opinions upon which he can depend. So he feels safe as a member of the gang and he feels independent, too, because he (and the rest of the gang) have become intolerant partisans of a music nobody else seems to like or enjoy. (This can lead to a dog-in-the-manger attitude which automatically casts doubt upon the purity of anyone else's interest in jazz. It can also lead to bursts of generosity.)

Parenthetically, this ambivalence or two-way drive may explain why jazz *aficionados* usually fasten upon one era and a few musicians with fanatical devotion and conduct a holy war upon all unbelievers. (For a while in the 'forties, crusading jazz cults were referring to each other as 'Fascists' and 'Communists'—terminology that is still revived occasionally.) To switch from the 'moldy figs' to the 'boppers,' that is, from the cult that is devoted to the style of the early 'twenties to the cult devoted to the style of the mid-'forties (or vice versa), is an unpardonable heresy. Such a deviation is a threat to the safety of the group and, at the same time, spoils the illusion of independence.

The jazz community reflects other adolescent qualities. The faddish clothes ('zoot' suits, bop ties, berets), the unusual personal appearance (goatees, beards, and even dyed hair), and the childishly exaggerated and poverty-stricken jargon ('the greatest,' 'the least,' 'the most') set the group apart from the rest of society and, at the same time, hold it safely together. Henry Jacobs' fake interview with a modern jazzman on the Folkways label (FP86-1) is so true that it is painful. Here again is the double illusion of independence and safety. Further, the excessive use of alcohol and narcotics, which on the surface defies public opinion and appears rebellious, may well be filling—and often becomes—a dependent need, an illusion of safety.

This two-way psychology which characterizes jazz, according to the psychiatrists, can become a trap in which the adolescent and the 'perpetual-adolescent' may be caught. Sociologist Bruce Cameron of Bradley University cites the extreme case of one jazzman's political attitude during World War II: 'Just let me *blow,* man. Just let me *blow.*' This is naïve egotism rather than selfishness. And examples can be found where the often-praised tolerance of jazzmen toward race, religion, and class seems to be due largely to indifference. A jazzman naïvely preoccupied with his art—and jazz can be a jealous mistress—can progress, however, from indifference to tolerance, and finally to acceptance of the problems of our time.

Meanwhile, the jazzman may be on an adolescent seesaw where, whether he feels too dependent or too independent, the result may be self-destructive. A great tenor saxophonist, who was playing with a big name band during World War II at the age of fourteen, spoke with an almost childish directness and simplicity when arrested for attempting unsuccessfully to hold up a drug-store with a fake gun and steal some heroin. (He was caught when he phoned to apologize.) Quoted at length by the New York *Post* he remarked: [2]

When I was only 13 I wanted to play a sax. Dad—he's a printer—went without his lunches for a year to have the money to get me the best he could. I didn't take any lessons. I just started playing on it . . .

I made up my mind I wanted to reach the top. I started fooling around with the stuff [heroin] several years ago . . . It's hard to explain why I did it. There were so many people listening I couldn't seem to detach myself from them. In this business I felt I had to create, to make something new and different.

When I tried it [drugs] it seemed to sort of close everybody out and I could concentrate better on my music . . . dope took every dime I had . . . I'm going to stop.

Here the same conflict is implicit: first, the desire to get away from a possibly unappreciative audience ('I couldn't seem to detach myself from them,' and, 'it seemed to sort of close everybody out and I could concentrate better on my music'); and second, the desire to be independently creative ('I felt I had to create, to make something new and different.').

As a matter of fact, the protest theory of the psychiatrists fits certain individuals—especially adolescents—like a glove. There is undeniable truth in it. And it goes far toward explaining the hysterical idiocy of the 'Go! Go! Go!' school of jazz appreciation. This group neither likes nor listens to the music—the music merely furnishes an occasion for socially sanctioned protest of the crudest variety. Similarly the adolescent behavior of the not-so-adolescent audiences at Jazz at the Philharmonic concerts enlarged upon the antics of the 'jitter-bugs' of the Benny Goodman era—the 'protesters' of the 'thirties. But they both seemed like responsible citizens compared to the 'rock-and-roll' addicts of the mid-'fifties.

During the late 'forties and early 'fifties, the Stuyvesant Casino and, later, the Central Plaza on Second Avenue, New York, witnessed scenes of what must have been the purest 'protest.' (The hectic, 'out-of-sync' short, *The Jazz Dance*, was filmed in one evening at Stuyvesant and captures unerringly the stereotype notion, held by the great American public, of frantic, abandoned calisthenics.) Significantly, the music is consistently Dixieland, a style pioneered by Negro musicians thirty years earlier, and the audience is consistently white. (I once saw a well-mannered Negro couple stranded at the Stuyvesant Casino in a state of near shock.)

Once in a while, some high-school girl will outdo her playmates by leaping up on a table and concentrating on some awkward but energetic bumps and grinds. The irony —and probably the saving grace—is that the youngster has no desire to appear 'sexy'; she is simply acting in the correct manner given the time, place, and music—only more so. Those not wrapped up in their own contortions glance at her with benign amusement, something like participants in a Haitian *vodun* ceremony, while she 'protests' happily and safely. She and her friends have found a much safer way than gang-wars to get rid of excess energy and, in a rather anaesthetic manner, 'rock-and-roll' may be helping to combat juvenile delinquency.

To the musician, who privately apologizes for the music he has to play in such acoustical traps, this is a living and not the first job he ever played that did not appeal to him. The same problem has beset jazzmen from the beginning and will probably continue until jazz becomes entirely respectable and adolescents therefore quit listening to it. Most musicians, as sociologist Howard S. Becker discovered, dislike the general public intensely.[3] The public is 'square' because it doesn't understand and thus, as the consumer, constitutes a threat. But the antics of adolescents— perhaps because they are sharing similar emotions—don't seem to reach or annoy the jazzman very strongly.

Still and all, even the psychiatrists admit that it is possible to take a mature interest in jazz. As Dr. Margolis writes: [4]

> . . . there is that group, who, although initially drawn to jazz by the adolescent storm, retain their interest even though they have grown emotionally to maturity, because they are able to derive from jazz an artistic and emotional satisfaction

which does stress its creative, individualistic, and self-expressive aspects.

In other words, jazz is an art and can be a rich and rewarding experience. Right here the limitations of the psychiatric approach become clear.

If it is possible for a jazzman to be interested in the music as a creative art, then jazz cannot be entirely a music of protest. If it is possible for people to be interested in jazz as mature, responsible adults—then jazz is not wholly protest music. The jazzman has a tremendous drive to express himself positively and creatively. In fact, one may ask whether any great art is created by people who are merely against this or that. The affirmative act of positive creation is not entirely protest.

Further, the theory that jazz is a protest music tends to ignore the complex web of socio-economic factors which cause general trends among large groups of people and which more or less dictate where, when, and for how much any jazzman may perform. The protest theory is simply one among many partly valid explanations of a very complicated art. Unquestionably, jazz reflects some of the sexual and other tensions of our culture. The same thing is true of German, Chinese, Eskimo, or any other popular music, for singing and dancing are some of the basic ways of expressing feeling.

No doubt jazz also runs headlong into some of our sacred cows and Puritan taboos. The American Negro, and therefore the whole of the United States, is heir to an elaborate and complex West African culture which, partly because it did not have a written language, is especially rich in music and dance. This culture also happens to express itself in powerful drum rhythms, a basic and universal manner of communication, which helps to explain its impact. Just because of their fundamental nature, these rhythms are difficult to ignore, although they lack social acceptance. In this sense, jazz is a challenge to our perception, a refreshing and revealing force in our culture.

There are positive reasons for the appeal of jazz. The Reverend Mr. Alvin L. Kershaw, famous for his TV appearances on the '$64,000 Question,' is disarmingly frank about it. 'True jazz,' he writes, '. . . is for me far more an act of worship than singing some of the so-called religious songs I learned back in Sunday School.' He finds listening to jazz a tremendously rewarding experience: [5]

> Jazz helps us be sensitive to the whole range of existence. Far from offering us rose-colored glasses . . . it realistically speaks of sorrow and pain . . . it helps us relate and interpret the variety of experiences we have had . . . jazz stimulates us to feel deeply and truthfully . . . jazz thunders a mighty 'yes' . . . it offers us an urgency to live fully . . .

These generalizations—because similar generalizations occur everywhere—seem almost meaningless. And yet they do point to certain truths.

Clearly, any great work of art—novel, symphony, painting, or whatever—should stimulate us to 'feel deeply and truthfully.' The practical point is whether we are accessible, that is, whether we are interested enough to make the effort of understanding which any work of art demands. It takes real work to fully understand Shakespeare, Beethoven, Leonardo da Vinci, and—to a lesser extent perhaps but just as surely—good jazz. As with the other arts, the student of jazz profits from his study of the subject in proportion to the amount of effort he puts into it.

The Reverend Kershaw says that jazz 'realistically speaks of sorrow and pain.' One of the basic characteristics of jazz is improvisation, and fine improvisation in any art is necessarily spontaneous, lively, and creative. And it is utterly impossible to conceal the *quality* of your improvisation in jazz, where you are judged on the spot by your peers. Hence fakery, insincerity, and pretentiousness are easily detected. The good jazzman must play from the heart—to use a hackneyed but meaningful phrase—he must be honest, he must play the way he truly feels. Above all, he must have something to say, or all the rest is a waste of time. 'Music is your own experience,' said Charlie Parker, 'your thoughts, your wisdom. If you don't live it, it won't come out of your horn.' [6] Hence good jazz is truly realistic and essentially honest.

In our time, jazz is debunking the myths of 'fine art' and the social pretensions of the concert hall. To allow that jazz should be granted a role in the world of art, for example, leads to disconcerting questions about who is really cultured in our society. A dramatic illustration of the healthy, realistic qualities of jazz is furnished by a comparison of the Prussian 'goose-step' and the free-swinging stride of the New Orleans march. Both are responses to military music but the difference is immense. Contrary to the robot-like motions of the goose-step, the New Orleans marcher enjoys a freedom of movement that mirrors the spirit of the music. The New Orleans marchers may appear relatively unorganized, but their motions permit greater individual expression and symbolize a truer community of interests.

On a more abstract level, jazz offers a common ground upon which the conflicting claims of the individual and the group may be resolved—a problem that has vexed our times. For the jazzman, the dancer, and even the sympathetic listener can express himself individually and, at the same time, participate freely in a creative whole. In other words, he can 'belong' by participating in collective improvisation, and simultaneously let off his own brand of steam, solo. Something like this takes place wherever folk

dances occur, but it takes place nightly and *en masse* at
the Savoy Ballroom in Harlem.

The Reverend Kershaw also speaks of jazz as 'an act of
worship,' and others (including Bunk Johnson) have called
it a way of life. Are these expressions vague generalizations? People have been deeply and strongly—and sometimes strangely—influenced by jazz. Jazz can be, indirectly,
a matter of life or death. Writing about her experiences in
Germany during the Second World War, the pianist Jutta
Hipp recalls: [7]

You won't be able to understand this, because you were
born here [in the U.S.A.] but to us jazz is some kind of religion. We really had to fight for it, and I remember nights
when we didn't go down to the bomb shelter because we listened to [jazz] records. We just had the feeling that you are
not our enemies, and even though the bombs crashed around
us . . . we felt safe.

However impractical Miss Hipp sounds—and her love for
jazz could have ended any 'way of life' whatsoever—the religious fervor of her actions is typical of the response that
jazz evokes in many people.

In his *Notes of a Native Son,* the Negro novelist James
Baldwin speaks of 'that depth of involvement and un-
spoken recognition of shared experience which creates a
way of life,' referring to the relation that Negroes bear to
one another. Significantly, a love of jazz seems to create
similar relationships. For jazz appears to proceed on an
emotional level of direct and immediate contact between
human beings, a contact that also seems to encourage self-
expression. In a society of increasingly mass-produced,
assembly-line entertainment, when every individual is
treated like an empty pitcher to be filled from above, jazz
retains something of the spirit of the handicrafts of yes-
teryear. The print of the human spirit warms it. Deep

down, jazz expresses the enforced and compassionate attitudes of a minority group and may well appeal to us because we all have blue moods and, in a fundamental sense, none of us is wholly free.

25 | Jazz and the Role of the Negro

The future of jazz will depend on the speed and direction of the musical blending. If the emphasis is upon European forms, while African rhythms as blended in the mambo are rejected, jazz may become very much like the music of our concert halls. The dance rhythm—and the swing—would be dropped (an experiment already tried by Stan Kenton and others) and the chances of acceptance and respectability increased. On the other hand, if the trend is toward 'Cuban' and other rhythms, jazz will remain a dance music, although perhaps not respectable. Both directions may be explored simultaneously, for that has been the pattern in the past.

In any event, the speed and direction of the musical blending will depend largely on the changing position of the Negro in our society, for the Negro has always been the chief innovator throughout the history of jazz. The famous semanticist S. I. Hayakawa is of the opinion that, if the Negro had been fully assimilated, we should have had no jazz; if the Negro had been completely unassimilated, his music would still be more or less African—as in Haiti today—and without much influence on the rest of our music.[1] Ironically, the fact that the Negro was partly accepted and partly rejected forced the fusing and resulted in a new music.

A perspective on this problem is furnished by Professor Morroe Berger of Princeton, who checked references to jazz in magazines and newspapers from 1919 to 1944.[2] He found, first, that leaders of white opinion (and a few Negro leaders), especially ministers and educators, opposed jazz on the grounds that it was 'primitive' and licentious—i.e. it was rejected for non-musical reasons. Secondly, he found that musicians not associated with jazz, that is, classical musicians, opposed it because it was new, played by musicians without orthodox training, and violated rules of the concert hall. These opinions are explicitly stated in *Etude*, a magazine for music teachers who, generally speaking, are the upholders of musical orthodoxy. (By 1935, *Etude* developed a sort of musical schizophrenia—because pupils wanted to play jazz or nothing—and recommended the heavily arranged, commercial kind of jazz, which it referred to as 'the better type.')

Berger's third finding is that the white North, judging by the comparative sales of recordings, was more favorable to jazz than the white South. Lastly, he found that jazz is not accepted as readily as the spiritual, for example, because the Negro jazzman does not conform to the happy and harmless stereotype associated with the spiritual. In concluding, Berger speculates about the fact that jazz brings Negro and white together in a relationship where the Negro is frequently the idol of the white, and asks why jazz continued to spread in spite of the bitter opposition of the leaders of opinion in the United States. The answer, he suggests, lies in the ideas the white man and the Negro have of themselves and of each other.

Here we get into fairly deep water. The question of what the white man and the Negro think and feel about themselves and each other is as complicated as human nature. Nevertheless, there are a few indications. We have already mentioned the excellent researches of Constance

Rourke, who, in the course of a wide investigation of all kinds of early Americana, concludes that the American public was consistently fascinated by novels, plays, skits, poems, memoirs, sermons, almanacs, and whatever about Yankee peddlers, frontiersmen, and Negroes. Especially the Negro. 'He became, in short,' she adds, 'a dominant figure in spite of his condition, and commanded a definite portraiture.' [3]

From the earliest times, then, everybody in our country seemed to enjoy hearing about the Negro. And, of course, the Negro was at the center of the conflict which resulted in the Civil War. As the slaveowners and dominant class, the whites were in a position to impose their attitudes about Negroes upon the Negroes, and a study of these attitudes as they appear in the literature of the day affords another clue. In Mark Twain's *Huckleberry Finn,* for example, Huck the white boy looks up to the colored man as an idol with almost magic powers. In the same way, the colored harpooner Queequeg, in Melville's *Moby Dick,* fascinates the other characters in the story—he is a 'devilish tantalization.' Melville's *The Confidence Man* affords another example. But why this confused preoccupation with the Negro? Here is a strong thread in the tapestry of American life and literature.

Perhaps the most helpful illustration is *Uncle Remus,* by Joel Chandler Harris—a subject brilliantly explored by Mr. Bernard Wolfe, the author with Milton Mezzrow of *Really the Blues.* In our time, stories by and about Uncle Remus are increasingly popular, from a full-length Disney feature through Hit Parade songs to a syndicated comic strip. On the surface, these stories tell how the weaker Rabbit outwitted the stronger Fox, Wolf, and Bear. The Rabbit, it seems clear, is a folk-hero of the Negroes, a symbol of how the Negro has survived by his mother-wit in a hostile environment.

Upon closer inspection, however, Wolfe writes, 'These

are very un-Aesopian creatures who speak a vaudeville dialect, hold candy-pulls, run for the legislature, fight and scheme over gold mines, compete for women in elaborate rituals of courtship and self-aggrandizement, sing plantation ditties about "Jim Crow," read the newspapers after supper, and kill and maim each other . . . coldbloodedly for prestige, plotting their crafty moves in advance and often using accomplices.' [4] As a matter of fact, Br'er Rabbit scalds the Wolf to death, sees to it that the innocent Possum dies in a fire, tortures the Bear, and causes the fatal beating of the Fox. He even tries to trick Mrs. Fox into eating her dead husband's head in some soup—all in the name of good, clean fun. What kind of stories are these?

Joel Chandler Harris himself collected the tales from country Negroes. Maybe his directions to a friend on how to procure these stories helps to explain what was taking place: tell a tale yourself first—preferably the 'Tar Baby' story—and then the Negroes will fall to laughing and slapping their thighs and forthwith tell you all the tales you can copy down. In this situation, the joke may well be on Harris, since the Negroes are telling tales in which the not-so-concealed point is that the clever Negro can always outwit the stupid white man. (Even the symbolism of the tar fits; it's black and yielding, and *almost* a trap for Br'er Rabbit.) Harris himself seems to have been partly aware of this, because he tried to explain it away.

Harris liked to call himself 'Uncle Remus,' enjoyed speaking Negro dialect, and loved 'to play minstrels'—identifying himself, in other words, with the Negro. On the other hand, he was painfully shy, lacking in confidence, and terribly frightened by society (he once escaped a party by jumping out a window). The point, of course, is that Harris was fascinated by and envious of the Negro, and wanted to be like him. But not as the Negro really is. Harris believed in the stereotype of the happy, uninhibited savage, and that's what he wanted to be. Once such a stereotype exists, the rest follows as the night the day, for this is one of the eternal fantasies of escape which appeals to all men.

Put the life and stories of Joel Chandler Harris together and you are faced with the conclusion that he was interested in the Negro because he fancied—incorrectly—that the Negro had the exact characteristics that he wanted for himself. Of course, Harris also had the Southerner's common conviction that the Negro is inferior. As Wolfe writes: [5]

The Remus stories are a monument to the South's ambivalence. Harris, the arche-typical Southerner, sought the Negro's love, and pretended he had received it (Remus's grin). But he sought the Negro's hate too (Br'er Rabbit), and revelled in it in an unconscious orgy of masochism—punishing himself, possibly, for not being a Negro, the stereotypical Negro, the unstinting giver.

Thus, like many white men, Harris thought of the Negro as a devoted child and a dangerous animal *at the same time,* and in a confused and paradoxical way was fascinated by and envied him, while looking down upon him.

Perhaps the most obvious example of this phenomenon in American theater is the minstrel show. White people took over Negro song and dance, blacked up their faces, and played at being Negroes—to the powerful and lasting enjoyment of white audiences. In a sense, the Negro had little or nothing to do with it at all—especially at the beginning. And here again, the audience was treated to—and loved—a stereotype: a happy, gifted, ignorant, and comic creature who bore no resemblance to the real Negro. It was the invention of the white man, a wishful characterization, a projection of what the white man wanted the Negro to be. It was also a fact—just as real as the pigmentation of skin—with which the Negro had to live, along with the bitter and contradictory fact of race prejudice.

It is difficult to realize the range and depth—and therefore its influence—of this Negro stereotype in American culture. The United States is flooded with stock portraits, pictures, and images of the Negro which are produced and consumed almost entirely in a white market. The Negro himself has nothing to do with it. Take a walk through any big department store and note the Gold Dust Twins, Cream of Wheat, Aunt Jemima's Pancakes, Wilson Hams, Uncle Ben's Rice, Golliwog Perfume, Hiram Walker Whiskey, Carioca Rum, Ballantine's Ale, as well as figurines, nylon stockings, women's underwear, bandanas, earrings, charm bracelets, ash trays, wallpaper, men's shorts, lamp shades, sweaters, napkins, dolls, toys, greeting cards —and so on and on.

In each case, the Negro is portrayed as happy and grinning, eager to be of humble service and offering something good to the public. In point of fact, a picture of a Negro on any product in this country—smiling and friendly— helps to sell it. And this white stereotype of the Negro conflicts sharply with the way the Negro is really treated. In other words, the attitude of many white men toward the Negro is ambivalent, a combination of attraction and repulsion, of acceptance and rejection. The Negro is alternately thought of, for example, as a loyal servant and a threatening beast. Inevitably, this white attitude was—and still is—a factor in molding the lives of the many Negroes who had to live in close and humiliating contact with it.

What is the effect of this attitude on the Negro and his music? The Negro was forced to play a part in which he sometimes came to believe (cf. Uncle Tom). He faked a friendly front in order to survive in a white world. If you weren't permitted to be yourself, it was much safer to pretend to be a happy child than a menacing savage. Gunnar Myrdal calls it 'the tyranny of expectancy.' At the same time, the Negro fought back against the way he was treated (there were at least 109 bloody uprisings before the Civil War). But mostly the Negro—unlike the American Indian —remained alive by pretending to be what he was expected to be—he donned a mask designed by the white man.

Wearing a mask, particularly a simple-minded façade expressing somebody else's confused notions, is not a comfortable way to live. The Negro novelist James Baldwin writes about the complexities of such a situation with deep insight: [6]

I knew very well what [white] Americans saw when they looked at me and this allowed me to play endless and sinister variations on the role which they had assigned me; since I knew that it was, for them, of the utmost importance that they never be confronted with what, in their own personalities, made this role so necessary and gratifying to them, I knew that they could never call my hand or, indeed, afford to know what I was doing; so that I moved into every crucial situation with the deadly and rather desperate advantages of bitterly accumulated perception, of pride and contempt.

The Negro employed his many talents at playing with the mask, adding to it, letting it slip on purpose, making fun of it. He would act a little differently than he was supposed to, pretending to be—and this was exciting and dangerous—just what the white man didn't expect or want. Or he could say indirectly exactly what he felt, covering up with comedy a lot of what might be insulting and hostile. Or he could make fun of the white man's fear and even his own resentment, lighting up the ludicrous paradoxes in the whole crazy, mixed-up situation.

During the late 'forties, for example, Fletcher Henderson worked in a production called the 'Cavalcade of Jazz' at the Royal Roost on Broadway. There was nothing new jazzwise, but Stump and Stumpy were one of the acts playing to a mixed audience. Two dark-skinned Negroes are sitting at a night-club table; behind the smaller one stands a huge, light-skinned, threatening bouncer. The smaller Negro can't see the bouncer behind him whose angry presence scares his buddy, and so he proceeds to cheer up his friend. 'Whatsa matter with you?' he demands loudly. 'You up No'th now, man!' The fact that he is utterly convinced that his troubles are over now that he is up North convulses the audience—the naïveté of such an attitude is a standing joke among Negroes. As the little fellow becomes insistently louder the bouncer glowers more and more threateningly behind him and his buddy tries more and more frantically to hush him, without success. 'You up No'th now,' he shouts with belligerent triumph.

At last his buddy catches his eye, nods fearfully at the bouncer, and the little fellow looks around—glaring at the huge figure towering menacingly above him. For a moment, his conviction does not falter. He pulls his buddy's sleeve, points dramatically at the bouncer, and commands: 'Straighten that fool out, man, straighten that fool out!' The inspired audacity is breathtaking and heartbreaking, and the audience is laughing hysterically. Here is the always dreamed-of repartee, the strong expression of true feelings, the whole man. The mask is off. Then the bouncer picks the little man up and thrashes him unmercifully while the audience screams.

In their way, Stump and Stumpy were kidding the country Negro who had just arrived up North—an experience that many Negroes share. But they were also kidding the whole tangled skein of Negro-white relationships—the little man thought, with the engaging optimism of everyman, that he didn't have to wear the mask after he got out of the South, and his belief led to predictable and well-worn results. His attitude is basically human—he hopes for the best. Above all, Stump and Stumpy were cutting through layers and layers of fakery and pretense in our society and, indeed, in human nature itself. They reassert the humanity of man.

Very early jazz in New Orleans was probably played without the mask. Although an imitation of white examples, the Negro marching band played music of, by, and for the Negro. The music has an open-air quality which is not entirely due to the fact that it was generally played out of doors. Perhaps the Latin-Catholic background with its lack of segregation created a more permissive environment; perhaps the code of conduct was so rigid that a Negro at least knew exactly what he could and what he could not do. When dealing with white people, on the other hand, the mask was probably well set. In any event, New Orleans jazz was a relatively serene adaptation to the mask without confusing reference to white attitudes.

In New Orleans, a musician couldn't depend upon jazz for a living—at first. As Zutty Singleton says: [7]

There were so many bands in New Orleans. But most of the musicians had day jobs, you know—trades. They were bricklayers and carpenters and cigar makers and plasterers. Some had little businesses of their own—coal and wood and vegetable stores. Some worked on the cotton exchange and some were porters.

And New Orleans jazz, as played for example by George Lewis, still has an unembattled, happy, and almost complacent sound in which the ensemble style of collective improvisation seems to mirror the stable life of a close-knit community in which jazz is not yet a full-time and competitive career.

New Orleans jazz is the music of a people drifting on the fringe of the bitter challenge of race prejudice. It couldn't last, not if the musician played the way he felt. Already Jelly Roll Morton was playing for white customers in

Storyville and resenting it. He cut a hole in the screen and watched while the girls performed. He played 'At the Animule Ball,' which begins to echo the conflicts of an angry ghetto, and in the lyrics he fantasied the destruction of his enemies. The well-known surgeon Dr. Edmond Souchon reports that King Oliver in the late 'teens, when asked by white teenagers the title of a tune just played, would answer invariably: 'Who Struck John.' Perhaps he was afraid someone would steal his stuff, but the surliness of his manner indicated resentment beneath the mask.

Soon New Orleans jazz had to make the transition from a more or less private music, played by Negroes for Negroes, to a public music which had to survive commercially in the white world at large. The music went indoors, shifting from march to dance music, and the musicians changed status from amateur to professional, playing a mixture more palatable to a white audience. At this early stage and long before the public heard about jazz, the mask was set.

When jazz reached a peak in its development in Chicago during the early 'twenties, a gradual change had taken place. The mask was slipping a little. Individual solos were becoming the fashion, and these solos were unusually assertive and—in the case of Louis Armstrong—almost explosive. In fact, they echoed the violence of the gangster-ridden days of Prohibition. Jimmy McPartland describes part of it: [8]

The mobsters would break a bottle over some guy's head, then jab it in his face, then maybe kick him. They made mincemeat of people. I never saw such a horrible thing in my life. But we kept playing . . .

The gifted singer, dancer, actress and entertainer, Edith Wilson, told me about a job in the early 'thirties in New York which turned out to be a heavily armed birthday party for Dutch Schultz. 'Whenever we worked for gangsters,' she said, 'we worried because we might accidentally get bumped off any minute, too.' She was escorted home by a gentleman named Lucky Luciano who had plans. 'He offered to get me off the dirty ol' stage and set me up in a clean new sportin' house,' she recalls. The environment was an occupational hazard that jazz somehow survived, and which paradoxically gave the jazzman a measure of freedom, while molding his style. The need to stay squarely behind the mask was diminishing.

The recordings of Louis Armstrong—especially the vocals—during the later 'twenties are documents in the creative handling of the mask. Armstrong was given the most banal of current tunes to record and, with impressive consistency, transformed them into something else, something intensely appealing. He accomplishes this, of course, by his fine musicianship, but the finishing touch is added by his sheer genius. He makes fun of the tune, sharing with the listener his insight into the silliness of the whole occasion, and at the same time, he improvises with such gusto and imagination that a tawdry ballad emerges as a thing of beauty.

For example, Armstrong's 1931 recording of 'All of Me' is a one-man cultural conspiracy. In the middle of his vocal, his accent goes insanely British (as Morton's does in 'The Animule Ball') and he roars in his gravelly voice '[I can't] get on *dee-ah*, without you!' These are the lyrics but the implications are many and various. On the surface, Louis is saying: 'This is as far as I can get with these corny lyrics without clowning, out of sheer embarrassment.' At the same time, by changes in the melody and by unusual accents in the rhythm, he makes the listener suddenly realize that he, Armstrong, is in full, double-edged control of the musical situation, embroidering beautifully on the stereotyped mask, and enjoying the whole affair hugely. In a word: he is the master—not of just the music but also of a complex and ironic attitude, a rare, honest way of looking at life. (Fats Waller excelled at the same thing.) Indeed, ironic nuances and implications occur in many fine jazz vocals.

Meanwhile, wherever jazz found an appreciative audience that would support it, the mask became less necessary. For many years, such an audience could only be found among the poorer Negroes, but the picture gradually changed. The high points can be suggested: New Orleans at the turn of the century; St. Louis and Memphis in the 'teens; Chicago in the 'twenties; Kansas City in the 'thirties; and New York in the 'forties. The West Coast may be next. In each case, prosperity preceded this supporting audience and migrations from the deep South contributed to the change.

During the late 'twenties and early 'thirties, for example, a tremendous development was taking place in Kansas City, almost entirely among Negro bands, and the mask was nearly thrown away. A real fellow-feeling sprang up, a group solidarity. Jo Jones says: [9]

Any place in Kansas City where there was a session the guys would just get up on the bandstand, and spiritually they knew when to come in . . . Nobody got tired . . . I just sat there and played the whole time for pure joy. And I never realized that an hour and a half had gone by.

There was no need for a mask here, except when playing for white dancers, and then a sort of watchful indifference could be substituted.

When Benny Goodman and the swing era arrived in the mid-'thirties, Negro musicians began to experiment restlessly with the mask. Occasions when it was not needed multiplied. Before the appreciative Negro audience at the Savoy Ballroom in Harlem, where white bands began to appear now and then for battles of music, the mask fell off. A mutual feeling of personal identity arose amid the teamwork that big-band arrangements made necessary. Meanwhile, Negro musicians were more and more idolized by white youngsters, and pioneering white bands began to feature Negro musicians. (Bookings down South were now flatly refused.)

During the early 'forties, the mask slipped completely and the bop and post-bop musicians emerged. The result was often unconcealed hostility. For a while, some played with their backs to the audience, walked off the stand after their own particular solos, and played it 'cool' to the point of commercial self-destruction. Some came back to their senses and made a living. Others, seconded by the hipster, went down and out, criticizing Louis Armstrong and Dizzy Gillespie in the same breath. The healthy part of the revolt lay in the determination not to play the role of the stereotype Negro entertainer, and the desire to be judged only by one's playing. Without the mask there were fewer alibis, but it was far better that way.

From the very beginning, perhaps the jazz musician's strongest motive was the desire for recognition and respectability. A man wants to better himself. In the mid-'forties, beneath the beret, the goatee, and the flamboyant clothes—a costume close to the left-bank Parisian of the 'nineties—was a real hunger for the musical and intellectual culture of the white community. This hunger was increasingly satisfied by long and serious study. Although generally speaking the Negro still creates the latest jazz products while the white man packages them, the cultural lag is closing and the mask is falling off.

When bassist Charles Mingus told me: 'It's time we Negroes quit crying the blues'—he didn't mean to stop using the 12-bar form. True enough, the Negro has had plenty to protest about and, in the sense that jazz reflects the attitudes of the Negro, jazz has been partly a music of protest. (There are, of course, additional reasons for this protest.) But the time should come when the need to protest lessens. Will jazz then disappear? I don't think so. By 1956, there were cool sounds that seemed a little less embattled, a little more fully attuned to entirely musical factors. The danger is that we may mistake this for weakness and lack of swing. The 'agony coefficient,' however, is noticeably decreasing, the mask is becoming unnecessary. Modern jazz can also be reasonably cheerful music.

Along with the painfully slow breakdown of the white stereotype of the Negro, the blending of the various components in jazz proceeds as best it can. But every day, the Negro is contributing more fully and freely. Perhaps the final irony is that the average white man's idea of the Negro, which often operates below the level of consciousness, stands for freedom—mental, moral, and physical. Without this complicated pattern, jazz might never have come into existence, but once free of it, the future is limitless.

26 | Postscript: The Future of Jazz

The study of jazz and its future—although full of paradoxes—may turn out to be of unexpected importance. For the growth and spread of jazz illustrates a key phenomenon in our civilization: the process of transculturation, or cross-culturation, or simply acculturation (specialists disagree on the term but agree that the process itself is of vast significance). In this case, it consists of the cross-influences of European and West African music upon each other as jazz evolved. If we establish the over-all pattern of this process by a study of jazz—one of the few likely subjects—we can better understand how various cultures influence each other, how our own society develops, and how the American character is formed.

As One World becomes a reality, jazz will continue to absorb, adapt, and re-create a variety of characteristics from the other musics of the world. This has been the pattern of the past: jazz takes whatever comes to hand and stamps it with a beat. Yet attempts by other traditions to absorb jazz—although this may be less true as time goes by—have consistently failed. Specifically, jazz and classical music were cradled in such different traditions that to most musicians they are mutually exclusive.

And yet, as Gunther Schuller, the French horn player with the Metropolitan Opera orchestra, says: 'The deeper blending of jazz and classical music is only a matter of time.' From the beginning, a mixing and merging has been going on without as yet producing a work of art—according to European standards. George Gershwin's 'Rhapsody in Blue' was neither jazz nor classical music, although it borrowed slightly from both. Igor Stravinsky's 'Ebony Concerto,' composed for the Woody Herman band, was a classical composition which had little to do with jazz. More recently, Robert Graettinger's 'City of Glass,' recorded by Stan Kenton, employed the most modern dissonances—but no jazz. The Rolf Liebermann 'Concerto for Jazz Band and Symphony Orchestra,' played by the Sauter-Finegan band within a symphony orchestra, allowed no improvisation but it may point the way to future success: a nucleus of jazzmen improvising within a symphony. The symphony men, of course, must know enough jazz not to interfere with the improvisation—they could even help produce the proper background.

The solo trumpeter with the Boston Symphony Orchestra, Roger Voisin, points to the trend: [1]

My father, who was born in France, hated jazz and couldn't play it; I love jazz but can't play it very well; I think my children will both enjoy and play jazz, as well as classical music.

Mr. Voisin is an ardent fan of Bobby Hackett's trumpet playing and a close and interested observer of the jazz scene. In a sense, his attitude is typical of the increased interest that symphony men show in jazz.

Socio-economic factors, however, complicate the picture crucially. Tin-Pan Alley and the production of Hit Parade tunes are a big business in which a large amount of money is invested. The investors, of course, want a good and, above all, a steady return on their investment. So they find out what will sell, reduce it to the most simple formula, and manufacture it on an assembly line like tin-cans. The booking of bands and the night-club business follow the same pattern. 'Once you get a job,' says bassist Tommy Potter who was thinking of quitting the business, 'the management never asks you to play good—they just keep ordering you to watch that schedule.' The irony is that Tin-Pan Alley, the bookers, and the night-club operators depend heavily upon the inspiration of the jazzmen.

The plight of the creative artist in a mercantile world—painter, author, composer, sculptor, or what not—is well known. The plight of the jazzman is not as well known but it is decidedly worse. He is playing music that leaders of public opinion hold in contempt—'red-light music.' The occupational hazards are notorious: the jazzman works while everyone else plays. What is more, the nature of jazz—with its stress on improvisation—makes plagiarism inevitable (how can you stop anyone from copying your recordings while he is improvising?). The creator in jazz seldom reaps the rewards of his creations, although he may see others do so with his material—diluted and commercialized. There is basis in fact for the tragedy of the 'young man with a horn.'

Where is the public for jazz? One of the editors of *Harper's*, Eric Larrabee, says: [2]

By the time the average jazz-lover settles down, has a family, and then returns to hear the music he used to love, the scene has changed so completely that he feels left out and condemns what he hears. Jazz is evolving so swiftly that it is difficult for it to develop an increasing public which understands what is happening.

Magazine editors in 1955 were hit by the same problem. In former years they felt that you didn't need an 'expert' to write about jazz. Then, as they realized that jazz is one of the arts in which people have deep and often irrational emotional investments, they chose writers who would write about Dixieland, the only music that the now middle-aged editors had experienced in their own youth and knew to be jazz. Meanwhile, the fanatic cults within modern jazz stirred up enough irrelevant dust to frighten any editor away from more contemporary music.

In spite of it all, jazz has continued to prosper. And judging by the last fifty years, the taste of the public will continue to improve. Expose the average person to all kinds of popular music and it is safe to say that, sooner or later, he will recognize the superior vitality and honesty of jazz. (Even jazz critics—the qualifications are nebulous—have been known to broaden in their tastes.) Better jazz is becoming better known. A few of the 'Rock and Roll' contingent of the mid-'fifties, for example, fell upon Count Basie's 'Every Day' (with Joe Williams singing the vocal) and graduated then and there. Each generation finds its own way.

In the future, the vanguard of jazz (and we are speaking here about the pioneers only in a very large field) will probably continue to consist of highly gifted individuals playing together in small groups where there is plenty of room for the free play of improvisation. Big bands, on the other hand, serve to consolidate and popularize the ideas of the pioneers. For with their necessary emphasis upon arrangements, big bands tend to incorporate—in a fairly elementary way—more European characteristics, sometimes at the expense of improvisation. (Sauter and Finegan insist that improvising should be subordinated to the piece as a whole.) Big bands also spelled the doom of soloists who could not read music and played entirely by ear. But they cost too much. By 1955, the small 'combo' of four to six musicians was riding high in nightclubs and on recordings.

As in the past, we may expect greater harmonic, melodic, and rhythmic complexity in jazz. As far as harmony is concerned, jazz is traveling the same path as classical music—toward the stone wall of atonality—but there is still a long way to go. Lennie Tristano's 'Intuition,' in which a small group of close friends play simultaneously whatever enters their heads, is a courageous step in this direction. The usual complaint is that it doesn't swing—a completely subjective criterion—although there is no reason why it shouldn't. Perhaps outstanding success along these lines needs the rare skill of musicians highly versed in both classical music and jazz and, of course, such an experiment would need some kind of financial support.

In the course of assimilating more and more elements of classical music—and thereby, incidentally, gaining social status—jazz generally turns to early classical forms, especially a free kind of counterpoint. (Nobody can miss the classical origin here.) The problem then is one of assimilation, maintaining the swing and improvising in an inspired fashion. By the mid-'fifties, both the Dave Brubeck Quartet and the Modern Jazz Quartet were achieving this in different ways. The Modern Jazz Quartet relied more on written scores and thus created a more unified and consistent whole; the Brubeck Quartet improvised almost entirely and thus created a music which relied on the inspiration of the moment. Both groups produced music of high quality.

The melody in jazz is also becoming more complex. The trend has been to lengthen the 'line,' or improvised tune, and to ignore the traditional rests, creating a new melody that overruns cadences. The standard 12, 16, and 32 bar forms of our popular music are being treated as points of departure for extemporaneous passacaglias and even sonatas. Much of this tendency took concrete form with the improvisations of altoist Charlie Parker. A further complexity was added with the adoption of more complex harmony.

As the modulations become more complicated, the improvisations above them follow suit.

Jazz rhythms are also becoming more complicated. In spite of the dislike, and perhaps dread, felt by the Dixieland and 'Cool' schools of jazz, Afro-Cuban rhythms have become a vital part—although not mechanically—of jazz since 1945. Here again, Charlie Parker added a split-second sense of timing that is the despair of many modern jazzmen—a rhythmic complication that seemed to grow up within jazz. Meanwhile, jazz drummers have visited Haiti and Africa and their influence has been strongly felt. Now their aim during a drum solo is to play a tune and to tell a story. There seems to be no end to the rhythmic complexity that jazz may absorb.

The time is coming when jazz will receive the study it deserves, when undergraduates at our colleges will be able to take courses, for credit, in American music (including jazz); when a course such as 'The World Origins of American Popular Music,' for example, will be offered in adult education centers from coast to coast; when visiting lectureships and endowed chairs in *American* music will be established at our leading universities; and when an organization such as the Institute of Jazz Studies, for example, will be able to launch a full-scale study of the role of jazz in American civilization. Then jazz will no longer be the stepchild of the arts.

CHAPTER 1

1. See R. A. Waterman, 'African Influence on the Music of the Americas' in *Acculturation in the Americas,* edited by Sol Tax (Chicago: Chicago University Press, 1952), pp. 207-18. See especially p. 211.

2. Rudy Vallee, *Vagabond Dreams Come True* (New York: Grosset & Dunlap, 1930) pp. 60-61.

3. John A. Lomax and Alan Lomax, *Folk Song U.S.A.* (New York: Duell, Sloan & Pearce, 1947), p. 338.

4. See Gilbert Chase, *America's Music from the Pilgrims to the Present* (New York: McGraw-Hill Book Company, 1955), pp. 22-40.

5. See Harriet Janis, album notes, 'Jazz a la Creole,' Circle Records, Album S-13.

6. See S. I. Hayakawa, 'Popular Songs vs. the Facts of Life,' *ETC.: A Review of General Semantics* (Winter, 1955), pp. 83-95.

7. See Alan Lomax, album notes, 'Run Old Jeremiah,' in the Library of Congress series *Folk Music of the United States* (AAFS), Album IV.

8. See R. A. Waterman, album notes, 'Tribal, Folk and Cafe Music of West Africa,' Arthur S. Alberts (ed.), Field Recordings, New York.

CHAPTER 2

1. See M. J. Herskovits, *The Myth of the Negro Past* (New York: Harper & Brothers, 1941), pp. 33-53.

2. As quoted in G. P. Jackson, *White and Negro Spirituals* (New York: J. J. Augustin, 1943), p. 254n.

3. See, for example, M. J. and F. S. Herskovits, *Trinidad Village* (New York: Alfred A. Knopf, 1947), pp. 327-31.

CHAPTER 3

1. See M. J. and F. S. Herskovits, *Suriname Folk-Lore* (New York: Columbia University Press, 1936), p. 517.

2. Harold Courlander, *Haiti Singing* (Chapel Hill: The University of North Carolina Press, 1939), p. 5 *et passim*.

3. Ibid. p. 5.

4. As quoted in *Jazzmen*, edited by Ramsey and Smith (New York: Harcourt, Brace & Company, 1939), p. 8.

5. See F. Ortiz, *La Africania de la Musica Folklorica de Cuba* (Havana, 1950), *passim*.

6. See Harold Courlander, album notes, 'Cult Music of Cuba,' Folkways LP 410.

7. See M. J. and F. S. Herskovits, *Trinidad Village* (New York: Alfred A. Knopf, 1947), *passim*.

8. This recording is in the archives of the Department of Anthropology at Northwestern University.

9. See M. W. Stearns, album notes, 'Religious Songs and Drums of the Bahamas,' Folkways LP 440.

10. H. E. Krehbiel, *Afro-American Folksongs* (New York: Schirmer, 1914), p. 134.

CHAPTER 4

1. See Charles Gayarré, *The History of Louisiana* (New York: W. J. Widdleton, 1867), and sources cited.

2. *Gumbo Ya-Ya*, edited by Saxon, Dreyer, and Tallant (Boston: Houghton Mifflin Company, 1945), pp. 224-5. Cf., however, W. A. Roberts, *Lake Pontchartrain* (Indianapolis: The Bobbs-Merrill Company, 1946), pp. 192ff.

3. G. W. Cable, 'The Dance in Place Congo,' *Century Magazine* (February 1886), p. 522.

4. M. J. Herskovits, *The Myth of the Negro Past* (New York: Harper & Brothers, 1941), p. 246.

5. Thomas Ashe, *Travels in America* (New York, 1811), p. 341.

6. Sir Charles Lyell, *A Second Visit to the United States of North America* (London, 1849), Vol. II, p. 113.

CHAPTER 5

1. Robert Tallant, *Voodoo in New Orleans* (New York: The Macmillan Company, 1946), p. 9.
2. Ibid. p. 18.
3. J. W. Buel, *The Mysteries and Miseries of America's Great Cities* (San Francisco: A. L. Bancroft and Company, 1883), pp. 524-5.
4. As quoted in Herbert Asbury, *The French Quarter* (New York: Alfred A. Knopf, 1936), p. 269.
5. C. D. Warner, *Studies in the South and West* (New York: Harper & Brothers, 1889), pp. 69-72.
6. Tallant, op. cit. pp. 57-8.
7. Ibid. pp. 66, 103.
8. Z. N. Hurston, *Mules and Men* (Philadelphia: J. B. Lippincott Company, 1935), p. 229.
9. Tallant, op. cit. pp. 223-4.
10. Asbury, op. cit. p. 243.
11. B. H. B. Latrobe, *Impressions Respecting New Orleans,* edited by Samuel Wilson, Jr. (New York: Columbia University Press, 1951), pp. 49-51.
12. G. W. Cable, 'The Dance in Place Congo,' *Century Magazine* (February 1886), pp. 517-32.
13. Thomas Jefferson, *Notes on the State of Virginia* (Philadelphia, 1803), p. 191n.

CHAPTER 6

1. F. L. Olmsted, *Journey in the Seaboard Slave States* (New York: Dix and Edwards, 1856), p. 552.
2. Rudi Blesh, *Shining Trumpets* (New York: Alfred A. Knopf, 1946), p. 155.
3. H. W. Odum, *Social and Mental Traits of the American Negro* (New York: Columbia University Press, 1910), pp. 98, 104ff.
4. W. E. B. Du Bois (ed.), 'Economic Co-operation among Negro Americans,' *Atlanta University Publications* (Atlanta, 1907), No. 12, p. 92. Also quoted in Herskovits, *Myth of the Negro Past* (New York: Harper & Brothers, 1941), p. 164.
5. M. J. Herskovits, *Dahomey* (New York: J. J. Augustin, 1938), Vol. I, p. 166.
6. *Gumbo Ya-Ya,* edited by Saxon, Dreyer, and Tallant (Boston: Houghton Mifflin Company, 1945), pp. 311-12.
7. Ibid. p. 301.

8. Alan Lomax, *Mister Jelly Roll* (New York: Duell, Sloan & Pearce, 1950), pp. 15-16.

9. *Gumbo Ya-Ya*, op. cit. pp. 306-8.

10. B. H. B. Latrobe, *Impressions Respecting New Orleans*, edited by Samuel Wilson, Jr. (New York: Columbia University Press, 1951), pp. 60, 138.

11. *Drums and Shadows*, Savannah Unit of the Georgia Writers Project, Georgia WPA (Athens: University of Georgia Press, 1940), p. 107.

12. Album notes, 'New Orleans Parade,' American Music Records, Nos. 101-3.

13. M. J. Herskovits, op. cit. pp. 357, 387.

14. Ibid. p. 402.

15. From an unpublished manuscript quoted by Grace King, *New Orleans, the Place and the People* (New York: The Macmillan Company, 1904), pp. 344-5.

16. Alan Lomax, op. cit. pp. 84-5.

CHAPTER 7

1. Tom Sancton, 'Trouble in Mind,' *The Second Line* (September 1951), p. 14.

2. 'Buddy Bolden,' *Jazz Hot* (Paris, December 1946), p. 7.

3. *Jazzmen*, edited by Ramsey and Smith (New York: Harcourt, Brace & Company, 1939), p. 12.

4. Alan Lomax, *Mister Jelly Roll* (New York: Duell, Sloan & Pearce, 1950), p. 60.

CHAPTER 8

1. J. W. Johnson, *God's Trombones* (New York: The Viking Press, 1927), p. 3.

2. Carter G. Woodson, *History of the Negro Church* (Washington, D. C.: Associated Publishers, 1921), p. 57.

3. W. H. Pipes, *Say Amen, Brother!* (New York: The William-Frederick Press, 1951), p. 65.

4. *The Journal of the Reverend John Wesley, A.M.* (New York: E. P. Dutton & Company, 1907), Vol. 2, p. 320.

5. Ibid. p. 304.

6. Gilbert Chase, *America's Music* (New York: McGraw-Hill Book Company, 1955), p. 81.

7. G. G. Johnson, *Ante-Bellum North Carolina* (Chapel Hill: The University of North Carolina Press, 1937), p. 395.

8. Morgan Edwards, 'Materials Towards a History of the Baptists in the Province of North Carolina,' *North Carolina Historical Review* (July 1930), VII, p. 386.

9 G. P. Jackson, *White and Negro Spirituals* (New York: J. J. Augustin, 1943), p. 285.

10. F. M. Davenport, *Primitive Traits in Religious Revivals* (New York: The Macmillan Company, 1905), pp. 75-7.

11. G. G. Johnson, op. cit. p. 406.

12. Lorenzo Dow, *History of Cosmopolite; or, The Four Volumes of Lorenzo's Journal* (New York: J. C. Totten, 1814), p. 197.

13. G. G. Johnson, op. cit. p. 399.

14. F. M. Davenport, op. cit. p. 92.

15. M. J. Herskovits, *The Myth of the Negro Past* (New York: Harper & Brothers, 1941), p. 231.

16. Hortense Powdermaker, *After Freedom* (New York: The Viking Press, 1939), p. 260.

CHAPTER 9

1. As quoted by Lydia Parrish, *Slave Songs of the Georgia Sea Islands* (New York: Creative Age Press, 1942), p. 199.

2. M. J. Herskovits, *The Myth of the Negro Past* (New York: Harper & Brothers, 1941), p. 161.

3. Sir Charles Lyell, *A Second Visit to the United States of North America* (London, 1849), Vol. I, pp. 327-8.

4. W. F. Allen, C. P. Ware, and L. M. Garrison, *Slave Songs of the United States* (New York, 1867), p. 89.

5. Ibid, p. 61.

6. Ibid. p. vii.

7. W. M. Doerflinger, *Shanty Men and Shanty Boys* (New York: The Macmillan Company, 1951), p. 97.

8. Ibid. p. 34.

9. H. W. Odum and G. B. Johnson, *Negro Workaday Songs* (Chapel Hill: The University of North Carolina Press, 1926), p. 89.

10. John A. Lomax and Alan Lomax, *Folk Song U.S.A.* (New York: Duell, Sloan & Pearce, 1947), pp. 293-4.

CHAPTER 10

1. J. W. Work, *American Negro Songs* (New York: Howell, Soskin & Company, 1940), pp. 34-5.

2. Lydia Parrish, *Slave Songs of the Georgia Sea Islands* (New York: Creative Age Press, 1942), p. 197.

3. F. L. Olmsted, *Journey in the Seaboard Slave States* (New York: Dix and Edwards, 1856), pp. 394-5.

4. H. W. Odum and G. B. Johnson, *Negro Workaday Songs* (Chapel Hill: The University of North Carolina Press, 1926), p. 263 *et passim*.

5. Nat Shapiro and Nat Hentoff, *Hear Me Talkin' to Ya* (New York: Rinehart & Company, 1955), p. 250.

6. William Broonzy, *Big Bill Blues* (London: Cassell & Company, 1955), pp. 88-9.

7. Wilder Hobson, *American Jazz Music* (New York: W. W. Norton & Company, 1939), p. 36.

8. Russell Ames, *The Story of American Folk Song* (New York, Grosset & Dunlap, 1955), p. 260.

9. Ibid. pp. 258-9.

CHAPTER 11

1. See Constance Rourke, *American Humor* (New York: Harcourt, Brace & Company, 1931), pp. 98-104.

2. *The New York Times*, 5 June 1881.

3. See M. H. Winter, 'Juba and American Minstrelsy,' *Chronicles of the American Dance*, ed. Paul Magriel (New York: Henry Holt & Company, 1948), pp. 39-63.

4. Charles Dickens, *American Notes* (1842) (London: Chapman & Hall, 1842), Vol. I, p. 218.

5. M. H. Winter, op. cit. p. 52.

6. *Theatrical Times* (London: August 1948), p. 500.

7. As quoted by Carl Wittke, *Tambo and Bones* (Durham: Duke University Press, 1930), p. 53n.

8. M. H. Winter, op. cit. p. 53.

9. Ralph Keeler, 'Three Years as a Negro Minstrel,' *Atlantic Monthly* (July 1869), Vol. XXIV, No. CXLI, p. 81.

10. As quoted by Rudi Blesh & Harriet Janis, *They All Played Ragtime* (New York: Alfred A. Knopf, 1950), p. 96.

11. Carl Wittke, op. cit. p. 147.

12. Ibid. p. 91.

13. W. C. Handy, *Father of the Blues* (New York: The Macmillan Company, 1944), p. 35.

14. Ibid. pp. 35-6.

15. M. H. Winter, op. cit. p. 60.

CHAPTER 12

1. The feeling and the content of the spiritual—and other types of Negro song—are discussed in John Greenway's *American Folksongs of Protest* (Philadelphia: University of Pennsylvania Press, 1953).

2. J. W. Work, *American Negro Songs* (New York: Howell, Soskin & Company, 1940), p. 17.

3. Gilbert Chase, *America's Music* (New York: McGraw-Hill Book Company, 1955), p. 237.

4. Ernest Borneman, *A Critic Looks at Jazz* (London: Jazz Music Books, 1946), p. 42.

5. John A. Lomax and Alan Lomax, *Folk Song U.S.A.* (New York: Duell, Sloan & Pearce, 1947), p. 335.

6. H. G. Spaulding, 'Under the Palmetto,' *Continental Monthly* (August 1863), Vol. 4, No. 2, pp. 196-8.

7. *The Nation* (30 May 1867), Vol. 4, pp. 432-3.

8. From an address delivered by J. Miller McKim in Philadelphia in 1862, as quoted by W. F. Allen, C. P. Ware, and L. M. Garrison, *Slave Songs of the United States* (New York, 1867), p. xviii.

9. Colonel T. W. Higginson, 'Negro Spirituals,' *Atlantic Monthly* (June 1867), Vol. 19, p. 692.

10. Frances A. Kemble, *Journal of a Residence on a Georgian Plantation* (1838–1839) (New York: Harper & Brothers, 1864), p. 218.

11. Allen, Ware, and Garrison, op. cit. p. v.

12. Sterling Brown, 'Negro Folk Expression: Spirituals, Seculars, Ballads, and Work Songs,' *Phylon* (January-April 1953), p. 49.

13. John A. Lomax and Alan Lomax, op. cit. p. 334.

CHAPTER 13

1. Dr. B. D. Simms and Ernest Borneman, 'Ragtime, History, and Analysis,' *The Record Changer* (October 1945), Vol. 4, No. 8, p. 8.

CHAPTER 14

1. Langston Hughes, *The Big Sea* (New York: Alfred A. Knopf, 1945), p. 254.

2. Wilder Hobson, *American Jazz Music* (New York: W. W. Norton & Company, 1939), p. 101.

3. John A. Lomax and Alan Lomax, *Negro Folk-Songs as Sung by Lead Belly* (New York: The Macmillan Company, 1936), pp. xii-xiii.

4. Ibid. p. 11.

5. W. C. Handy, *Father of the Blues* (New York: The Macmillan Company, 1944), p. 184.

6. Ibid. p. 74.

7. Ibid. pp. 76-7.

8. Nat Shapiro and Nat Hentoff, *Hear Me Talkin' to Ya* (New York: Rinehart & Company, 1955), p. 93.

9. Louis Armstrong, *Swing That Music* (New York: Longmans, Green & Company, 1936), pp. 52-4

CHAPTER 15

1. Abel Green and Joe Laurie, Jr., *Show Biz from Vaude to Video* (New York: Henry Holt & Company, 1951), p. 317.

2. Paul Whiteman and Mary Margaret McBride, *Jazz* (New York: J. H. Sears & Company, 1926), p. 94.

3. Ibid. p. 104.

4. Lawrence Gilman, 'Music,' New York *Tribune*, 13 February 1924.

5. 'When Armstrong Came to New York,' *The Jazz Record*, 1 April 1943, No. 4, p. 4.

6. Jack Bland, 'The Kazoo Comes On,' *The Jazz Record*, 1 June 1943, No. 8, p. 3.

7. Bing Crosby, *Call Me Lucky* (New York: Simon & Schuster, 1953), p. 80.

8. Ibid. pp. 73, 75.

9. Nat Shapiro and Nat Hentoff, *Hear Me Talkin' to Ya* (New York: Rinehart & Company, 1955), p. 120.

10. Hoagy Carmichael, *The Stardust Road* (New York: Rinehart & Company, 1946), p. 42.

11. Ibid. pp. 6-7.

12. Ibid. p. 53.

13. Shapiro and Hentoff, op. cit. p. 116.

14. George Johnson, 'The Wolverines and Bix,' *Frontiers of Jazz*, edited by Ralph de Toledano (New York: Oliver Durrell, 1947), pp. 129, 131.

CHAPTER 16

1. Nat Shapiro and Nat Hentoff, *Hear Me Talkin' to Ya* (New York: Rinehart & Company, 1955), p. 282.

2. Langston Hughes, *The Big Sea* (New York: Alfred A. Knopf, 1945), p. 229.

3. Barry Ulanov, *Duke Ellington* (New York: Creative Age Press, 1946), p. 28. See also Charles Edward Smith, 'The Duke Steps Out,' *Jazz* (January 1943), Vol. 1, Nos. 5-6, p. 12.

4. Rudy Vallee, *Vagabond Dreams Come True* (New York: Grosset & Dunlap, 1930), pp. 163-4.

5. Langston Hughes, op. cit. p. 258.

6. Shapiro & Hentoff, op. cit. p. 238.

7. Ibid. p. 235.

8. Bing Crosby, *Call Me Lucky* (New York: Simon & Schuster, 1953), p. 50.

9. F. L. Allen, *The Big Change* (New York: Harper & Brothers, 1952), p. 184.

10. Shapiro and Hentoff, op. cit. pp. 295-6.

11. Dave E. Dexter, Jr., album notes, 'Kansas City Jazz,' Decca Records, Album A-214, p. 9.

12. Ibid. p. 2.

13. Shapiro and Hentoff, op. cit. p. 360.

14. Nat Hentoff, 'Jazz and the Intellectuals: Somebody Goofed,' *Chicago Review* (Fall 1955), Vol. 9, No. 3.

15. Hughes Panassié, *The Real Jazz* (New York: Smith & Durrell, 1942), pp. vii-viii.

CHAPTER 17

1. Benny Goodman, *The Kingdom of Swing* (Harrisburg: Stackpole Sons, 1939), p. 138.

2. Ibid. pp. 161-2.

3. Ibid. pp. 241-2.

4. Quoted from a talk given to the author's class at the New School during the fall of 1955.

5. Benny Goodman, op. cit. pp. 151-2.

6. As quoted in Shapiro and Hentoff, *Hear Me Talkin' to Ya* (New York: Rinehart & Company, 1955), p. 278.

7. Ibid. p. 278.

8. Benny Goodman, op. cit. p. 129.

9. Ibid. pp. 198-9.

10. Quoted from a talk given to the author's class at New York University in 1954.

11. Shapiro and Hentoff, op. cit. p. 304.

12. Ibid. p. 302.

13. In conversation with the author in 1952.

CHAPTER 18

1. 'Bop Will Kill Business unless It Kills Itself First,' *Down Beat,* 7 April 1948, p. 2.

2. Nat Shapiro and Nat Hentoff, *Hear Me Talkin' to Ya* (New York: Rinehart & Company, 1955), p. 340.

3. From a conversation at Cornell University during 1948.

4. Shapiro and Hentoff, op. cit. p. 346.

5. André Hodeir, *Hommes et problèmes du jazz* (Paris, 1954), p. 128; American edition: *Jazz: Its Evolution and Essence,* translated by David Noakes (New York: The Grove Press, 1956).

6. From the liner to 'Hampton Hawes Trio,' Contemporary Records LP C3505, quoted by Lester Koenig (26 August 1955).

7. Shapiro and Hentoff, op. cit. p. 354.

8. *Metronome* (June 1947), p. 16.

9. *Down Beat* (2 November 1955), p. 14.

10. In conversation with the author in 1948.

11. Leonard Feather, *The Encyclopedia of Jazz* (New York: Horizon Press, 1955), p. 30.

12. Hodeir, op. cit. p. 145.

13. *Metronome* (June 1955), p. 25.

14. *Down Beat* (11 August 1954), p. 8.

15. Shapiro and Hentoff, op. cit. pp. 396-7.

16. As quoted by Hal Holly (Charles Emge) in *Down Beat* (9 March 1955).

CHAPTER 19

1. Told to the author at Music Inn, Lenox, Massachusetts, during the summer of 1954.

2. The story of the Tico Tico dance comes from Mr. Gabriel Oller, proprietor of the Spanish Music Center, 1291 Sixth Avenue, New York City.

3. *Metronome* (January 1947), p. 46.

4. In conversation with the author in 1951.

CHAPTER 20

1. As quoted by W. T. Bartholomew, *Acoustics of Music* (New York: Prentice-Hall, 1946), p. 184.

CHAPTER 21

1. Quoted in M. J. Herskovits, *Man and His Works* (New York: Alfred A. Knopf, 1948), p. 436.
2. Ibid. p. 437.

CHAPTER 22

1. N. Curtis-Burlin, *Negro Folk Songs* (New York: Schirmer, 1918), pp. 9-10.
2. Milton Metfessel, *Phonophotography in Folk Music* (Chapel Hill: University of North Carolina Press, 1928).
3. Ibid. p. 135n.
4. Natalie Curtis, *Songs and Tales from the Dark Continent* (New York: Schirmer, 1920), p. 9.
5. Winthrop Sargeant, *Jazz: Hot and Hybrid* (New York: E. P. Dutton & Company, 1946), p. 160.

CHAPTER 23

1. From a letter to the author (18 January 1956).
2. From a letter to the author.
3. This, and much of the following material, was furnished to me by the staff of *The New York Times* while I was writing a piece (never published) for the Sunday Magazine.
4. *The New York Herald Tribune* (27 November 1952).
5. *The New York Times* (23 October 1953).
6. *The New York Times* (17 February 1952).
7. *St. Louis Post-Dispatch* (10 July 1955).
8. A. Truhlar, *Mlada Fronta* (25 December 1955).
9. *The New York Times* (1 January 1956).
10. *The New York Times* (2 September 1955).
11. *The Christian Science Monitor* (9 January 1956).
12. Clifton Daniel, *The New York Times Magazine* (17 April 1955).
13. Digested and translated in *The Current Digest of the Soviet Press* (28 December 1955), Vol. VII, No. 46, pp. 5-6, 11.
14. *Holiday* (June 1950).

15. *Down Beat* (18 June 1952).
16. *Down Beat* (4 June 1952).
17. *Down Beat* (4 November 1953).
18. *Down Beat* (27 January 1954).
19. *U.S. News & World Report* (2 December 1955), pp. 54ff.
20. *The New York Post* (3 October 1955).
21. *The New York Times* (6 November 1955).
22. From a letter to the author.
23. From a letter to the author.
24. *Down Beat* (27 January 1954).

CHAPTER 24

1. Norman M. Margolis, 'A Theory on the Psychology of Jazz,' *The American Imago*, Vol. II, No. 3 (Fall 1954), pp. 372-3. See also Aaron H. Esman, 'Jazz—A Study in Cultural Conflict,' *The American Imago*, Vol. VIII, No. 2 (1951), pp. 3-10.
2. *The New York Post* (16 February 1954), p. 28.
3. 'The Professional Dance Musician and His Audience,' *American Journal of Sociology* (September 1951), pp. 136-44.
4. Margolis, op. cit. p. 282.
5. *The Church Tower* (January 1956), pp. 30-32; reprinted from *The Intercollegian* (November 1955).
6. Nat Shapiro and Nat Hentoff, *Hear Me Talkin' to Ya* (New York: Rinehart & Company, 1955), p. 405.
7. In a letter to the author.

CHAPTER 25

1. 'Reflections on the History of Jazz,' Dr. S. I. Hayakawa of Illinois Institute of Technology in a privately printed 8-page pamphlet with a headnote reading: 'The following article was a Poetry Magazine Modern Arts Series lecture, given Saturday, March 17, 1945, at the Arts Club of Chicago . . .' p. 2.
2. 'Jazz: Resistance to the Diffusion of a Culture Pattern,' *Journal of Negro History* (October 1947), pp. 461-94.
3. Constance Rourke, *American Humor* (New York: Harcourt, Brace & Company, 1931), p. 79.
4. Bernard Wolfe, 'Uncle Remus and the Malevolent Rabbit,' *Commentary* (July 1949), p. 32.
5. Ibid. p. 41.
6. James Baldwin, *Notes of a Native Son* (Boston: The Beacon Press, 1955), p. 45.

7. Nat Shapiro and Nat Hentoff, *Hear Me Talkin' to Ya* (New York: Rinehart & Company, 1955), p. 17.
8. Ibid. p. 129.
9. Ibid. p. 291.

CHAPTER 26

1. In conversation with the author in August 1955.
2. In conversation with the author in July 1955.

Compiled by Robert George Reisner

BIOGRAPHIES AND AUTOBIOGRAPHIES

Allen, Walter C. and Brian A. L. Rust. *King Joe Oliver.* Belleville, New Jersey, Allen and Rust, 1955. 162 p. discography.

Antrim, Doron K., Paul Whiteman, Jimmy Dorsey, etc., give their secrets of dance band success, New York, Famous Stars Pub. Co., 1936. 87 p. illus.

Armitage, Merle, editor. *George Gershwin.* New York, Longmans, Green, 1938. 252 p.

Armstrong, Louis. *Satchmo.* New York, Prentice-Hall, 1954. 240 p. illus. Paperback ed. New York, Signet, 1955. 191 p. illus.

Armstrong, Louis, *Swing that Music.* New York, Longmans, Green, 1936. 136 p. illus.

Broonzy, William. *Big Bill Blues,* William Broonzy's story as told to Yannick Bruynoghe. London, Cassell, 1955. 139 p. illus. discography.

Carmichael, Hoagy. *The Stardust Road.* New York, Rinehart, 1946. 156 p. illus.

Condon, Eddie and Thomas Sugrue. *We Called It Music.* New York, Holt, 1947. 341 p. illus. discography.

Crosby, Bing and Pete Martin. *Call Me Lucky.* New York, Simon & Schuster, 1953. 344 p. illus. Paperback ed. New York, Pocket Books, Inc., 1954. 309 p. illus.

Crosby, Ted. *The Story of Bing Crosby.* Cleveland, World Pub. Co., 1946. 239 p. illus. discography.

Eaton, Jeanette. *Trumpeter's Tale: The Story of Young Louis Armstrong.* New York, Morrow, 1955. 191 p. illus.

Ewen David. *A Journey to Greatness: The life and music of George Gershwin.* New York, Holt, 1956. 384 p. illus. discography.

Ewen, David. *Men of Popular Music.* 2nd ed. New York, Prentice-Hall, 1949. 213 p. illus. discography. (1st ed., Ziff-Davis, 1944.)

Ewen, David. *The Story of George Gershwin.* New York, Holt, 1943. 211 p. illus. discography.

Ewen, David. *The Story of Irving Berlin.* New York, Holt, 1950. 179 p. illus.

Goffin, Robert. *Horn of Plenty: The Story of Louis Armstrong.* New York, Allen, Towne & Heath, 1947. 304 p. illus. (French ed. Louis Armstrong, *Le Roi du jazz.* Paris, P. Seghers, 1947. 304 p. illus.)

Goldberg, Isaac. *George Gershwin, A Study in American Music.* New York, Simon & Schuster, 1931. 305 p. illus.

Goodman, Benny and Irving Kolodin. *The Kingdom of Swing.* Harrisburg, Stackpole, 1939. 265 p. illus.

Graham, Alberta P. *Strike Up the Band! Bandleaders of Today.* New York, Nelson, 1949. 160 p.

Handy, William C. *Father of the Blues; An Autobiography.* New York, Macmillan, 1941. 317 p. illus.

Harrison, Max. *Charlie Parker.* Cranbury, A.S. Barnes. 1961. 84 p. illus.

Holiday, Billie with Bill Dufty. *Lady Sings the Blues.* New York, Doubleday, 1956. 250 p. illus.

Horne, Lena. *In Person, Lena Horne;* as told to Helen Arstein and Carlton Moss. New York, Greenberg, 1950. 249 p. illus.

Hughes, Langston. *The Big Sea: An Autobiography.* New York. Knopf, 1945. 335 p.

James, Burnett. *Bix Beiderbecke.* Cranbury, A.S. Barnes. 1961. 90 p. illus.

Kahn, Ely J. *The Voice.* New York, Harper, 1947. 125 p. illus.

Kaminsky, Max, and V. E. Hughes. *My Life in Jazz.* New York, Harper, 1963. 242 p. illus.

Lambert, G. E. *Duke Ellington.* Cranbury, A. S. Barnes. 88 p. illus.

Lomax, Alan. *Mister Jelly Roll.* New York, Duell, Sloan and Pearce, 1950. 318 p. illus. discography. (Reprinted: New York, Grove Press, 1956.)

Lyttelton, Humphrey. *I Play as I Please.* London, MacGibbon & Kee, 1954. 200 p. illus.

Manone, Wingy and Paul Vandervoort. *Trumpet on the Wing.* Garden City, N. Y., Doubleday, 1948. 256 p. illus. discography

McCarthy, Albert. *Louis Armstrong.* Cranbury, A. S. Barnes. 1961. 85 p. illus.

Mezzrow, Milton and Bernard Wolfe. *Really the Blues.* New York, Random House, 1946. 388 p. Paperback ed. New York, Dell, n.d. 384 p.

Mize, John T. H. *Bing Crosby and the Bing Crosby Style: Crosbyana thru biography, photography, discography.* Chicago, *Who's Who in Music,* 1948. 174 p. illus.

Oliver, Paul. *Bessie Smith.* Cranbury, A. S. Barnes. 1962. 88 p.

Ortiz Oderigo, Néstor R. *Perfiles del jazz.* Buenos Aires, Ricordi Americana, 1955. 189 p.

Panassié, Hugues. *Louis Armstrong.* Paris, Éditions du Belvédère, 1947. 107 p. illus. discography.

Panassié, Hugues. *Les Rois du jazz, notes biographiques et critiques sur les principaux musiciens de jazz.* Genève, C. Grasset, 1944. 2 v. 252 p.

Preston, Denis. *Mood Indigo* [Duke Ellington]. Egham, Surrey, Eng., Citizen Press, 1946. 84 p.

Ray, Harry. *Les Grandes Figures du jazz.* Brussels, Les Cahiers Selection, 1945. 46 p.

Robinson, Julien L. *Band Leaders,* by Julien Vedey [pseud.]. London, Rockliff, 1950. 202 p. illus.

Shaw, Artie. *The Trouble with Cinderella.* New York, Farrar, Straus and Young, 1952. 394 p.

Spellman, A. B. *Four Lives in the Bebop Business.* New York, Pantheon, 1966. 241 p.

Trazegnies, Jean de. *Duke Ellington.* Brussels, Hot Club de Belgique, 1946. 80 p. illus.

Ulanov, Barry. *Duke Ellington.* New York, Creative Age, 1946. 322 p. illus. discography. (Spanish ed. Buenos Aires, Editorial Estuardo, 1946. 400 p.)

Ulanov, Barry. *The Incredible Crosby.* New York, Whittlesey House, 1948. 336 p. illus. discography.

Vallée, Rudy. *Vagabond Dreams Come True.* New York, Dutton, 1930. 262 p. illus.

Waters, Ethel and Charles Samuels. *His Eye Is on the Sparrow.* Garden City, N. Y., Doubleday, 1951. 278 p. illus. Paperback ed. New York, Bantam, 1952, 342 p.

Williams, Martin. *Jelly Roll Morton.* Cranbury, A. S. Barnes. 1962. 88 p.

Woollcott, Alexander. *The Story of Irving Berlin.* New York, Putnam, 1925. 237 p. illus. discography.

DISCOGRAPHIES

Aasland, Benny H. *The 'Wax Works' of Duke Ellington.* Stockholm, Foliotryck, 1954. n.p. discography.

Blackstone, Orin. *Index to Jazz.* New Orleans, Gordon Gullickson, 1947. 4 v.

Carey, Dave and Albert McCarthy. *The Directory of Recorded Jazz and Swing Music.* Fordingbridge, Hampshire [Eng.], Delphic Press, 1949–   . v. 1-3.

Delaunay, Charles. *Hot Discography.* Paris, Hot Jazz, 1936. 271 p.

same 1938. 408 p. *Hot Discographie*. Paris, Hot Jazz, 1943. 540 p. *Hot Discography*. 1940 ed. New York, Commodore Record Co., 1943. 416 p.

Delaunay, Charles. *Hot Discographie encyclopédique*, 1951– Avec la collaboration de Kurt Mohr. Paris, Éditions Jazz disques, 1952?–

Delaunay, Charles, *New Hot Discography*, ed. by Walter E. Schaap & George Avakian. New York, Criterion, 1948, 608 p.

Lange, Horst H. *Die Deutsche Jazz-Discographie*. Berlin, Ed. Bote & G. Bock, 1955. 651 p.

Mello, Edward J. and Tom McBride. *Crosby on Record, 1926–1950*. San Francisco, Mello's Music, 1950. 101 p. illus.

Mohr, Kurt. *Discographie du jazz*. Geneva, Vuagnat, 1945. 84 p. discography.

Møller, Børge J. C. *Dansk Jazz Discography*. Copenhagen, Artum Musikforlag, 1945. 94 p.

Møller, Børge J. C. *Parlophone Bio-Discografi*. Copenhagen, A/S L. Irich's Bogtrykkeri, 1946. 64 p.

Nicolausson, Harry. *Svensk jazzdiskografi*. Stockholm, Nordiska musikförlaget [1953]. 115 p.

Panassié, Hugues. *Discographie critique des meilleurs disques de jazz, 1920–1951*. Paris, Corrêa, 1951. 371 p.

Panassié, Hugues. *Histoire des disques swing*. Geneva, Ch. Grasset, 1944. 117 p. discography.

Panassié, Hugues. *Petit guide pour une discothèque de jazz*. Paris, R. Laffont, 1955. 147 p.

Pensoneault, Ken and Carl Sarles. *Jazz Discography*. New York, The Needle, 1944. 145 p.

Ramsey, Frederic, Jr. *A Guide to Longplay Jazz Records*. New York, Long Player Publications, 1954. 263 p. illus.

Schleman, Hilton R. *Rhythm on Record*. London, Melody Maker, 1936. 333 p. illus. discography.

Schwanniger, A. and A. Gurwitch. *Swing Discographie*. Genève, Grasset, 1945. 200 p.

Smith, Charles E. and Frederic Ramsey, Jr. and others. *The Jazz Record Book*. New York, Smith & Durrel, 1942. 515 p. illus.

Wante, Stephen and Walter De Block. *V-Disc Catalogue*. Antwerp, Willem Van Laerstraat, n.d. 83 p.

Wilson, John, S. *Collector's Jazz, Traditional and Swing*. Philadelphia, Lippincott, 1958. 318 p.

Woodward, Woody. *Jazz Americana*. Los Angeles, Trend Books, 1956. 128 p. illus. discography.

ENCYCLOPEDIAS & OTHER REFERENCE WORKS

Allen, Stuart S. *Stars of Swing*. London, British Yearbooks, 1947.

76 p. illus. discography.

American Society of Composers, Authors and Publishers. *The ASCAP biographical dictionary of composers, authors and publishers.* New York, Crowell, 1952. 636 p.

Bannister, Lawrence H. *International Jazz Collectors' Directory.* Worcestershire, Bannister, 1948. 76 p.

Berendt, Joachim E. *Jazz Optisch.* Munich, Nymphenburger Verlagshandlung, 1945. 72 p. illus.

Burley, Dan. *Dan Burley's Original Handbook of Harlem.* New York, 1944. 158 p. illus.

Burton, Jack. *Blue Book of Tin Pan Alley.* Watkins Glen, N. Y., Century House, 1951. 520 p. illus.

Claxton, William. *Jazz West Coast: A Portfolio of Photographs.* Hollywood, Calif., Linear Productions, 1955. unpaged. illus.

Down Beat. Bouquets to the Living. Chicago, Down Beat Pub. Co., 195-. 32 p. illus.

Egg, Bernhard. *Jazz-fremdwörterbuch.* Leipzig, W. Ehrler, 1927. 47 p. illus.

Feather, Leonard. *The Encyclopedia of Jazz.* (rev. ed.) with *Encyclopedia of Jazz in the Sixties.* New York, Horizon Press, 1966.

Gold, Robert. *Jazz Lexicon.* New York, Knopf, 1964. 363 p.

Handy, William C. and Abbe Niles. *A Treasury of the Blues.* New York, C. Boni, 1949. 258 p. illus. (First ed. pub. in 1926 under title: *Blues, An Anthology.*)

Heerkens, A. *Jazz: Picture Encyclopedia.* Alkmaar, Holland, Arti [1954?]. 64 p. illus. (Text in Dutch, English, French, & German.)

Jackson, Edgar and Leonard Hibbs. *Encyclopedia of Swing.* London, The Decca Record Co., 1941. 83 p.

The Jazzfinder; containing permanent reference material. New Orleans, 1949. 152 p. illus.

Kristensen, Sven Møller and John Jørgensen, Erik Wiedemann, Børge Roger Henrichsen. *Jazzens Hvem, Hvad, Hvor: Politikens Jazzleksikon.* København, Politikens forlag, 1953. 384 p. illus.

Laade, Wolfgang and W. Ziefle, D. Zimmerle. *Jazz-Lexikon.* Stuttgart, G. Hatje, 1953. 186 p. illus.

Merriam, Alan P. *A Bibliography of Jazz.* Philadelphia, American Folklore Society, 1954. 145 p. (With the assistance of Robert J. Benford.)

Miller, Paul Eduard, editor. *Down Beat's Yearbook of Swing 1939.* Chicago, Down Beat Pub. Co., 1939. illus. discography.

Miller, Paul Eduard. *Miller's Yearbook of Popular Music.* Chicago, PEM Pub., 1943. 195 p. illus. discography.

Noble Peter, editor. *Yearbook of Jazz, an Illustrated 'Who's Who' of Jazz Personalities.* London, The Citizen Press, 1945. 99 p. illus.

Panassié, Hugues and Madeleine Gautier. *Dictionnaire du jazz.* Paris,

R. Laffont, 1954. 366 p. illus.

Poole, Gene. *Enciclopedia de swing*. Buenos Aires, Academia Americana, 1939. 92 p.

Reisner, Robert George. *The Literature of Jazz, A Preliminary Bibliography*. New York, New York Public Library, 1954. 53 p.

Rose, Al, Edmond Souchon. *New Orleans Jazz: A Family Album*. Baton Rouge, La. State. 1967.

Shelly, Low, editor. *Hepcats Jive Talk Dictionary*. Derby, T.W.O. Charles, 1945. 50 p.

Ténot, F. *Dictionnaire du Jazz*. New York, Larousse, 1967. 256 p. illus.

Testoni, Gian Carlo and Arrigo Polillo, Giuseppe Barazzetta, Roberto Leydi Pino Maffei. *Enciclopedia del jazz*. Milano, Messaggerie Musicali, 1953. 500 p. illus. discography.

Treadwell, Bill. *Big Book of Swing*. New York, Cambridge House. 1946. 130 p. illus.

THEORY, HISTORY, AND CRITICISM

American Jazz Annual 1956 (Newport Edition). New York, Hemisphere Press, 1956. 98 p. illus.

Arntzenius, Louis M. G. *Amerikaansche Kunstindrukken*. Amsterdam, A. de Lange, 1927. 190 p. illus.

Back, Jack. *Triumph des Jazz*. Vienna, Alfa-Edition, 1949. 239 p. illus.

Baresel, Alfred. *Das Jazz-Buch*. Leipzig, J. H. Zimmermann, 1926. 34 p. illus.

Baresel, Alfred. *Das neue Jazzbuch*. Leipzig, J. H. Zimmermann, 1929. 98 p. illus.

Berendt, Joachim E. *Der Jazz; eine zeitkritische Studie*. Stuttgart, Deutsche Verlags-Anstalt, 1950. 96 p.

Berendt, Joachim E. *Das Jazzbuch*. Frankfurt, Fischer Bücherei, 1953. 237 p. illus. discography.

Berendt, Joachim. *New Jazz Book*. (tr. by Dan Morgenstern.) rev. ed. New York, Hill & Wang, 1970. 314 p.

Bergh, Øivind. *Moderne Dansemusikk*. Oslo, Musikk-Huset, 1945. 146 p. illus.

Bernhard, Edmond and Jacques de Vergnies. *Apologie du jazz*. Bruxelles: Les Presses de Belgique, 1945. 234 p. discography.

Bernhard, Paul. *Jazz, eine musikalische Zeitfrage*. München, Delphin-Verlag, 1927. 109 p. illus.

Bettonville, Albert. *Paranoia du jazz*. Brussels, Cahiers du Jazz, 1939. 40 p.

Biedermann, Felix. *Jazz, Wiener Roman*. Wien, E. Strache, 1925. 325 p. (Author's pseud., Felix Dormann, at head of title.)

Blesh, Rudi. *Shining Trumpets, a History of Jazz*. New York, Knopf, 1946. 365 p. illus. discography.

Blesh, Rudi and Harriet Janis. *They All Played Ragtime*. (rev. ed.)

New York, Oak, 1966. 347 p. illus. discography.

Bohlander, Carlo. *Das Wesen der Jazzmusik.* Frankfurt a/M., Grahl & Niclas, 1954. illus.

Borneman, Ernest. *A Critic Looks at Jazz.* London, Jazz Music Books, 1946, 53 p.

Bouvier-Ajam, Maurice. *Connaissance du jazz.* Paris, Durand, 1952. 43 p. illus.

Bragaglia, Anton G. *Jazz Band.* Milano, Edizioni 'Corbaccio,' 1929. 291 p. illus.

Brunn, Harry O. *Story of the Original Dixieland Jazz Band.* Baton Rouge, La. State, 1961. 268 p.

Burian, E. F. *Jazz.* Praha, Aventinium, 1928. 208 p.

Caraceni, Augusto, *Il jazz delle origini ad oggi.* Milano, Edizioni Suvini Zerboni, 1937. 179 p. illus. discography. (Reprinted: *Jazz.* Roma, Zampardi 1945. 173 p.)

Cerri, Livio. *Antologia del jazz.* Pisa, Nistri-Lischi, 1955. 353 p. illus.

Cerri, Livio. *Jazz, musica d'oggi.* Milano, R. Malfasi, 1948. 269 p. illus.

Coeuroy, André. *Histoire générale du jazz; strette, hot, swing.* Paris, Éditions Denoël, 1942. 256 p. discography.

Coeuroy, André and André Schaeffner. *Le Jazz.* Paris, C. Aveline, 1926. 150 p.

Columbia Records. *The History of Jazz on the Columbia Records.* Tokyo, Nippon Columbia Co., 194-. 185 p. illus. Text in Japanese.

Condon, Eddie and Richard Gehman, editors. *Eddie Condon's Treasury of Jazz.* New York, Dial, 1956.

Cosmetto, Cléon. *La Vraie Musique de jazz.* Lausanne, J.-F. Chastellain, 1945. 49 p. illus.

Criel, Gaston. *Swing: présentation de Jean Cocteau et Charles Delaunay.* Paris, Éditions Universitaires Françaises, 1948. 91 p. illus.

David, Jean. *Le Jazz et les hommes d'aujourdhui.* Brussels, Éditions de l'Onyx, 1946. 80 p.

Deitch, Gene. *The Cat.* New York, The Record Changer, 1948. 32 p. 46 cartoons. (Commentary by George Avakian.)

Delaunay, Charles. *De la Vie, et du jazz.* Lausanne, Éditions de l'echiquier, 1939. 70 p.

De Toledano, Ralph, editor. *Frontiers of Jazz.* 2nd ed. New York, Ungar, 1962. 178 p.

Dexter, Dave, *Jazz Cavalcade.* New York, Criterion, 1946. 258 p. illus.

Dexter, Dave. *Jazz Story.* New York, Prentice-Hall, 1964. 176 p. illus.

Dorigné, Michel. *La Guerre du jazz.* Paris, E. Buckner, 1948. 151 p. illus.

duPont, Jean. *Introduction à la musique de jazz.* Vaucluse, France, 1945. 90 p.

Edwards, Paul. *Notions élémentaires sur le jazz.* Liège, Club de

Belgique, 1945. 75 p.

Enefer, Douglas S. *Jazz in Black and White*. London, Alliance Press, 1945. 63 p.

Esquire's Jazz Book, 1944–1947. New York, Smith & Durrell, 1944–7. 4 v. illus. discography.

Esquire's World of Jazz. ed. by William Hayes. New York, Grosset, 1962. 224 p. illus.

Feather, Leonard. *Inside Be-bop*. New York, J. J. Robbins, 1949. 103 p. illus. discography.

Ferand, Ernst T. *Die Improvisation in der Musik*. Zurich, Rhein-Verlag, 1938. 464 p. illus.

Finkelstein, Sidney. *Jazz: A People's Music*. New York, Citadel, 1948. 278 p. illus. discography. (German ed. *Jazz*. [Aus dem Amerikanischen ubertragen von Elke Kaspar] Stuttgart, G. Hatje, 1951. 200 p. illus.)

Frankenstein, Alfred. *Syncopating Saxophones*. Chicago, R. O. Ballou, 1925. 103 p. illus.

Gilbert, Douglas. *Lost Chords, the Diverting Story of American Popular Songs*. Garden City, N. Y., Doubleday, 1942. 377 p.

Gilbert, Will G. *Rumbamuziek, Volksmuziek van de Midden-Amerikaansche Negers*. 's-Gravenhage, J. P. Kruseman [1947?] 119 p. illus.

Gilbert, Will G. and C. Poustochkine. *Jazzmuziek*. 's-Gravenhage, J. P. Kruseman, 1939. 116 p. illus.

Gilbert, Will G. and C. Poustochkine. *Jazzmuziek, inleiding tot de Volksmuziek der Noord-Amerikaanse Negers*. Den Haag, J. P. Kruseman [1948?] 142 p. illus.

Gitler, I. *Jazz Masters of the Forties*. New York, Macmillan, 1966. 290 p.

Goffin, Robert. *Aux Frontières du jazz*. Paris, Éditions du Sagittaire, 1932. 256 p. illus.

Goffin, Robert. *Jazz, from the Congo to the Metropolitan*. Garden City, N. Y., Doubleday, 1944. 254 p. (French ed. *Histoire du jazz*. Montreal, Parizeau, 1945. 337 p.)

Goffin, Robert. *Nouvelle Histoire du jazz*. Bruxelles, L'Écran du monde, 1948. 334 p. illus.

Goffin, Robert. *La Nouvelle-Orléans, capitale du jazz*. New York, Éditions de la Maison française, 1946. 269 p.

Goffin, Robert and Charles Delaunay, editors. *Jazz '47*. Paris, Intercontinental du livre, 1947. 76 p. illus.

Goldberg, Isaac. *Jazz Music, What It Is and How To Understand It*. Girard, Kansas, Haldeman-Julius, 1927. 64 p.

Goldberg, Isaac. *Tin Pan Alley*. New York, John Day, 1930. 341 p. illus.

Goldberg, Joe. *Jazz Masters of the Fifties*. New York, Macmillan, 1966. 246 p.

Grossman, William L. and Jack W. Farrell. *The Heart of Jazz*. New York, New York University Press, 1955.

Guinle, Jorge. *Jazz Panorama*. Rio de Janeiro, Livraria Agir Editôia, 1953. 184 p. illus.

Hadlock, Richard. *Jazz Masters of the Twenties*. New York, Macmillan, 1965. 255 p.

Hame, Olli. *Rytmin Voittokulku-Kirja Tanssimusükista*. Helsinki, Frazier's Musicstore, 1949. 222 p.

Harris, Rex. *Jazz*. Harmondsworth, Middlesex, Penguin Books, 1952. 224 p. illus. (Expanded: *Jazz*. New York, Grosset & Dunlap, 1955. 280 p. discography.)

Helander, Olle. *Jazzens väg en bok om blues och stomps, deras upphovsmän och utövare*. Stockholm, Nordiska musikförlaget, 1947. 346 p. illus. discography.

Heuvelmans, Bernard. *De la Bamboula au be-bop; esquisse de l'évolution de la musique de jazz*. Paris, Éditions de la Main' jetée, 1951. 193 p.

Hibbs, Leonard. *21 Years of Swing Music on Brunswick Records*. London, A. White, 1937. 80 p. illus.

Hirsch, Arthur Z., Jr. *Black and Tan Fantasy* (The Sociology of Jazz Music). 1946. (Manuscript Copy in Schomburg Collection of The New York Public Library.)

Hobson, Wilder. *American Jazz Music*. New York, W. W. Norton, 1939. 230 p. illus. discography.

Hodeir, André. *Hommes et problèmes du jazz*. Paris, Au Portulan, chez Flammarion, 1954. 412 p. illus. discography. (English trans: *Jazz, Its Evolution and Essence*. New York, Grove, 1956. 295 p. discography.)

Hodeir, André. *Introduction à la musique de jazz*. Paris, Libraire Larousse, 1948. 128 p.

Hodeir, André. *Le Jazz, cet inconnu*. Paris, Collection Harmoniques, 1945. 220 p. discography.

Howe, Martin. *Blue Jazz*. Bristol, Perpetua Press, 1934. 33 p.

Hughes, Langston. *The First Book of Jazz*. New York, F. Watts, 1955. 65 p. illus. discography.

Le Jazz. Souillac (Lot) Mulhouse, 1952. 47 p. illus. discography. (*Le Point;* revue artistique et litteraire, 40).

Jazzways: a Year Book of Hot Music. v. 1, ed. by G. S. Rosenthal. Cincinnati, 1946. 120 p. illus. discography.

Johnson, Frank and Ron Wills, editors. *Jam;* An Annual of Swing Music. Sydney, New South Wales, Tempo Pub., Co., 1938. v. 1 48 p. illus.

Jones, Le Roi. *Black Music*. New York, Morrow, 1967. (paper ed. New York, Apollo). illus.

Jones, Max, editor. *Jazz Photo Album*. London, British Yearbooks, 1947. 96 p. illus.

Keepnews, Orrin and Bill Grauer. *A Pictorial History of Jazz*. New York, Crown, 1955. 282 p. illus.

Keil, Charles. *Urban Blues*. Chicago, Univ. of Chicago, 1966. 231 p.

illus.

Koebner, Franz W. *Jazz und Shimmy*. Berlin, Eysler, 1921. 122 p. illus.

Kristensen, Sven Møller. *Hvad Jazz Er*. København, E. Munksgaard, 1938. 94 p. illus.

Kristensen, Sven Møller. *Jazzen og dens Problemer*. København, Athenaem, 1946. 120 p. illus.

Lang, Iain. *Background of the Blues*. London, Workers Music Association, 1943. 55 p. discography.

Lang Iain. *Jazz in Perspective; the Background of the Blues*. London, Hutchinson, 1947. 148 p. illus. discography. (Italian ed. *Il jazz*. Trans. by Roberto Leydi.)

Legrand, Gérard. *Puissances du jazz*. [Paris] Arcanes, 1953. 218p. illus.

Leonard, Neil. *Jazz and the White Americans*. Chicago, Univ. of Chicago 1962. 215 p.

Levi, Ezio and Gian Carlo Testoni. *Introduzione alla vera musica di jazz*. Milano, Edizione Magazzino musicale, 1938. 115 p. discography.

Lucas, John. *Basic Jazz on Long Play*. Northfield, Minnesota, Carleton Jazz Club, 1954. 103 p. discography.

McCarthy, Albert, editor. *Jazzbook 1947*. London, Nicholson & Watson, 1948. 171 p. illus.

McCarthy, Albert, editor. *Jazzbook 1955*. London, Cassell, 1955. 173 p. illus.

McCarthy, Albert, editor. *PL Jazzbook 1946*. London, Nicholson & Watson, 1946. 188 p. illus.

McCarthy, Albert. *The Trumpet in Jazz*. London, The Citizen Press, 1945. 82 p. illus. discography.

McCarthy, Albert and others. *Jazz on Record: The First Fifty Years 1917–1967*. New York, Oak, 1968. 416 p.

McRae, Barry. *Jazz Cataclysm*. Cranbury, A. S. Barnes. 1967. 184 p.

Mendl, Robert W. S. *The Appeal of Jazz*. London, P. Allan, 1927. 186 p. illus.

Metronome Yearbook. New York, Metronome, 1950, 1951. 1953–6.

Nelson, Stanley R. *All About Jazz*. London, Heath, Cranton, 1934. 190 p. illus.

Newport Jazz Festival 1955. Program. n.p., J. Willaumez, 1955. 97 p. illus. (note: succeeding issues expected annually.)

Niemoeller, Adolp F. *The Story of Jazz*. Girard, Kansas, Haldeman-Julius Publications, 1946. 32 p.

Noble, Peter. *Transatlantic Jazz, A Short History of American Jazz*. London, The Citizen Press, 1945. 96 p. illus. discography.

Oliver, Paul. *Meaning of the Blues*. New York, Collier, 1963. 383 p.

Ortiz Oderigo, Néstor R. *Estetica del jazz*. Buenos Aires, Ricordi

Americana, 1951. 203 p. discography.

Ortiz Oderigo, Néstor R. *Historia del jazz*. Buenos Aires, Ricordi Americana [1952] 285 p.

Osgood, Henry O. *So This Is Jazz*. Boston, Little, Brown, 1926. 258 p. illus.

Panassié, Hugues. *Douze Années de jazz (1927–1938) souvenirs*. Paris, Corrêa, 1946. 281 p. illus.

Panassié, Hugues. *Hot Jazz*. New York, M. Witmark, 1936. 363 p. discography. (English trans. of *Le Jazz hot*.)

Panassié, Hugues. *Le Jazz hot*. Paris, Corrêa, 1934. 432 p. illus. discography.

Panassié, Hugues. *Jazz panorama*. Paris, Deux Rives, 1950. 283 p. discography.

Panassié, Hugues. *The Real Jazz*. New York, Smith & Durrell, 1942. 326 p. discography. (Condensed as: *La Musique de jazz et le swing*. Paris, Corrêa, 1945. 172 p. discography. Reprinted as: *La Véritable Musique de jazz*. Paris, R. Laffont, 1946. 298 p. illus. discography.)

Patanè, Giuseppe. *Be-bop ou pas be-bop? Ou, A la decouverte du jazz*. Genève, Éditions Sabaudia, 1951. 130 p. illus.

Peck, Ira, ed. *New Sound, Yes*. New York, Four Winds, 1966. 133 p. illus.

Porto, Sergio. *Pequena história do jazz*. Rio de Janeiro, Ministério da Educação e Saúde, Serviço de Documentação [1953] 117 p. illus. discography.

Ramsey, Frederic, Jr. and Charles Edward Smith, editors. *Jazzmen*. New York, Harcourt, Brace, 1939. 360 p. illus.

Sargeant, Winthrop. *Jazz: Hot and Hybrid*. New York, Dutton, 1946. 287 p. revised ed. illus. discography.

Schuller, Gunther. *Early Jazz: Its Roots and Musical Development*. New York, Oxford. 1968. 401 p.

Schwerké, Irving. *Kings Jazz and David (Jazz et David rois)*. Paris, Privately printed by Les Presses Modernes, 1927. 259 p.

Shapiro, Nat and Nat Hentoff, editors. *Hear Me Talkin' to Ya*. New York, Rinehart, 1955. 432 p.

Simon, George T. *Big Bands*. New York, Roy Pub., 1963. 93 p.

Skaarup, Victor and Martin Goldstein. *Jazz*. Copenhagen, E. Pedersen, 1934. 128 p.

Slawe, Jan. *Einführung in die Jazzmusik*. Basel, Verlag National-Zeitung, 1948. 135 p.

Smith, Hugh L., Jr. *The Literary Manifestation of a Liberal Romanticism in American Jazz*. Albuquerque, University of New Mexico (doctoral dissertation) 1955.

Soby, Olaf. *Jazz Kontra Europaeisk Musikkultur*. Copenhagen, Levin and Munksgaard, 1935. 96 p.

Sonner, Rudolf. *Musik und Tanz; Vom Kulttanz zum Jazz.* Leipzig, Quelle and Meyer, 1930. 124 p.

Spaeth, Sigmund. *A History of Popular Music in America.* New York, Random House, 1948. 729 p.

Specht, Paul L. *How They Became Name Bands.* New York, Fine Arts Publications, 1941. 175 p. illus.

Thoorens, Leon. *Essai sur le jazz.* Liege, L'Horizon Nouveau, 1942. 36 p.

Trienes, Walter. *Musik in Gefahr.* Regensburg, G. Bosse, 1940. 150 p. illus.

Twittenhoff, Wilhelm. *Jugend und Jazz; ein Beitrag zur Klärung.* Mainz, Verlag Junge Musik [1953] 134 p.

Ulanov, Barry. *A History of Jazz in America.* New York, Viking, 1952. 382 p.

Vaal, Hans de. *Jazz: van Oerwoudrhythme tot Hollywoodsymphonie.* Amsterdam, J. van Campen, 194-. 90 p. illus.

Vémane, Henri. *Swing et moeurs.* Lille, Editions des Marchenelles, 1943. 31 p.

Vica, Carl. *Du Classicisme au jazz.* Paris, Marcel Vigne, 1933.

Von Haupt, Lois. *Jazz: An Historical and Analytical Study.* New York, New York University Graduate School, 1945. 131 type-written pages. illus. Thesis (M.A.).

Walles, Erik. *Jazzen Anfaller.* Stockholm, Natur och kultur, 1946. 128 p. illus. discography.

Whiteman, Paul and Leslie Lieber. *How To Be a Bandleader.* New York, McBride, 1941. 144 p. illus. discography.

Whiteman, Paul and Mary Margaret McBride. *Jazz.* New York, J. H. Sears, 1926. 298 p. illus.

Willems, Edgar. *Le Jazz et l'oreille musicale; étude psychologique.* Genève, Editions 'Pro musica,' 1945. 48 p.

Williams, Martin T. *The Jazz Tradition.* New York, Oxford U. P., 1970. 250 p.

Williams, Martin T., ed. *The Art of Jazz.* New York, Oxford U. P., 1959. 256 p. illus.

Williams, Martin T. *Jazz Masters of New Orleans.* New York, Macmillan, 1967. 287 p.

Williams, Martin, ed. *Jazz Panorama.* New York, Macmillan, 1962. 287 p.

Wilson, John S. *Jazz: The Transition Years, 1940–1960.* New York, (Appleton) Meredith, 1966. 185 p. illus.

Witmark, Isidore and Isaac Goldberg. *The Story of the House of Witmark: from Ragtime to Swingtime.* New York, L. Furman, 1939. 480 p. illus.

JAZZ FICTION

Allen, Steve. *Bop Fables.* New York, Simon & Schuster, 1955. 68 p.

illus.

Baker, Dorothy. *Young Man with a Horn*. New York, Houghton, Mifflin, 1938. 243 p. Paperback ed. New York, Penguin, 1945. 184 p. also New York, New American Library.

Bontemps, Arna. *Lonesome Boy*. Boston, Houghton, Mifflin, 1955. 28 p. illus.

Borneman, Ernest. *Tremolo*. New York, Harper, 1948. 224 p.

Burlin, Natalie (Curtis). *Hampton Series Negro Folksongs*. New York, G. Schirmer, 1918–19. 4 v.

Burlin, Natalie (Curtis). *Songs and Tales from the Dark Continent*. New York, Schirmer, 1920. 170 p. illus.

Chase, Gilbert. *America's Music*. New York, McGraw-Hill, 1955. 733 p.

Courlander, Harold. *Haiti Singing*. Chapel Hill, The University of North Carolina, 1939. 273 p. illus.

Doerflinger, William M. *Shantymen and Shantyboys; Songs of the Sailor and Lumberman*. New York, Macmillan, 1951. 374 p. illus.

Georgia Writers Project. Works Projects Administration. Savannah Unit. *Drums and Shadows; Survival Studies among the Georgia Coastal Negroes*. Athens, University of Georgia Press, 1940. 274 p. illus.

Green, Abel and Joe Laurie. *Show Biz, From Vaude to Video*. New York, Holt, 1951. 613 p.

Greenway, John. *American Folk Songs of Protest*. Philadelphia, University of Pennsylvania, 1953. 348 p. discography.

Herskovits, Melville J. *Dahomey*. New York, J. J. Augustin, 1938. 2 v. illus.

Herskovits, Melville J. *Man and His Works*. New York, Knopf, 1948. 678 p.

Herskovits, Melville J. *The Myth of the Negro Past*. New York, Harper, 1941. 374 p.

Herskovits, Melville J. and Frances S. *Suriname Folk-lore*. New York, Columbia University Press, 1936. 766 p. illus.

Herskovits, Melville J. and Frances S. *Trinidad Village*. New York, Knopf, 1947. 351 p. illus.

Jackson, George P. *White and Negro Spirituals*. New York, J. J. Augustin, 1943. 349 p.

Johnson, James Weldon. *God's Trombones; Seven Negro Sermons in Verse*. New York, Viking, 1927. 56 p. illus.

Johnson, James Weldon, ed. *Books of American Negro Spirituals*. 2 v. in 1. New York, Viking, 1940. 187 p. 189 p.

Krehbiel, Henry E. *Afro-American Folksongs*. New York, Schirmer, 1914. 176 p. illus.

Landeck, Beatrice. *Echoes of African Folk Songs of the Americas*. rev. ed., New York, McKay, 1969. 184 p.

Locke, Alain. *The Negro and His Music*. Port Washington, Kennikat, 1936. 142 p.

Lomax, John A. and Alan Lomax. *Folk Song: U.S.A.* New York, Duell, Sloan & Pearce, 1947. 407 p.

Metfessel, Milton. *Phonophotography in Folk Music.* Chapel Hill, University of North Carolina Press, 1928. 181 p. illus.

Odum, Howard W. and Guy B. Johnson. *Negro Workaday Songs.* Chapel Hill, University of North Carolina, 1926. 278 p.

Ortiz Fernández, Fernando. *La Africania de la musica folklorica de Cuba.* Habana, Ministerio de Educación, Dirección de Cultura, 1950. 477 p. illus.

Ortiz Oderigo, Néstor R. *Panorama de la musica Afro-Americana.* Buenos Aires, Editorial Claridad, 1944. 298 p. illus. discography.

Parrish, Lydia. *Slave Songs of the Georgia Sea Islands.* New York, Creative Age Press, 1942. 256 p. illus.

Pipes, William H. *Say Amen, Brother!* New York, William-Frederick Press, 1951. 210 p.

Rourke, Constance. *American Humor; a Study of the National Character.* New York, Harcourt, Brace, 1931. 315 p. (Reprinted: N.Y., Anchor books, 1953. 253 p.)

Saxon, Lyle, Edward Dreyer, and Robert Tallant. *Gumbo Ya-Ya.* Boston, Houghton Mifflin, 1945. illus.

Tallant, Robert. *Voodoo in New Orleans.* New York, Macmillan, 1946. 247 p.

Tax, Sol, editor. *Acculturation in the Americas.* Chicago, University of Chicago, 1952. 339 p.

Wittke, Carl. *Tambo and Bones.* Durham, N. C., Duke University Press, 1930. 269 p.

Work, John W. *American Negro Songs.* New York, Howell, Soskin, 1940. 259 p. illus.

CURRENT MAGAZINES

Australian Jazz Quarterly (Melbourne).
Bulletin du Hot Club de France (Toulouse).
Bulletin du Hot Club de Genève (Geneva).
Discophile (England).
Down Beat (Chicago).
Estrad (Stockholm).
Hot Club of Japan Bulletin (Tokyo).
International Discophile (Los Angeles).
Jazz-Echo (Hamburg).
Jazz Hot (Paris).
Jazz Journal (London).
Jazz Magazine (Buenos Aires).
Jazz Magazine (Paris).
Jazz Monthly (London).
Jazzbladid (Reykjavik).
Melody Maker (London).

Metronome (New York).
Musica Jazz (Milan).
Orkester Journalen (Stockholm).
Record Research (New York).
Rhythme (Eindhoven).
Rytmi (Helsinki).
Second Line (New Orleans).

A SYLLABUS OF FIFTEEN LECTURES

─────────── ON THE HISTORY OF JAZZ ──────────

Illustrative Recordings: Folkways Jazz Series, 2801–11 (these eleven LP's constitute the best-edited and widest-ranging series on jazz to date); the best single introductory LP is Leonard Bernstein's 'What Is Jazz,' Columbia 919; see also Riverside's 'History of Classic Jazz,' SDP 11; 'The History of Jazz,' Capitol 793–96; Leonard Feather's 'Encyclopedia of Jazz,' Decca DFX 140; and Langston Hughes' 'The Story of Jazz,' Folkways FC 7312. (See Bibliography for details on books listed.)

The text of *The Story of Jazz* contains close to four hundred references to a broad selection of recorded material deriving from many sources. As an aid to reference and for group, individual, and class study of *The Story of Jazz,* all musical examples have been put on tape in exact sequence of the text—by chapter, page, and line.

The *Guide Track to the Story of Jazz* has been produced on an experimental, educational basis by the Institute of Jazz Studies, Rutgers University. The taped selections have been re-recorded from originals in public and private archives, and from the Archive of the Institute of Jazz Studies, as collected and established by the late Marshall Stearns, author of *The Story of Jazz* and founder of the Institute.

Copies will be available to accredited institutions and libraries. A descriptive catalog of *A Guide Track to the Story of Jazz* lists all recorded selections and demonstrates organization of the material.

Requests and inquiries about use of the *Guide Track* should be made
to the Institute of Jazz Studies, Rutgers University, New Brunswick,
New Jersey, 08903.

LECTURE 1: DEFINITIONS

A.   Jazz and academic music; jazz as a separate and distinct art with
    separate and distinct standards.
B.   Jazz and the musics of the world: harmony, melody, rhythm,
    timbre, form, and blue tonality.
C.   A tentative definition of jazz in terms of its origins, age, and dis-
    tinctive characteristics.

Readings: The Story of Jazz, chaps. 1, 20, 21, 22; 'Harpsichords and
Jazz Trumpets' in De Toledano, *Frontiers of Jazz;* Finkelstein, *Jazz,*
chap. 1; Sargeant, *Jazz Hot & Hybrid,* chap. 2; Feather, *The Book of
Jazz,* chap. 22 (improvisation); Gunther Schuller, *Early Jazz,* chap. 1,
New York, 1968.

Recordings: Folkways Jazz Series, vol. I; cf. also Folkways P–402, 417,
418, 429, 441, 500, 502, and FP–651, 652, 653; suggested contrasts: Jose
Iturbi and Pine Top Smith playing boogie-woogie, plus Erroll Garner
(rhythm); Perry Como and Mahalia Jackson singing 'Silent Night'
(melody), and John Lee Hooker and any barber-shop group (harmony).

LECTURE 2: JAZZ PREHISTORY

A.   The background and musical heritage of the African, the question
    of provenience, and pertinent details of the slave trade.
B.   The halfway mark: Haiti, Trinidad, Brazil, Cuba, the Bahamas,
    Dutch Guiana, Martinique—retentions and reinterpretations of
    African culture according to social, religious, and musical factors.
C.   The African heritage in the U. S. A. and varying social, religious,
    and musical climates.

Readings: The Story of Jazz, chaps. 2, 3; Herskovits, *The Myth of the
Negro Past, Dahomey, Trinidad Village, Life in a Haitian Valley;*
Canot, *Adventures of an African Slaver;* Courlander, *Haiti Singing* (a
greatly revised edition is in preparation).

Recordings: Folkways 403, 407, 432 (Haiti); 410 (Cuba); 461 (Jamaica); 440 (Bahamas). Cf. also 'Belgian Congo,' Commodore 30005;
'Steel Bands,' Cook 1042; Library of Congress, Archive of American

Folk Songs, vols. 12, 13; Riverside 4001-02 (Africa: Coast and Congo).

LECTURE 3: NEW ORLEANS

A. The early background and variety of Old World cultures; the roles of the slave, the free Negro, and the Creoles of Color.

B. The musical melting pot: Protestant hymns, German and French marches, and their harmonies; 'Latin' and West Indian rhythms; Italian, French, Spanish, Central European, and Scotch-Irish melodies.

C. The marching band; the process of blending; the emergence of patterns, forms, and styles.

Readings: The Story of Jazz, chaps. 4, 5, 6; Ramsey and Smith, *Jazzmen,* chaps. 1, 2, 3; Charters, *Jazz in New Orleans;* Asbury, *The French Quarter; Saxon,* Dreyer and Tallant, *Gumbo Ya-Ya;* Cable, *The Grandissimes*; Shapiro and Hentoff, *Hear Me Talkin' to Ya,* Part I; Hurston, *Mules and Men;* Armstrong, *Satchmo.*

Recordings: Folkways Jazz Series, vol. 3; Folkways 2461–4; selections from Bunk Johnson (talking) AM 643; Kid Ory, 'Tailgate,' Good Time Jazz 12022; George Lewis, Blue Note 7027–28; see also Good Time Jazz LP's 12004–05, 12008, 12016; Folkways 2462 and Pax 9001 offer examples of the Eureka Brass Band; 'Creole Reeds,' Riverside 12–216.

LECTURE 4: THE BLUES

A. Origins: cries and hollers, work songs, ring-shouts, sermons and shouting spirituals; the blues form.

B. The blues as social document: socio-economic factors in the deep South after the Civil War.

C. The blues as literature: the quality of the experience communicated.

Readings: The Story of Jazz, chaps. 8, 10, 12; Big Bill Broonzy, *Blues;* W. C. Handy, *Father of the Blues;* Niles, *A Treasury of the Blues;* Botkin, *Lay My Burden Down;* Shapiro and Hentoff, *Hear Me Talkin' to Ya,* Part III; Laing, *Jazz in Perspective,* pp. 102–41; Sterling Brown, *Negro Caravan;* Russell Ames, *The Story of American Folk Song;* Ethel Waters, *His Eye Is on the Sparrow.*

Recordings: Folkways Jazz Series, vol. 2; Negro prison songs, Tradition 1020, Folkways 475; Ma Rainey, 'Blues,' Riverside 12–108; 'The Bessie

Smith Story,' Columbia 503–05; Blind Lemon Jefferson, Riverside 12–125; Bill Broonzy, Folkways 2326, 3586; Blind Willie Johnson, Folkways 3585; Leadbelly, Folkways 241–42; 'American Street Songs,' Riverside 12–611; Robert Johnson, Columbia CL 1654; cf. also Mahalia Jackson.

LECTURE 5: JELLY ROLL MORTON

The life and times of Ferdinand 'Jelly Roll' Morton, his environment, travels, fellow musicians—in his own words. An estimate of his many-sided contribution to jazz as a composer, arranger, and soloist. (This might tie in with Lecture 3.)

Readings: Alan Lomax, *Mister Jelly Roll; The Story of Jazz,* chap. 7 *et passim;* Morton. 'I Discovered Jazz' in De Toledano, *Frontiers of Jazz;* Blesh, *Shining Trumpets,* pp. 243–53; Schuller, *Early Jazz,* chap. 4.

Recordings: The Library of Congress material issued on Riverside 9001–12 constitutes several lectures in itself. See especially the discussion of funerals, marching bands, discourse on jazz, the Robert Charles riot, voodoo, and the demonstrations of 'Maple Leaf' and 'Tiger Rag.' See also 'The King of New Orleans,' RCA Victor LPM 1649; 'Stomps and Joys,' RCA Victor LPV 508; 'Classic Jazz Piano,' Riverside 12–111; Milestone 56020.

LECTURE 6: RAGTIME

A. A definition of ragtime; the origin of its form and rhythm in march music and minstrel banjo.
B. The evolution of styles: Sedalia, St. Louis, New Orleans, and (ragtime based) New York.
C. The transition from piano to orchestra, perfected by Morton around 1926, and the relationship to rent-party, barrelhouse, and boogie-woogie piano.

Readings: The Story of Jazz, chap. 13; Blesh and Janis, *They All Played Ragtime;* Wittke, *Tambo and Bones;* Ramsey and Smith, *Jazzmen,* chap. 8; Ross Russell, 'Grandfather of Hot Piano' (James P. Johnson) in De Toledano, *Frontiers of Jazz; Record Changer,* October, 1945.

Recordings: Folkways Jazz Series, vol. X; Riverside 12–110, 12–126 (Joplin, Scott, Turpin, *et. al.*); selections from Tony Parenti, Riverside

12–205; Wally Rose, Good Time Jazz 3; Ralph Sutton, Verve 1004; Fats Waller, Riverside 12–109; James P. Johnson, Riverside 12–105; Willie "The Lion" Smith, Dot 3094.

LECTURE 7: NORTH TO CHICAGO

A. Pioneering jazzmen in the transitional era of minstrelsy, tent-shows, carnivals, and vaudeville, and their early and wide-spread travels.

B. New Orleans, World War I, and the migration North to Chicago by land or on riverboats.

C. The arrival and impact in Chicago: Keppard, Noone, Dodds, King Oliver and others; the first big bands, and the effect of the new environment on the music.

Readings: The Story of Jazz, chaps. 11, 14; Armstrong, *Swing That Music,* chaps. 4, 5, 6; Manone, *Trumpet on the Wing,* pp. 1–35; Ramsey and Smith, *Jazzmen,* pp. 59–100; Laing, *Jazz in Perspective,* chap. 3; Schuller, *Early Jazz,* chaps. 6, 7.

Recordings: Folkways Jazz Series, vol. V; 'Young Louis Armstrong,' Riverside 12–101, 12–122, Milestone 2006, Epic 16003 (all with King Oliver); 'Jazz Odyssey—The Sound of Chicago,' vol. II, Columbia C3L 32, record 1. Suggested novelty: Morton's 'Steamboat Stomp.'

LECTURE 8: CHICAGO AND THE JAZZ AGE

A. General backgrounds—the popular scene: Paul Whiteman's Aeolian Hall Concert in 1924 (see his book for the program) and the effect of coast-to-coast publicity.

B. The main stream: Louis Armstrong's Hot Five and later groups; the beginning of a fifteen year reign.

C. The New Orleans Rhythm Kings, the Wolverines (with Bix Beiderbecke), and the Austin High gang.

Readings: The Story of Jazz, chap. 15; Ramsey and Smith, *Jazzmen,* chaps. 4–7; Armstrong, *Swing That Music;* George Johnson, 'The Wolverines and Bix,' in De Toledano, *Frontiers of Jazz;* selected passages in Carmichael, Condon, Mezzrow; Hodes in Gleason, *Jam Session* (also Gleason on Hines); Schuller, *Early Jazz,* chaps. 3, 5.

Recordings: Folkways Jazz Series, vols. V, VI; 'Jazz Odyssey—The Sound of Chicago,' vol. II, Columbia C3L 32; 'Louis Armstrong Story,' Columbia CL 851–54; 'V.S.O.P.,' Epic EE 22019; 'Rare Batch of Satch,'

RCA Victor LPM 2322; 'Rare Items (1935-1944),' Decca 79225; 'Satchmo,' Decca 8604–07; 'The Bix Beiderbecke Story,' Columbia 844–46; 'Thesaurus of Classical Jazz' Columbia C4L 18; 'The Immortal Johnny Dodds,' Milestone 2002; 'Johnny Dodds, New Orleans Clarinet,' Riverside 12–104; 'Earl Hines—at Apex Club,' Decca 79235.

LECTURE 9: BIG BANDS IN NEW YORK

A. The pull to New York as it becomes the focal point of the sheet music, radio, recording, and booking business.
B. Fletcher Henderson, Don Redman and the evolution of big bands in Harlem (Chick Webb, Luis Russell, Charlie Johnson, Sam Wooding, Cecil Scott, Elmer Snowdon *et al.*)
C. The arrival and emergence of the Duke Ellington orchestra, its aims, accomplishments, and unique contribution.

Readings: The Story of Jazz, chap. 16; Ulanov, *Ellington;* Laing, *Jazz in Perspective,* chap. 7; *Jazz Record Book,* pp. 90–117 (commentary); Shapiro and Hentoff, *Hear Me Talkin' to Ya,* pp. 167–201; Otis Ferguson in Gleason, *Jam Session;* Henderson and Ellington in Shapiro and Hentoff, *The Jazz Makers;* Schuller, *Early Jazz,* chaps. 6, 7.

Recordings: Folkways Jazz Series, vol. VII; 'Jazz Odyssey—The Sound of Harlem,' vol. III, Columbia C3L 33; 'The Fletcher Henderson Story,' Columbia C4L 9; Henderson (1924-31) Decca 79227, (1931-34) Decca 79228; Don Redman, RCA Victor LPV 520; Jimmie Lunceford, Columbia CS 9515; Chick Webb (1929-36) Decca 79222, (1937-39) Decca 79223; 'Duke Ellington—Beginnings 1926-28,' Decca 79224; 'Hot in Harlem,' Decca 79241; 'Ellington Era,' vol. I, Columbia C3L 27; vol. II, Columbia C3L 39; 'In a Mellotone,' RCA Victor LPM 1364; 'At His Very Best,' RCA Victor LPM 1715; 'Indispensable Duke Ellington,' RCA Victor LSP 3906; Coleman Hawkins, RCA Victor LPV 501; 'The Perry Bradford Story,' Crispus Attucks 101.

LECTURE 10: SWING IS KING

A. The Depression and its effect on jazz in the late twenties and early thirties.
B. Isolated jazzmen in big commercial bands and radio studios; the beginnings of swing with the Dorsey Brothers and Casa Loma bands reaching an Eastern public.
C. The trials and triumph of pace-setting Benny Goodman, who finally scores a triumph at the Palomar Ballroom in 1935.

Readings: The Story of Jazz, chap. 17; Goodman, *The Kingdom of Swing;* Dexter, *Jazz Cavalcade,* chap. 7; Ramsey and Smith, *Jazzmen,* pp. 214–54; Hobson, *American Jazz Music,* chap. 8; Shapiro and Hentoff, *Hear Me Talkin' to Ya,* pp. 313–34; Frazer, 'Homage to Bunny,' in Gleason, *Jam Session;* Shapiro, 'Benny Goodman' in Shapiro and Hentoff, *The Jazz Makers.*

Recordings: Folkways Jazz Series, vol. VIII; 'B.G.—1927-34,' Decca 54010; 'B.G.—The Small Groups,' RCA Victor LPV 521; 'Benny Goodman,' RCA Victor LSP 4005; 'King of Swing,' Columbia OSL 180. On single records, contrast Moten's 'Lafayette' (1932) with Goodman's 'Sweet Sue' (1938) for perspective.

LECTURE 11: KANSAS CITY AND THE COUNT

A. The Southwest in general, World War II, and mass migrations North, supplying both musicians and audience from Texas to Colorado.

B. Kansas City and environs under the Pendergast machine (1927–38); prosperity in Prohibition acting as a magnet for musicians: Alphonse Trent, Bennie Moten, and others.

C. The emergence of Count Basie in New York in 1936 and the impact of the band upon the jazz world in person and on recordings.

Readings: The Story of Jazz, chaps. 17, 18; Dexter, *Jazz Cavalcade,* pp. 70–76; Shapiro and Hentoff, *Hear Me Talkin' to Ya,* pp. 284–312; Horricks, *Count Basie and His Orchestra;* Shapiro on Basie in *The Jazz Makers;* various articles by Frank Driggs in jazz magazines (to be assembled in book form).

Recordings: Folkways Jazz Series, vols. VII, X; 'Territory Bands—Zach Whyte, Alphonse Trent,' Historical 5829–24; Bennie Moten, Historical 5829–9, RCA Victor LPV 514; 'The Best of Count Basie,' Decca DBX 170; 'Kansas City Jazz,' Decca 8044; 'Lester Young Memorial,' Epic SN 6031; 'Lester Young and Kansas City Six,' Mainstream 6012; Jay McShann, Decca 79236.

LECTURE 12: BOP

A. The socio-economic background: the record ban (1942–44), World War II, the tax on dancing, and the effect of the microphone to sell vocal groups.

B. The evolution of bop: Dizzy Gillespie, Charlie Parker, Thelonious Monk, Kenny Clarke and others at Mintons.

C. The New Orleans Revival on the West Coast; the influence of King Oliver's recordings, Bunk Johnson, Kid Ory, and others.

Readings: The Story of Jazz, chap. 18; Feather, *Inside Bebop;* Ross Russell's series in the *Record Changer;* Ulanov, *History of Jazz;* Shapiro and Hentoff, *Hear Me Talkin' to Ya,* Part IV; Robbins in Gleason, *Jam Session;* Parker, Gillespie, Young, and Christian in Shapiro and Hentoff, *The Jazz Makers.*

Recordings: Folkways Jazz Series, vols. IV (A), X (B5), XI (B7); 'Harlem Jazz Scene 1941,' Counterpoint 5548; 'Norvo's Jam Session,' Parker PLP 408; Dizzy Gillespie (with Charlie Parker), 'Groovin' High,' Savoy 12020; 'Carnegie Hall Concert,' Roost 2234; 'Jazz at Massey Hall,' Fantasy 86003; 'The Greatest Dizzy Gillespie,' RCA Victor LPM 2398; Charlie Parker, Savoy 12000, 12001, 12009, 12014, 12079, Parker PLP 407, Roost 2210, Verve 84004–06; a wide sampling of The New Orleans Revival on Good Time Jazz 12001–03, 12005–07.

LECTURE 13: AFRO-CUBAN JAZZ

A. The very early days: New Orleans to Los Angeles, Miami, and New York via Morton's 'Spanish Tinge' and 'Latin' dance hits recorded by various jazzmen including Armstrong's 'Peanut Vendor.'
B. The Cuban-American factor: Noro Morales in Harlem in the thirties; Del Campo, Machito, Puente, and others in the forties.
C. The fusing: Cab Calloway, Duke Ellington, Kenton, Herman, Gillespie and Chano Pozo; the modern trend to integrated drum suites and rhythm sessions.

Readings: The Story of Jazz, chap. 19; Slonimsky, *Music of Latin America;* one of the few sources of information on this subject can be found in liner notes to record albums.

Recordings: 'Sunday Jazz a la Lighthouse,' Contemporary 3501; Clark Terry, 'Swahili,' Emarcy 36007; Machito, 'Kenya,' Roulette 52006; 'Drum Suite,' Victor 1279; Art Blakey, 'Orgy in Rhythm,' Blue Note 1554–55; 'Candido,' ABC-Paramount 180; Puente, 'Night Beat,' Victor 1447, 1449; Blakey, 'Drum Suite,' Victor 1002.

LECTURE 14: COOL AND MODERN JAZZ

A. Cool jazz: origins and definition; the influence of Lester Young and other members of the Basie band.
B. The (so-called) West Coast school: Dave Brubeck, Shorty Rogers,

Jimmy Giuffre, Chet Baker, Gerry Mulligan and others, their aims and accomplishments; the roles of Tristano and Getz.

C. The Miles Davis recordings of 1949 and thereafter: Charlie Mingus, Art Blakey, Thelonious Monk, Sonny Rollins and their groups.

Readings: The Story of Jazz, chaps. 18, 26; Gleason, 'The Cool Coast,' in *Jam Session; Jazz West Coast,* ed. Richard Bock; Dave Brubeck, 'Jazz Perspective,' in Gleason, *Jam Session;* Shapiro and Hentoff, *Hear Me Talkin' to Ya,* pp. 391–404; Morgan and Horricks, *Modern Jazz;* Hodeir, *Jazz: Its Evolution and Essence,* pp. 116–38.

Recordings: (See Lecture 11 for examples of Lester Young); Gerry Mulligan, 'Quartet,' Fantasy 8082; 'Genius of Gerry Mulligan,' Pacific 20140; 'Jimmy Giuffre 3,' Atlantic 1254; Dave Brubeck, 'Jazz Impressions,' Columbia 984; Lennie Tristano, Atlantic 1224; 'Subconscious-Lee,' Prestige 7250; Stan Getz, 'The Brothers,' Prestige 7252; Charlie Mingus, 'Pithecanthropus Erectus,' Atlantic 1237; 'Tijuana Moods,' RCA Victor LSP 2533; 'Mingus Live at Monterey,' Fantasy JWL 1001–02; Miles Davis, 'Birth of the Cool,' Capitol T 1974; 'Bags' Groove,' Prestige 7109; ' 'Round About Midnight,' Columbia 8469; Thelonious Monk, Blue Note 81509–11; 'Blue Monk,' Prestige 7508; Monk, 'Music, with Coltrane,' Riverside 3004; John Coltrane, 'Giant Steps,' Atlantic 1311; 'My Favorite Things,' Atlantic 1361; Sonny Rollins, 'Saxophone Colossus,' Prestige 7326.

LECTURE 15: THE FUTURE OF JAZZ

A. The appeal of jazz, the role of the Negro, and jazz and the social scientists (the mask).

B. The increasing importance of the arranger-composer in modern jazz and the trend toward classical concepts with a jazz vocabulary.

C. The scene today: jazz and popular music and the general public. Is taste changing?

Readings: The Story of Jazz, chaps. 23–26; Hodeir, *Jazz: Its Evolution and Essence,* pp. 267–82; Feather, *The Book of Jazz,* chaps. 5, 23; Gleason, 'Toward a New Form,' in *Jam Session;* G. V. Kennard, S. J., 'To Swing Is to Affirm,' in *Jam Session;* Henry Pleasants, 'What Is This Thing Called Jazz,' in *Jam Session;* Gleason, 'Rhythm and Blues Make the Grade,' in *Jam Session.*

Recordings: 'The Modern Jazz Quartet,' Atlantic 1265; 'European Concert,' Atlantic 2–603; Miles Davis, 'Miles Ahead,' Columbia 1041; 'Kind of Blue,' Columbia 8163; 'Miles Smiles,' Columbia 9401; Teddy Charles Tentet, Atlantic 1229; George Russell, RCA Victor 1372; 'Music for Brass,' Columbia C28 831; Ornette Coleman, 'The Shape of Jazz to Come,' Atlantic 1317; 'Free Jazz,' Atlantic 1364; 'At Stockholm,' Blue Note 84224–25; 'Rock and Roll Forever,' (a sampler), Atlantic 1239.